The Pocket Guide to
Italian Food and Wine

THE POCKET GUIDE TO
Italian Food and Wine

Spike and Charmian Hughes

FIRESIDE

A Fireside Book
Published by Simon & Schuster, Inc.
New York

Library of Congress Cataloging-in-Publication Data

Hughes, Spike
The Pocket Guide to Italian Food and Wine
"A Fireside book."
1. Gastronomy. 2. Cookery, Italian 3. Wine and
winemaking—Italy. I. Hughes, Charmian II. Title.
TX641.H84 1986 641'.0945 86-24859

ISBN 0-671-63877-7

A Fireside Book
Published by Simon & Schuster, Inc.,
Simon & Schuster Building
Rockefeller Center
1230 Avenue of the Americas
New York, New York 10020

Fireside and colophon are registered trademarks of
Simon & Schuster, Inc.

Originally published in 1987 by
Xanadu Publications Ltd.,
5 Uplands Road, Hornsey, London N8 9NN

Printed and bound in Spain.

CONTENTS

INTRODUCTION

It is because, apart from our home in the South of England, we would rather be in Italy than anywhere else in the world, and because we both always feel so well on it, that we are constantly frustrated and depressed by the average tourist's belief that Italian food is always covered with a thick oily tomato sauce smelling to high heaven of garlic. This is simply not true, of course, but it is an illusion that still persists strongly enough to discourage far too many travellers, when literally in Rome, from eating as the Romans do, and so finding out that if they will only be a little more adventurous they can really eat very well indeed.

One of the great differences between eating in Italy and eating in France is that in France there are about 250 ways of cooking chicken and each of them is called by a name which will at any rate be understood by anybody who can read French (even if only professional cooks and some experienced eaters will immediately recognize its gastronomic significance); whereas in Italy, if there are 250 different ways of serving spaghetti there will be a dozen or more regional names for each of them which only natives of those particular regions will understand.

Regional dialects in Italy are very much live languages, and a century of political unity has so far done nothing to affect their everyday use or to lessen regional pride and insularity. While this means that every region has its own gastronomic specialities, it also means that every region has its own name for many dishes which are common to all parts of Italy.

As a result, where most Italians will recognize the 'high' Italian word for mussels – *muscoli* or *mitili* – a Venetian who calls them *peoci* will not necessarily know what a speaker from the Marches, who calls them *pidocchi* ('lice') is talking about.* As if this sort of thing were already not confusing enough, we find that the fish stew called *cacciucco* in Tuscany is known as *brodetto* on the Adriatic coast, but that *brodetto* in Florence is an Eastertide soup of broth, bread and beaten eggs and lemon juice.

Such is the intenseness of regional pride that a young lady we met in Mantua, for instance, assured us that something or other *alla mantovana* was quite different from the same dish cooked *alla bolognese*. What difference there was proved to be so slight as to be hardly worth commenting on. To our friend,

---

* The etymological origin of the English word, 'piddock' a bivalve mollusc, is said by the Concise Oxford Dictionary to be unknown. It obviously comes from *pidocchio*, but how did it get from the Adriatic into the English language?

however, anything from Bologna was foreign, and she believed that it couldn't possibly be as good as anything *alla mantovana*.

This belief, of course, is the basis for the whole Italian attitude towards food. For although the legal position of women in Italy has improved greatly over the last two decades, it is still rare, though known, for *babbo* to turn his hand to the cooking – never the washing up of course! – and in the family it is still basically *mamma* who runs the show. She forms her children's taste in food so firmly that it remains with them all their lives, and it is heartbreaking to hear Italians one knows complaining that when they stopped in Paris they couldn't find anywhere to eat.

The one good thing about the Italian's inability to eat anything but the food that *mamma* cooks, is that when he leaves his native region to live and work in another he and his fellow exiles insist on being provided for; which means that all over Italy you can find restaurants specialising in 'foreign' food.

This can be a help to the traveller who may find himself in a region whose food he does not greatly care for, although much of the joy of eating out in Italy lies in sampling the infinite local variations on basic national themes. In any restaurant whose proprietor proclaims that he comes from Bologna (or the region Emilia) or from Tuscany, or which sports the words *bolognese, emiliano* or *toscano*, not only will the cooking be as good as local raw material will allow, but the menu will include excellent 'imported' ham and *salami*. On the same principle, wines from the Florentine house of Antinori and the Sicilian red and white Corvo di Salaparuta are ubiquitous and reliable, even in railway dining cars.

The highly developed invidivualism of Italian cooks makes it difficult for those who, like us, are trying to describe how it is done. All one can do is to describe what a dish should be made of – the referees for this being Ada Boni's *Talismano della felicità* (the earlier, fuller editions) and Pellegrino Artusi's witty and authoritative classic, *L'arte del mangiar bene*, which was written in the 1890's and has now run into well over 70 editions. And, of course, Elizabeth David.

We had cooked and eaten from her *Italian Food* ever since it was first published, but it was not until we came to consult it on questions of detail when we were writing this book that we realized how magnificently she had managed to sort out and make sense of that bewildering thing called *la cucina italiana*. We were not surprised to find a restaurant in Italy which told us proudly that 'Elizabeth David ate here'.

Referees for the more widely encountered 'standard' Italian dishes were comparatively easy to find; when it came to the less generally known regional specialities it was another matter, and in the end – where we had inevitably been unable to taste all the dishes ourselves (who could?) – we had to rely on information officially supplied by the region concerned.

Inevitably since writing this book we have met natives of one region or another who disagree entirely with the recipe told us; but that is probably because their particular *mamma* exercised her artistic right to adapt the recipe as she felt inclined.

Regional food plays such an important part in the life of the Italians and thus of all who visit their country, that we have made a point of including a separate section on the subject which we hope will encourage you to try the specialities of the regions you are visiting. We have therefore divided this book into two main sections. The first section is called ON THE MENU, and it is concerned with what one may regard as 'standard' Italian food – that is, those dishes likely to be encountered in the averagely good restaurant and trattoria up and down the country. The second, THE REGIONS OF ITALY, deals with regional specialities as a guide to making the most of what local, and often unfamiliar, cooking has to offer.

It must be understood that in the regional sections we are not necessarily recommending everything we have listed; some of the dishes, indeed, are included almost as a warning – in case you do not relish eating some of the less appetizing parts of sheep and goat which the poorer districts of Italy have to make do with. Typically, Italians swear by their *pesce fresco* (fresh fish) which is indeed usually very good. The pollution along much of the coastline (the Lagoon of Venice is notorious) and the spate of scare stories every summer might, however, counsel a little caution here, though we have never come to any harm ouselves. Of the twenty regions of Italy only five have no contact with the sea – and they are all in the fertile meat-producing north.

It is the Italian custom to list the regions in a kind of west-to-east geographical sequence starting always with Piedmont and ending with Sardinia. As we have never been able to remember whether Basilicata comes before or after Puglia we have decided to do the simple and obvious thing: list the regions in alphabetical order. The traveller who is not certain which region he is in can check his bearings with the map on page 000

Where we have been absolutely powerless to help the tourist who eats in Italy is in describing the hundreds of thousands of dishes concocted by restaurant proprietors all over the country and named after themselves or their establishments. Here individualism runs riot, and in trying to distinguish *spaghetti* cooked *alla Mario* by one gentleman of that name in Milan and another in Taormina your guess is as good as ours or a million Italians'. If your Italian is not up to asking how these irregular dishes are cooked and you'd rather not risk eating them 'blind', as it were, there are usually enough other things to eat on even the most modest menu.

Unfortunately, the more imaginative cooks and proprietors are not content merely to call their creations after themselves, and leave it at that; they begin to think up fancy names for dishes which have a convincing classical ring about them.

We encountered one such item on a seaside menu which puzzled us for a long time; *spaghetti alla capitana* sounded authentic enough. It proved, after reference to the Accademia Italiana della Cucina, to have been thought up by a former head cook of a ship belonging to the Compagnia di Navigazione Italiana, and in the Accademia's opinion was only of *reclamistico* interest.

Although they frequently appear on menus and we have often eaten them in one part of Italy or another, four dishes have been left out altogether because they are never by any chance cooked the same way twice running, and since their names appear nowhere in any of the books by the three referees we have mentioned we cannot even find out what they are supposed to consist of.

The dishes in question are *pasta* or *risotto* served *alla barcaiola, alla boscaiola, alla montanara* and *alla contrabbandiera* – respectively in the manner of the boatman, the woodman, the mountaineer and the smuggler; or their wives. The ambiguity of the Italian words is such that the dishes may indeed be cooked in the manner of the boatwoman, the woodwoman, the mountaineeress and the smugglerette. One thing seems to be pretty consistent about these picturesque creations – namely, that the dishes associated with woods and mountains are likely to contain mushrooms, while those associated with boats and smugglers are likely to contain fish. To this extent, at any rate, the names are faintly helpful.

Holidaymakers in Europe have in recent years increasingly deserted the pension and the hotel for the rented villa or flat (to say nothing of tents and caravans), and in doing their own marketing and cooking have in consequence had to concern themselves with the raw materials of Italian food. In recent years the proliferation of excellent self-service supermarkets (*supermercati*), even in quite small towns, has made self-catering a lot easier.

However, for the more venturesome of these holiday-makers we have compiled a special section on shopping which we have called SHOPPING GUIDE. This includes a list of Italian names for the different food shops; tables of weights and measures; a list of the meat, fish, fruit and vegetables from which to compile your own shopping list before setting out for the shops – or market, wherever possible – to buy the ingredients for your meals at home or your beach picnic.

The idea of what might be called a pre-selected shopping list composed before you go out, is that by writing down the items, together with the weight or number of each item required, you can hand the list to the shopkeeper and so save yourself a lot of unnecessary and sometimes embarrassing skirmishes with the Italian language – which you will get to know better anyway, merely with the expereince of writing down a daily shopping list. If you are lucky enough to have rented a villa with a *domestica* laid on, there is no better or quicker way of learning Italian than making out shopping lists and doing the accounts with her.

In conclusion, it cannot be stressed too strongly that this is not a cookery book; nor are we setting ourselves up as 'experts' on Italian food. It is written strictly from the point of view of two consumers who hope that others who don't know Italy or the Italian language as well as they might wish, will find it a help and an encouragement to explore and enjoy the pleasures and adventure of discovering how to eat well in Italy.

Phonetic System

The phonetic symbols which appear in brackets after each dictionary entry provide an effective shorthand guide to Italian pronunciation for those with little or no knowledge of the language. Pronounce each phonetic syllable as you would in English and the word comes out sounding as it should in Italian. The result won't be perfect every time, but it will always come close enough to get your meaning across and to avoid major disasters.

Italian is a stressed language, so remember to give emphasis to the phonetic syllable in each word that is CAPITALISED. Syllables joined by hyphens should be sounded together as smoothly as possible. But be sure to give each syllable full and distinct pronunciation. Don't say sp'getee as in English, but spa-GET-tee. There are no nasal sounds in Italian, so be careful with the letter 'n' in words like Mango (mango). Say MAN-go, pronouncing the 'n' clearly, not nasally as in the English bank or bang. Double consonants must also be given separate pronunciation in Italian, but stick closely to the phonetic symbols and you should have no trouble with these.

All of the phonetic symbols used are composed of ordinary letters from the English alphabet. A bar over a vowel means that the sound is long rather than short. The following table gives the required English pronunciation for symbols that might prove confusing.

a	as in	*lard* (but see below)
ā	as in	*cake* (but see below)
ay	as in	*bay* (but see below)
ch	as in	*cherry*
e	as in	*lemon*
ee	as in	*peel*
g	as in	*garnish*
i	as in	*pie*
j	as in	*jelly*
o	as in	*cork*
ō	as in	*hotel*
oo	as in	*food*
r	(see below)	
s	as in	*salad*
y	as in	*yam* (but see below)

There is no Italian sound that does not have a near equivalent in English. However, some Italian syllables and vowel sounds may prove tricky to pronounce at first. The table below gives detailed explanation of the phonetic symbols used for these.

a The Italian 'a' is always given a broad *ah* pronunciation, but less broad than the English 'a' in fat. Try for a sound mid-way between lard and fat and you'll be just about right. If this sounds difficult at first, stay with lard. The exact sound will come eventually with practice.

ā Represents one of the two Italian 'e' sounds. It is pronounced almost exactly like the long English 'a' in cake, but as you become more comfortable with the language try to chop it off short and give it a slight 'eh' sound. Doing this will greatly facilitate pronunciation when a appears unstressed in the middle of words.

ay Represents the Italian dipthong 'ei' and should be given a full, long 'a' pronunciation, as in bay, with extra emphasis on the *ee* sound at the end.

yo Represents the Italian dipthong 'io' and should be pronounced as a single sound like 'yo' in yolk. *Ya, ya, ye, yo,* and so on, represent similar Italian dipthongs and should again be pronounced singly as in papaya, yale, yellow, yorkshire pudding, etc.

cho represents *'cio'* and should be pronounced as a single sound, not unlike the *'cho'* in artichoke. Note that there is no *'ž'* or *'y'* sound: the letter *'ž'* in the word merely softens the preceding consonant.

wo Represents the Italian dipthong *'uo'* and should be pronounced as a single sound like the *'wo'* in woke. *Wa, wa, wi* and so on, represent similar dipthongs and should again be pronounced singly as in guava, waiter, wine, etc.

r The Italian *'r'* is always trilled, rather like the Scottish *'r'* in 'porridge' or 'partridge'.

dz and *ts* represent the two Italian *'z'* sounds and should be pronounced respectively like the *'ds'* in beds and the *'ts'* in beets – even if they come at the beginning of a word! (The familiar English z sound, as in maize, is one of the *'s'* sounds in Italian)

SECTION ONE

On The Menu

LISTA del GIORNO

Pane e coperto   Servizio 12%

ANTIPASTI

Salame toscano
Prosciutto crudo di Parma
Prosciutto cotto
Bresaola di Chiavenna
Ventresca di tonno
Magri misti

MINESTRE

Lasagne verdi al forno
Tagliatelle alla bolognese
Spaghetti alle vongole
Spaghetti alla amatriciana
Risotto
Minestrone di riso
Zuppa alla pavese
Zuppa di verdura

BOLLITO

Menzo
Pollo
Testina
Lingua
Salse varie

PESCE

Sogliole dorate
Scampi e calamari fritti
Coda di rospo

PIATTI DEL GIORNO

Spezzatini di vit. con piselli
Trippa alla fiorentina
Saltimbocca romana
Pollo novello al forno
Involtini con piselli
Vitello tonnato
Asparagi a piacere
Agnello al forno

Manzo brasato con lenticchie
Petto di tacchina 'Duchessa'
Arrosto di vitello con patate

PIATTI da FARSI

Bistecca alla fiorentina
Cervella dorata
Fegato alla veneziana
Rognoni trifolati
Paillard di vitello
Fegatini di pollo salvia
Costolette alla milanese
Fegato alla griglia
Filetto di bue ai ferri
Piccata al prezzemolo
Fritto cervella e carciofi

CONTORNO/LEGUMI/VERDURE

Patate arroste
Scorzanera
Fagioli toscani
Spinaci al burro
Finocchi al burro
Cavolfiore
Zucchine ripiene
Barbabietole
Peperonata

INSALATA

Finocchi
Cipolle cotte
Fagiolini
Bietole rosse
Radicchi

DOLCI

FORMAGGI assortiti

FRUTTA fresca di stagione

GELATI

ON THE MENU

Whether you will in fact be given a menu to look at at all in Italy may depend on the type of place you eat in.

Some of the best eating we have ever enjoyed there was done entirely by ear – in a *trattoria* off the Piazza della Signoria in Florence which was run by father, mother, son, and a little old man who did the washing up and fanned the tiny charcoal grill and had the face of one of the figures on Ghiberti's doors of the Baptistry. The son, Marcello, who acted as waiter, taught Greek at the University of Florence, and found the tips at his parents' restaurant a great help. It was a *trattoria* which had been a great meeting-place for artists, writers and musicians (Stravinsky had been a frequent customer); the Vanucci family made a speciality of buying superb home-made *salami* from around the Tuscan countryside and you chose your food from Marcello's recital of the day's dishes. The Vanuccis have now retired, and we are hungrier for it.

The *trattoria* was typical of what are in the end the best places to eat at in Italy – the small family-run restaurant where the *pasta* is likely to be home-made, the wine from a relation's vineyard, the customers friendly and deafeningly talkative, where there is often the sort of long communal table you find in a London club that anybody can sit at and where nobody asks the price of anything. We have found places like this whenever we have stayed in an Italian town for more than a couple of meals; the second time you go back to one you are no longer a tourist but a regular *cliente*.

Most establishments in Italy do provide a menu to look at (sometimes the only copy may be hung up outside, where, like any menu on display, it should be consulted before entering). When typewriters are used for these menus the spelling and typing may prove to be a little less – shall we say? – sophisticated than in France. Abbreviations abound – VIT. or even 'v;' for vitello, MOZZ. for mozzarella – and grave and acute accents are represented by apostrophes after the letters they belong to. The words which took us longest to decipher were ASCE' and SOUTTE'. We worked out in the end that they were the typewritten Italianized forms of *Haché* and *Sauté* – French words one hardly expected to find so far from home as Bari.

The average Italian *ristorante* (where waiters wear white coats) considers itself higher class than the *trattoria* (where the family serve you in shirt-sleeves); it has a menu (sometimes printed) that may be headed *Lista delle vivande* or *Lista delle pietanze*, both of which mean a list of dishes; and there will probably be baskets of fruit on the sideboard and a *Lista dei vini* incorporated in the menu. If the wine list is printed separately then the prices will be high and the more cosmopolitan the whole thing begins to look, sound and smell; the staff will talk English to you and tell you how they worked at Claridge's for seven years and lived at Herne Hill, or about their uncle in Brooklyn.

In many less pretentious *ristoranti*, especially on the main tourist routes, it is possible to eat a *prezzo fisso* or opt for the *menu turistico* (not as horrendous as it sounds), but the fixed-price menu is not encountered quite so often in Italy as in France. What is a prominent feature of nearly all *ristorante* menus, however, is a section marked *Piatti del giorno* (dishes of the day) and another marked *Piatti da farsi* (dishes to order), while some include a category, *Piatti pronti* (dishes ready). As it would be quite impossible to list all the dishes likely to crop up under these headings without duplicating more than two-thirds of the contents of this book, we have paid the hungry reader the compliment of assuming that he will quickly be able to identify the dishes he wants to know about by referring to the Index, or just thumbing though sections on Meat (page 68), Fish (page 58), Poultry and Game (page 94) and so learning whether what he's faced with is flesh, fowl or good red herring.

In the case of *Piatti freddi* (cold dishes), which is a category encountered far too seldom in a boiling Italian summer, we have listed the dishes most often found under this heading – though never, it seems, when one really needs them. (The Italians' delight in tucking into a steaming *minestrone* in an evening temperature of well over 80 is something that never ceases to amaze us). On the other hand, Italians do not share our predilection for 'piping hot' food and you may find main courses, and particularly accompanying vegetables, on the tepid side.

One problem frequently faces the traveller in Italy and that is finding somewhere to eat only what you want, and not what you're expected to want. Restaurant-owners are naturally not too pleased by the arrival of customers who occupy valuable table space and then, owing to loss of appetite, lack of exercise, the heat, financial embarrassment, general holiday lassitude or all five, order a plate of scrambled eggs and a salad.

For the traveller in search of a little *ad hoc* food a *rosticceria* can be a godsend. You may have to eat standing up (if all the stools at the counter are occupied), but you can get hot food and cold food (and delicious cold veal to take away for your picnic) and the prices are normally reasonable.

Other types of eating place include the *pizzeria* which has spread widely over Italy from Naples, and where you can find other things besides *pizza* to eat (on reflection, another good place to look for a one-dish meal); the *latteria*, which is a dairy and caters for the sort of teashop appetite we ourselves have never suffered from, though some *latterie*, especially in the north, may provide a wider range of snacks or even a full meal.

The five classes of eating places we have mentioned – the *ristorante*, the *trattoria*, the *rosticceria*, the *pizzeria*, the *latteria* – should between them provide the hungry or unhungry traveller with all he needs. In choosing any of them it is essential that you choose one which is crowded and busy, for that is a sure sign of quality. The 'quiet little place round the corner' may be all very well here but in Italy, as in France, an empty restaurant means that it's a bad restaurant and is to be avoided.

Credit cards such as Access, Eurocard, Mastercard, Visa and of course American Express are accepted by many hotels (the Michelin guide, an essential for all manner of travellers, whether motorists or not, will tell you which). We find them useful towards the end of a holiday. We find them less useful in restaurants, as the cheaper and more congenial 'family' type of restaurant or *trattoria* is less likely to take them, though most of the smarter ones will.

One word about the restaurants that straddle the *autostrade*. They are good and very crowded; but as they offer a 24-hour service, by avoiding the rush hour – 12 noon till 1.30 or so – you can eat in comfort. You may eat a *prezzo fisso* or *alla carta*, and along the Autostrada del Sole the Motta chain of restaurants makes a point of serving regional specialities. This comes as a pleasant surprise, for driving along an *autostrada* one has very little feeling of being in any region at all, only of rushing though a landscape. The red Michelin guide marks these *autostrada* restaurants on its map of the country's principal roads. It also tells you when their listed restaurants in any town are open. The problem with Michelin, as often outside France, is that their choice of restaurants tends towards the up-market and obvious.

Generally speaking, most places will close for at least two weeks in August and on one day a week, which will usually be signalled on the door: eg *chiuso il giovedì* (closed Thursdays). As a rule of thumb, most that open on Sundays close Mondays. It is therefore a good idea to make a priority of mastering the Italian words for the days of the week: *Lunedí* (Monday), *martedí, mercoledí, giovedí, venerdí, sabato, domenica*.

Before you Begin

Coperto   – Cover charge.
Coperto e pane – Cover charge and bread.
S.Q.   – Secondo quantità – according to quantity.
S.G.   – Secondo grandezza – according to size.
S.S.   – Secondo stagione – according to season.
a piacere   – As you please. *Sogliole a piacere:* sole cooked in any manner you please.

Pasta

If you ask for what is generally known to English-speakers nowadays as pasta it is wise to specify *pasta asciutta*, or dry *pasta* served with a sauce. At the evening meal asking simply for *'pasta'* can often result in your being brought a plate of *Pasta in brodo,* a soup with any of a hundred differently shaped kinds of small *pasta* in it.

Mustard

Ask for *senape*, not *mostarda* which is a sweet-sour pickle.

Caution

Fritto misto. To those of us who have asked for a *fritto misto* for years in Italian restaurants in London or New York, the order has usually brought a mixed fry of lamb cutlets, liver, brains, sweetbreads, artichokes, zucchini, and anything else that happens to be going. When we first returned to Italy after the war and ordered our first *fritto misto* we were given a plateful of what can only be described as assorted rubber rings that tasted faintly of fish.

We were eating in Lerici and it didn't occur to us that to the local restaurant a *fritto misto* was a mixed fry of octopus, squids and the rest of those unbecoming uglies that would really be better used as a bait to catch something edible and more easily chewed. We should have made a point, of course, of stipulating that we wanted a *fritto misto di carne* – a mixed fry of meat. We wouldn't have got it, as later on it was explained to us that it was really a winter dish. We have subsequently discovered, of course, that our first experience in Lerici was pure bad luck: a tasty and masticable *fritto misto di pesce* is to be found on most seaside menus, and often inland as well.

Zuppa inglese. It is possible that out of the corner of his eye the English traveller may once have seen this dish listed somewhere on a menu and have decided to order it next time he was homesick for Brown Windsor Soup. *Zuppa inglese,* however, is not a soup; careful study of the menu shows that it is in fact always listed under *Dolci* (sweets) and is the Italian name for their version of trifle. The Italian for Brown Windsor, according to a menu of 1910 we saw the other day, is *Potage Windsor.*

Casalinga

This adjective is used about anything home-made and is especially to be recommended when applied to *salami.*

Cafés, etc

Perhaps the greatest asset the foreign traveller to Italy can take with him is a pregnant wife and/or young children, especially babes in arms or toddlers. The Italians love children, and revere pregnant women in a way you rarely find in other countries. A pregnant wife or girlfriend will get you swiftly through Customs, her presence will immediately produce a table in an otherwise full restaurant, and everything will be done to make her comfortable in shops, cafés, trains, buses – wherever you happen to go. Children in Italian families are not considered a race apart, as they are elsewhere, where hotels often advertise 'No children under 12 accepted' as an added amenity.

But in Italy children, even the unweaned, not only always eat with the rest of the family at home but are taken to restaurants as well, where they eat what the grown-ups eat, though maybe a *mezza porzione* (half-portion). And of course there is no nonsense in Italy about children not being allowed on licensed premises. You can take them to cafés and bars, where they will have the time of their lives, with exotic ices and soft drinks. To save a lot of questions, ices *(gelati)* are usually visible or illustrated on the enormous refrigerator that contains them, and you can choose one simply by pointing at what you want. And instead of being described as a 'lemon drink' or an 'orange drink' (what do they put or not put in them, that they have to be excused in this way?), a lemonade or orangeade in Italy is *una limonata* or *un'aranciata,* but there is always Coke, if you must . . .

For the adult, what you drink depends on the time of day (though the bars are always open). Before lunch or dinner, the obvious drink is an *aperitivo.* Though it may be an acquired taste, the most effective appetizer we have found to be Campari.

Campari-soda, un This may be sold ready-mixed in small conical bottles, or the Campari will be served neat into a glass and soda added to taste. It loses nothing of its strong, aperitive qualities for being expensively advertised in France as a 'long drink' (another example of Franglais the French Academy has been powerless to suppress).

Americano, un Campari and red vermouth, with ice, a shaving of lemon peel, and topped up with soda.

Negroni, un Like an American plus gin and soda (the vermouth should be Punt e Mes: see below).

Vermouth Provides a more direct way of putting an edge on the appetite.

A Neat *Martini Rosso* does more for your appetite than anything we know except possibly an *Americano*.

The white so-called *Martini Dry* is a pleasant pre-meal drink to linger over, but without the aperitivo properties of its red stable-companion.

The Cinzano vermouths are too sweet for our taste – the *bianco* notoriously so, and the *rosso* lacking the bitter-sweet subtlety of the Martini red.

The most unusual vermouth of all is *Carpano's Punt e Mes*, a very effective and strongly-flavoured aperitivo, and reminiscent (among other flavours) of Cooper's pre-war bitter Oxford marmalade.

After all this appetite stoking you may find by the end of a meal that you need a *digestivo*. There are innumerable brands on the market of which the best-known, Cynar, is made of artichokes. You are unlikely to want to try any of these more than once, though some, famously Fernet Branca, have a limited value as short-range hangover cures.

If you are merely thirsty, Italian beer, a kind of weak, gaseous lager, may do the trick if properly chilled. It can sometimes be found on draught *(alla spina)* but more usually in a bottle or can. Ask for *una birra italiana* or *nazionale* or you may get a well-known foreign brand (Carlsberg or Heineken as a rule) – *'birra estera'* – brewed under licence in Italy and indistinguishable, except in price, from the local *Nastro Azzurro*. In the north-east, German-speaking part of the country excellent local beers can be found.

If you want unsweetened fruit juice, ask for *una spremuta d'arancia/di limone/di pompelmo* (freshly squeezed orange/lemon/grapefruit juice). A *succo di frutta* (fruit-juice) tends to denote a small bottle of very thick, sweet, pear or apricot pulp, very good but not very refreshing. Tomato juice *(succo di pomodoro)* is also more viscous than elsewhere and will come of course from a bottle or can.

There are probably occasions during the day when you would rather have a cup of coffee than anything else (tea is usually weak and invariably made with a bag). Italians drink more coffee without than with milk, and they drink it standing up in bars, knocked back like a glass of vodka. This of course is the *espres-*

so, for the people in a hurry (such as commercial travellers, who rate this as breakfast): a small, squat cup half-full of very strong coffee. If there is anywhere to sit at the bar (it costs you a little more to drink anything at a table, a lot more if the table is outside and in Venice or Capri) and you are not in all that much of a hurry, try asking for a 'long' or 'high' coffee *(caffe lungo/alto)*. This is an *espresso* in the same squat cup, made with a little more water and filled nearly to the top. You will notice hardly any difference in taste, for it will still be a cup of very strong coffee. For coffee with milk, ask for a *cappuccino* – so called because it is the colour of the habits worn by Capucin monks. It is normally served in a large cup with the milk aerated by the steam of the *espresso* machine. *Caffe-latte* is a vague term, in hotels usually eliciting a large empty cup with a pot of coffee and a jug of hot milk, in bars anything from the same to a flat *cappuccino*. *Un caffe corretto al rhum* or *alla grappa* is worth remembering on a cold day, being *espresso* 'corrected' with a dash of rum or *grappa*.

Tipping

If you travel by train in Italy, stations (in theory) display prominently (somewhere) the official railway tariff per piece of luggage carried by a porter *(facchino)*. The tariffs vary and are lower in, say, Sicily than in Milan or Turin. In any case it is wise to add a few hundred lire to your official tip.

In restaurants, the service (usually 12 to 15 per cent) will have been added to the bill. Here again, it is customary to leave a few hundred lire on the plate when you have paid the bill; you are supposed to take the bill away with you, incidentally, or a receipt at any rate, under a government provision to cut down tax-evasion among restauranteurs – don't lose any sleep over this one!). In cafés the situation is more fluid: if leaning at the bar a small coin, or nothing; if sitting outside you could ask *servizio compreso?* with a rising inflection, and leave some ten per cent if the answer is *no*.

The first Italian phrase every foreigner should learn to say is 'thank-you' – either *grazie tante* (many thanks) or *mille grazie* (a thousand thanks), neither of which is too effusive and both of which will be answered by a courteous *prego*. The next phrase you must learn is the Italian for please – *per favore* – or, if you are asking the way from a stranger, start your question with the words *mi scusi, signore/signora*. To summon a waiter, Italians generally shout *Senta!* (Listen!) but this might be considered rather cheeky from a foreigner with no further command of the language.

ANTIPASTI — HORS-D'ŒUVRE AND FIRST COURSES

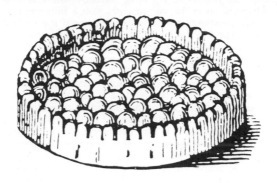

We have always found that where in France the hungry eye tends to focus first on the main dishes of a menu – on the fish, the *rôtis*, or the *specialités de la maison* – in Italy one thinks of nothing in the way of 'afters' until one has considered the *antipasti*. The reason for this, we think, is that while a lot of very good French *hors-d'oeuvres* find their way abroad, very few of even the most de luxe restaurants elsewhere can ever hope (or even try) to offer you *salami* or ham as fresh as it is in the smallest *trattoria* in Italy. Until you have eaten it in Italy, indeed, you have never known what good *salami* can taste like.

The luridly coloured Danish approximation to be found in so many sandwich bars and the monstrously expensive slivers of hard, sometimes rancid and greasy *salami* that still surface in some restaurants at home have probably prejudiced many travellers on their first visit to Italy against ever trying to eat *salami* again.

We therefore urge those who may have been put off by eating *salami* at home, to forget their unhappy experience and believe us when we assure them that the variety, character and quality of Italy's local hams and sausages are one of the glories of what remains of Western civilisation. Not only every region, but almost every village in the country will claim to produce the best *salami* in Italy, and if the claim itself may usually be regarded with some scepticism, it nevertheless pays to test it at first hand.

But ham and *salami* are by no means the only attraction of the *Antipasti* menu. By the sea there are end-

NB. In the catalogue of *antipasti* that follows we have included a number of dishes which are eaten less in restaurants than as supper dishes or snacks with a glass of wine in *pizzerie*, *rosticcerie* and such.

less varieties of shellfish, crabs, prawns, and cephalo-
pods the like of which you have probably never set
eyes on outside an aquarium. Finally, there are the
numberless vegetable dishes – stuffed aubergines
and pimentos, olives, courgettes, mushrooms and
tomatoes.

Except in the smarter restaurants, *hors-d'oeuvres* in
Italy are not brought round to you on a trolley; when
they are, the menu will announce the fact as *Assortiti
al carrello*. As in France, the individual items are listed
and priced separately on the menu so that you can
choose exactly what you want and can afford. If you
would like to have the choice made for you, nearly
every *Antipasti* section of an Italian menu includes
one of the following ways of saying so:

Antipasti assortiti

Antipasto di lusso (a relatively grand *hors-d'oeuvre*)

Antipasto misto

Magri assortiti (without meat)

Magri misti (the same)

Acciughe *(at-CHOO-gā)*   Anchovies.

Affettati misti   A mixture of sliced cold meats, ham,
sausages, etc.

Agoni *(a-GŌ-nee)*   Freshwater shad from the Lom-
bard lakes.

Alici *(a-LEE-chee)*   Anchovies.

Antipasti di molluschi *(an-tee-PAS-tee dee mōl-LOOS-
kee)*   A plate of assorted shellfish.

Antipasto alla genovese *(an-tee-PAS-tō al-la jen-ō-VĀ-
zā)*   A dish of raw young broad beans, salami and
cheese *(sardo)*.

Antipasto di pesce *(dee PESH-ā)*   Hors-d'oeuvre of
fish.

Aringa sott'olio, Filetti di *(fee-LET-tee dee a-REEN-ga
sōt-ŌL-yō)*   Fillets of herring in oil.

Asparagi *(as-PAR-a-jee)*   Asparagus. Sometimes
served with poached egg *(see pp 100-101)*.

Baccelli *(bat-CHĀL-lee)*   Raw, broad beans, often
eaten with pecorino cheese *(see also antipasto alla
genovese)*.

Bagna caoda *(BAN-ya ka-Ō-da)* (Piedmont)   A hot
sauce of butter, oil, garlic, anchovies and white truffles into which you dunk pieces of fresh vegetable
such as celery, artichoke, pimentos and cardoons.

Barchette *(bar-KET-tā)*   The same as the French barquettes – small pastry cases filled with almost anything suitable as hors-d'oeuvre.

Bondiola di Parma *(bōn-DYŌ-la dee PAR-ma)* Pork sausage from Parma; also other parts of northern Italy.

Botargue *(bō-TAR-gwa)* or **Bottarga** *(bōt-TAR-ga)* Smoked or dried tunny or mullet roe, served with oil and lemon.

Bresaola *(bra-sa-Ō-la)* (Lombardy) Dried salt beef, served with oil, lemon, chopped parsley.

Bruschetta *(broos-KET-ta)* Slices of white bread baked crisp, rubbed with garlic and eaten with olive oil.

Buttariga *(boot-ta-REE-ga)* Tunny or mullet roe.

Calamaretti *(ka-la-ma-RET-tee)* Baby octopus or squids.

Capocollo *(ka-po-KOL-lō)* Cured neck of pork; speciality of Parma.

Caponata *(ka-pō-NA-ta)* See *melanzane alla siciliana* (page 29).

Caponata alla marinara *(al-la ma-ree-NA-ra)* Hard biscuits that have been soaked and are covered with oil, garlic, anchovies, black olives, onions, marinated aubergine *(egg plant)* and pimentos, and herbs.

Caponatina *(ka-pō-na-TEE-na)* See *melanzane alla siracusana* (page 31).

Carciofi *(kar-CHŌ-fee)* Artichokes. (Unless otherwise indicated 'artichokes' means globe artichokes throughout this book).
    Arrostiti *(ar-rōs-TEE-tee)* Roast, with garlic, olive oil and parsley.
    Bolliti *(bōl-LEE-tee)* Boiled and served either hot or cold with a dressing.
    Contadina, alla *(al-la kōn-ta-DEE-na)* Stuffed with such things as breadcrumbs, garlic, anchovies, capers; well seasoned and stewed in oil.
    Dorati *(dō-RA-tee)* Dipped in egg and flour and fried.
    Fiorentina, alla *(al-la fyōr-en-TEE-na)* Artichoke hearts masked with a cheese sauce, mushrooms and cauliflower.
    Forno, al *(al FŌR-nō)* Baked in a covered pan with olive oil, garlic and parsley.
    Fritti *(FREET-tee)* Fried artichoke hearts.
    Funghi, con *(kōn FOON-gee)* Stuffed with mushrooms, breadcrumbs, onion and herbs.
    Giudia, alla *(al-la JOO-dya)* Roman speciality of very young, but not necessarily small, artichokes, fried whole in olive oil; when they are cooked they

look like open flowers and are brown and crisp to eat.

Maionese, alla *(al-la ma-yō-NĀ-zā)* Artichoke hearts with mayonnaise.

Milanese, alla *(al-la mee-la-NĀ-zā)* With butter and cheese.

Ripieni *(ree-PYEN-ee)* 'Ripieni' means stuffed, and artichokes are stuffed with many things in Italy, including rice, tunny fish, anchovies, sweetbreads and sometimes a creamy cheese sauce.

Romana, alla *(al-la rō-MA-na)* Stewed in oil, flavoured with mint and garlic.

Tortino di carciofi *(tōr-TEE-nō dee kar-CHŌ-fee)* This is really an artichoke omelette; the artichokes, when cooked, are covered with beaten egg, and when the eggs are done it is served to you rather like a flan.

Veneziana, alla *(al-la vā-net-TSYA-na)* Stewed in oil and white wine.

Vino bianco, al *(al VEE-nō BYAN-kō)* Stewed in oil, white wine and herbs.

Carciofini all'olio *(kar-chō-FEE-nee al-LŌL-yō)* Very young artichokes, with the outside leaves removed, served in oil.

Carpaccio *(kar-PAT-chō)* Raw beef fillet sliced translucently thin; may be served with a piquant sauce; with oil, lemon and little chunks of parmesan and/or rucola. Can also be eaten as a main course.

Caviale *(kav-YA-lā)* Caviar.

Cestini *(chās-TEE-nee)* Small cases of puff or flakey pastry with a savoury filling.

Cetriolini *(chāt-ree-yō-LEE-nee)* Gherkins.

Chizze *(KEET-tsā)* Squares of pastry filled with anchovy or cheese.

Ciambotta/Ciamforta *(cham-BŌT-ta/cham-FŌR-ta)* Dialect for melanzana *(egg plant)* in Naples.

Cipolline in agrodolce *(chee-pōl-LEE-nā een a-grō-DŌL-cha)* Sweet and sour baby onions.

Cocktail di pesce *(KŌK-tāl dee PESH-ā)* Fish 'cocktails' of all sorts appear on many menus, but mostly at seaside resorts where there are tourists. (See coppa di gamberetti below).

Coppa *(KŌP-pa)* A variety of *salame* made from pig's head, neck, muscles and rind.

Coppa di gamberetti *(dee gam-bā-RET-tee)* Prawn cocktail.

Coppa romana/Coppa di testa *(dee rō-MA-na/dee TES-ta)* Brawn.

Coppa veneta *(VEN-e-ta)* In the Veneto a kind of meat loaf with ham, tongue, mortadella *(qv)*.

Cozze *(KÔT-tsā)* One name for mussels (Naples).

Cozze, impepata di *(eem-pā-PA-ta dee)* Mussels highly flavoured with pepper.

Cozze in salsa piccante *(een SAL-sa peek-KAN-tā)* Mussels in a well-flavoured sauce.

Crespone di Milano *(krās-PŌ-nā dee mee-LA-nō)* See under *salame di Milano* (p. 32).

Crostini *(krōs-TEE-nee)* These are small pieces of bread, fried bread or toast, covered or spread with things like cheese, pâté, shellfish, or in Florence, with chickens' livers. Usually served hot.

Crostini di provatura *(dee prō-va-TOO-ra)* Rounds of bread with a thick slice of provatura cheese baked in the oven, with an anchovy and oil sauce poured over them.

Culatello di Zibello *(koo-la-TEL-lō dee dzee-BEL-lō)* (or **di Parma** *(dee PAR-ma)* Rump of pork cured like ham. Very good indeed.

Cuscinetti *(koo-shee-NET-tee)* Baked cheese sandwiches.

Datteri di mare *(DAT-tā-ree dee MA-rā)* 'Sea dates' – delicious little shellfish the shape and size of a date found along the Ligurian coast. Eaten raw or like *moules marinière*.

Datteri marinati *(DAT-tā-ree ma-ree-NA-tee)* Datteri di mare (see above) served with oil, vinegar, sage and garlic.

Dōratini di ricōtta *(dōr-a-TEE-nee dee ree-KŌT-ta)* Cheese fritters, served with or without sugar, according to which end of the meal you eat them.

Fagioli *(fa-JŌ-lee)* White beans
    Toscana col tonno, alla *(al-la tos-KA-na kol TON-no)* With tunny fish.

Fagiolini col tonno *(Fa-jō-LEE-nee kol TŌN-nō)* French beans with tunny fish.

Fegatelli di pollo al marsala *(fä-ga-TEL-lee dee POL-lo al mar-SA-la)* Chicken livers with Marsala.

Finocchiona toscana *(fee-nōk-KYŌ-na tōs-KA-na)* See under salame (p 31).

Fiori di zucca *(FYŌ-ri dee TZOO-ka)* Flower of the marrow, sometimes stuffed and fried, or just fried.

Fonduta *(fōn-DOO-ta)* (Piedmont) Melted fontina cheese, egg yolks, butter and milk served with white truffles.

Fragoline di mare *(fra-gō-LEE-na dee MA-rā)* 'Little sea strawberries' – tiny squids used as an ingredient of *frutti di mare* ('sea fruits').

Fritelle *(free-TEL-lā)* This seems to cover everything from meat rissoles to pancakes or fritters filled with cheese or other savoury things and fried. You can also get *fritelle* with sweet fillings.

Frittata *(freet-TA-ta)* See under Eggs (p. 54).

Frittatine imbottite *(freet-ta-TEE-nā eem-bot-TEE-tā)* Pancakes stuffed with many different things including cheese, ham, meat and vegetables.

Frittatine ripiene *(...ree-PYEN-ā)* Same as *frittatine imbottite.*

Frutti di mare *(FROO-tee dee MA-rā)* Dish of small shellfish and polypods.

Funghetti alla giudia *(foon-GET-tee al-la JOO-dya)* Mushrooms in oil with garlic and parsley.

Funghi *(FOON-gee)* Mushrooms (see under Vegetables, p. 102)

Insalata *(een-sa-LA-ta)* Salad
  Carni, di *(dee KAR-nee)* A meat salad, but when we have had it, has been unlike any meat salad known in England, as the meat is chopped up and mixed with cold cooked vegetables, hard-boiled egg as well as lettuce and perhaps raw celery.
  Frutti di mare, di *(dee FROO-tee dee MA-rā)* Shellfish salad.
  Lingua di bue, di *(dee LEEN-gwa dee BOO-wā)* Beef tongue, chopped vegetables, oil, lemon juice.
  Mascherata *(mas-kā-RA-ta)* A mixed salad masked with mayonnaise.
  Pesce, di *(dee PESCH-ā)* Fish salad of white fish and shellfish.
  Russa, alla *(al-la ROOS-sa)* Chopped, cold, cooked vegetables with a mayonnaise. If you find it on the menu under Pesce *(fish)* it will include white fish and mayonnaise; if under the Carne *(meat)* section it will have cold chicken and mayonnaise with it.

Tonno, di *(dee TŌN-nō)* Tunny-fish salad, probably with cold vegetables like *insalata russa* above.

Lingua piccante *(LEEN-gwa peek-KAN-tā)* Spiced or pickled tongue.

Lingua con salsa verde *(kōn SAL-sa VER-dā)* Tongue with a 'green' sauce: parsley, oil, lemon juice, capers and anchovies.

Lonza *(LŌN-dza)* Cured fillet of pork.

Lumache *(loo-MA-kā)* Snails
  Borgogna, alla *(al-la bōr-GŌN-ya)* Our old friend, bourguignonne (boor-GEEN-yōn) – Stuffed with garlic butter.
  Francese, alla *(al-la fran-CHĀ-zā)* With a filling of onion, carrot, celery, parsley, butter, garlic, breadcrumbs and leeks. Served in their shells *à la francaise*.
  Romana, alla *(al-la rō-MA-na)* With chopped anchovies, oil, garlic, tomatoes, mint.

Mazzancolle *(mat-tsan-KŌL-lā)* Very large prawns cooked as scampi *(grilled, boiled or fried)*.

Melanzane *(mā-lan-DZA-nā)* Eggplant, aubergines.
  Agrodolce, in *(een a-gro-DŌL-chā)* In a sweet-sour sauce.
  Farcite *(far-CHEE-tā)* Stuffed.
  Finitese, alla *(al-la fee-nee-TĀ-zā)* (Calabria) With grated cheese and basil, coated with flour and egg and fried.
  Forno, al *(al FŌR-nō)* Cut in half, stuffed with things like meat, onion, cooked rice, cheese, herbs, tomatoes or anything else the cook feels like, and cooked in the oven in olive oil. On your lucky day this can be very good.
  Funghetti, ai *(î foon-GET-tee)* Small pieces fried in oil with garlic and chopped parsley.
  Genovese, alla *(al-la jen-ō-VĀ-zā)* Stewed in oil with onion and tomatoes. Beaten egg is then added.
  Marinara, alla *(al-la ma-ree-NA-ra)* (Naples) Cold boiled aubergine dressed with vinegar and oil, garlic, and well seasoned.
  Napoletana, alla *(al-la na-pō-lā-TA-na)* Baked in the oven with cheese and tomato sauce.
  Parmigiana, alla *(al-la par-mee-JA-na)* A piece of egg plant, *mozzarella* cheese, tomato sauce, covered with grated parmesan (but see also p 133).
  Pomidoro, al *(al pō-mee-DŌR-ō)* Really the same thing as *al forno*, above.
  Ripiene alla calabrese *(ree-PYEN-ā al-la ka-la-BRĀ-zā)* Stuffed with a mixture of mince, onion, chopped basil, rice or breadcrumbs, grated cheese and a tomato sauce, and baked in the oven.

Romagna, alla *(al-la rō-MAN-ya)* Sliced, dipped in egg and fried. Placed in a dish with alternating slices of cheese, browned in the oven.

Romana, alla *(al-la rō-MA-na)* Slices baked with a meat sauce, basil and cheese.

Siciliana, alla *(al-la see-cheel-YA-na)* With chopped meat and tomato sauce, beaten egg and grated cheese.

Siciliana, alla (caponata) *(ka-pŏ-NA-ta)* An elaborate dish of aubergine, olives, celery, capers, hard-boiled egg, baby octopus, lobster, prawns, smoked tunny-fish roe and swordfish, all covered with a sweet-sour sauce made of almonds, olive oil, bread, anchovies, orange juice, sugar, grated chocolate and vinegar.

Siracusana, alla (caponatina) *(al-la see-ra-koo-ZA-na (ka-pŏ-na-TEE-na)* A mixture of aubergine, celery, capers, green olives, sugar, vinegar and grated chocolate cooked together in olive oil.

Melone *(Mā-LŌ-nā)* Melon

Mortadella *(Mōr-ta-DEL-la)* A large pink sausage from Bologna with peppercorns and squares of white fat in it.

Moscardini *(Mŏs-kar-DEE-nee)* Very small members of the squid family.

Mozzarella in carozza *(mŏt-tsa-REL-la een ka-RŌT-tsa)* A sandwich of bread and mozzarella, the famous buffalo-milk cheese from Naples, the whole thing dipped in beaten egg and fried.

Mozzarella milanese *(Mee-la-NĀ-zā)* A slice of mozzarella cheese dipped in egg and breadcrumbs and fried.

Olive *(ō-LEE-vā)* Olives

Condite con capperi *(kōn-DEE-ta kōn KAP-pā-ree)* Olives with capers, which, though you find them nearly everywhere, are a Sicilian speciality.

Ripiene d'acciughe *(ree-PYEN-ā dat-CHYOO-gā)* Olives stuffed with anchovies.

Ostriche *(ŌS-tree-kā)* Oysters.

Pandorato *(pan-dōr-A-tō)* Slices of bread soaked in egg and milk, then fried a golden brown.

Pâte di fegato *(pa-TĀ dee fā-GA-tō)* Liver pâté.

Pâte di fegato di pollo *(dee PŌL-lō)* Chicken-liver pâté.

Peperonata *(pā-pā-rŏ-NA-ta)* (Lombardy) Sliced red pimentos, tomatoes and onions cooked in oil and butter.

Peperoncini *(pā-pā-rŏn-CHEE-nee)* Small hot peppers.

Peperoni *(pā-pā-RŌ-nee)* Sweet peppers, pimentos.

Arrostiti *(ar-rōs-TEE-tee)* Roasted on or under a flame, peeled and dressed with oil and vinegar.

Forno, al *(al FOR-nō)* Baked in the oven with olive oil.

Gratinati *(gra-tee-NA-tee)* Stuffed with cheese, tomato, anchovies and spices, rolled in bread-crumbs and cooked in the oven (Campania).

Imbottiti *(eem-bōt-TEE-tee)* Stuffed pimentos which can be filled with many things, including fish, meat, rice, cheese.

Ripieni *(ree-PYEN-ee)* See imbottiti, above.

Sott'aceto *(sōt-ta-CHE-tō)* In vinegar.

Sott'olio *(sōt-OL-yō)* In oil.

Pesce in carpione *(PESH-ā een kar-PYŌ-nā)* Fish first fried in oil then marinated with onions in vinegar (see also under Fish section).

Petits pâtés *(pe-TEE pa-TĀ)* Little pastry cases filled with savoury mixtures.

Pizza *(PEET-tsa)* The *pizza* is eaten to begin a meal instead of *pasta*, or as a supper dish with a glass of wine. It has become very popular all over the world in the last ten years or so. It is the shape and roughly the size of a pancake, but made with bread dough, baked in the oven and eaten at once. In Naples, where we first ate them, they are cooked in an open wood-fired bake oven in front of you and are very good but they can be very indigestible. We have listed a few of the better-known forms of *pizze* below; there are many others.

Calzone *(kal-TSŌ-nā)* A crisp-topped folded-over pizza, the filling on the inside.

Mozzarella, alla *(al-la mōt-tsa-REL-la)* Tomato and mozzarella cheese.

Napoletana *(na-pō-lā-TA-na)* This is the famous one with tomato, mozzarella cheese, anchovies, chopped basil, wild marjoram *(origano)* and olive oil.

Pomodoro, al *(al pō-mō-DO-rō)* With tomato. It is the cheapest and has no cheese.

Rosmarino, al *(al roz-ma-REE-no)* This is always made of pastry, not bread dough; it is well sea-soned with salt, pepper and rosemary and is very good.

Rustica *(ROOS-tee-ka)* This is different, as it is a flan filled with a mixture of cheese, eggs and ham or sausage in a cream sauce. It is called a *pizza* nevertheless.

Pomodori ripieni *(pō-mō-DO-rō ree-PYEN-ee)* Stuffed tomatoes. They are sometimes stuffed with *carne* (meat), *funghi* (mushrooms), *tonno* (tunny fish), *capperi e acciughe* (capers and anchovies); very often with breadcrumbs or rice, sometimes even macaroni. Usually highly flavoured with garlic and oil basil, parsley or mint, which is often used with them in Rome. The district round Parma is famous for its beautiful tomatoes, so eat them in Emilia.

Pompelmo *(pōm-PEL-mō)*   Grapefruit.

Prosciutto *(prō-SHOOT-tō)*   Ham.
  Affumicato *(af-foo-mee-KA-tō)*   Smoked.
  Cinghiale, di *(dee choon GYA-lā)*   Ham from a wild boar.
  Cotto *(Kō-tō)*   Cooked ham.
  Crudo *(KROO-do)*   Raw ham.
  Fichi, con *(kon FEE-kee)*   With ripe figs.
  Langhirano, di *(dee lan-gee-RA-nō)*   A fine ham from the province of Parma.
  Melone, con *(kon ma-LŌ-nā)*   Raw ham with melon.
  Montagna, di *(dee mōn-TAN-ya)*   Ham from a mountain district.
  Parma, di *(dee PAR-ma)*   The most famous ham of all.
  San Daniele, di *(dee san dan-YEL-ā)*   From Udine, but found in shops and restaurants as far away as Ventimiglia, and exceptionally good.
  Speck *(spek)*   Speciality from Alto Adige.

Radiche *(RA-dee-kā)* or **Rapanelli** *(ra-pa-NEL-lee)*   Radishes.

Rane dorate *(RA-nā dō-RA-tā)*   Frogs' legs dipped in egg and fried in olive oil.

Ricci di mare *(REE-chee dee MA-rā)*   Sea urchins. Served raw with lemon.

Salame *(sa-LA-mā)*.
  Fabriano *(fa-bree-YA-nō)*   A *salame* from the Marches which is a mixture of pork and veal.
  Felino, di *(dee fā-LEE-nō)*   Pure pork from the village of Felino near Parma. Very expensive.

Finocchiona *(fee-nōk-KYŌ-na)* A delicious spiced *salame* from Tuscany flavoured with fennel seed.

Fiorentina *(fyør-en-TEE-na)* *Salame* from Florence, made of pure pork.

Genovese *(jen-ō-VĀ-zā)* A mixture of pork, veal and pork fat, well flavoured.

Milano, di *(dee mee-LA-nō)* The small-grained *salame* of pork, beef and pork fat that you find in every shop outside Italy that sells Italian food; also called **crespone** *(krās-PŌ-nā)*.

Napoletano *(na-pō-lā-TA-nō)* This sausage from Campania is the same as Milan *salame*, but more highly flavoured.

Toscana *(tōs-KA-na)* Same as *fiorentina* (see above).

Ungherese *(oon-ga-RĀ-zā)* Hungarian *salame* of pork and beef, well flavoured. Much liked by the Italians.

Salmone affumicato *(sal-MŌ-nā af-foo-mee-KA-tō)* Smoked salmon. We have never tried this in Italy so we can make no comment. It is usually the same sort of price as the best *prosciutto*.

Salmone scozzese *(sal-MŌ-nā skōt-TSĀ-zā)* Scotch salmon.

Salsiccia luganica *(sal-SEET-cha loo-GA-nee-ka)* Sausage from the north-east of Italy (Friuli-Venezia Giulia); fried, grilled, or eaten raw when dried.

Salumi nostrani *(sa-LOO-mee nōs-TRA-nee)* Local *salami*.

Sardine all'olio *(sar-DEE-nā al-LŌL-yō)* Sardines in oil.

Soppressata *(sōp-prās-SA-ta)* Highly flavoured sausage.

Sott'aceti *(sōt-ta-CHET-ee)* Mixed vegetable pickles in plain vinegar.

Succo di pomodoro *(SOOK-kō dee pō-mō-DƟ-rō)* Tomato juice.

Tonno sott'olio *(TŌN-nō sōt-ŌL-yō)* Tunny-fish in oil; served with lemon. See also *ventresca di tonno* below.

Tostini arlecchino *(tos-TEE-nee ar-lāk-KEE-no)* Gaily coloured savoury toasts.

Tostini di ricotta *(tos-TEE-nee dee ree-KŌT-ta)* Best described as Cottage Cheese Croquettes.

Trote affumicate *(TRŌ-tā af-foo-mee-KA-tā)* Smoked trout.

Uova *(WŌ-va)* Eggs.

Fredde con salsa maionese *(FRĀ-dā kon SAL-sa ma-yō-NĀ-zā)* Egg mayonnaise.
Ripiene *(ree-PYEN-ā)* Stuffed eggs.

Uova di tonno *(WŌ-va dee TŌN-nō)* (Sardinia) Dried and salted tunny-fish roe.

Ventresca di tonno *(ven-TRES-ka dee TŌN-nō)* The stomach of the tunny-fish, and by far the best part. See under Fish, p 66.

Vitello tonnato *(vee-TEL-lō ton-NA-tō)* See under *Piatti freddi*, p000.

Vongole *(VON-gō-lā)* Clams

Zucchini *(zoo-KEE-nee)* Baby marrows, courgettes.
Agrodolce, in *(een ag-rō-dōl-chā)* Stewed in oil and served with a sweet-sour sauce.
Fiori di zucchini *(FYOR-ee dee zoo-KEE-nee)* The flowers of marrow dipped into a batter and fried.
Fritti *(FREET-tee)* Cut into small pieces, dipped into egg and breadcrumbs or flour and fried.
Indorati *(een-dō-RA-tee)* Slices dipped in flour and then into a mixture of beaten egg and grated cheese, and fried in oil.
Montanara, alla *(al-la mōn-ta-NA-ra)* Slices are stewed slowly in butter. Breadcrumbs soaked in milk, and grated cheese are added at the last moment.
Napoletana, alla *(al-la na-pō-lā-TA-na)* Baked in the oven with a tomato sauce and *mozzarella* cheese.
Parmigiana, alla *(al-la par-mee-JA-na)* Fried zucchini, tomato sauce and grated cheese, baked in a casserole in the oven.
Parmigiano, al *(al par-mee-JA-nō)* Fried in butter and served with parmesan.
Ripieni *(ree-PYEN-ee)* Stuffed.
Ripieni alla napoletana *(al-la na-pō-lā-TA-na)* Stuffed with a savoury mixture and baked in the oven with tomato sauce and grated cheese.
Ripieni alla siciliana *(al-la see-cheel-YA-na)* Stuffed with a mixture of breadcrumbs, anchovies, garlic and parsley, and baked.
Salsa piccante, in *(een SAL-sa peek-KAN-tā)* Fried, served cold with a piquant sauce (Tuscany).
Stufato, in *(een stoo-FA-tō)* Stewed in olive oil with onions.
Toscana, alla *(al-la tōs-KA-na)* Minced pork, tomato, onion and baby marrow cooked together and served with grated cheese.

MINESTRE – SOUPS

Originally *minestra (mee-NES-trā)* meant a meal (a *minestrone* being a big meal), but today it has come to mean not only a good nourishing soup, but is the heading on an Italian menu under which you may also find listed any of the hundreds of different farinaceous dishes which the Italians eat before settling down to their main meat, fish or poultry course.

That Italian soups should be known as *minestre* is hardly surprising, for most of them are almost meals in themselves. In many cases they are so solid that they can be eaten with a fork – minestrones, soups of rice and beans, pasta and lentils, peas and rice, and numberless other combinations of natural and compounded carbohydrates.

On many menus you will find some sort of *pasta* served *'in brodo'* (in broth or consommé) – *quadrucci, pastina, raviolini, tagliolini,* or, in Parma, *anolini.* These are normally small shapes or stuffed envelopes of *pasta* and are eaten at the evening meal.

We have divided this part of ON THE MENU into two sections. The first consists of those liquid and less-liquid soups and broths and near-stews which Italians enjoy, icy winter and scorching summer alike. The second section is shown as PASTA ASCIUTTA and FARINACEI, two terms sometimes seen on menus which do not lump all their farinaceous dishes together under MINESTRE and leave you to sort it all out for yourself.

The farinacei include rice and *polenta* (maize) dishes, *gnocchi* (dumplings) and one or two items featuring the starchier legumes.

Note: Some Italian soups are eaten cold or warm *(semi-freddo).*

Acquacotta *(ak-kwa-KŌT-ta)* (Tuscany)   This means literally 'cooked water'; it is a thick vegetable broth poured over slices of bread soaked in beaten egg.

Brodetto *(brō-DET-tō)*   See under Fish, p 66.

Brodetto pasquale *(brō-DET-tō pas-KWA-lā)*   A broth of meat, vegetables and herbs, thickened with egg yolks and served with grated cheese.
    Crostini, con *(kən crōs-TEE-nee)*   Served with croutons and cheese.
    Misto *(MEES-tō)*   Chicken, beef and vegetable broth.
    Pollo, di *(dee PŌL-lō)*   Chicken broth.

Brodo *(BRŌ-dō)*   Broth or consommé.
    Ristretto di bue *(rees-TRET-tō dee BOO-wā)*   Concentrated beef broth.
    In tazza *(een TAT-tsa)*   Served in a cup.
    Rombetti alla giardiniera, con *(kən rōm-BET-tee*

al-la jar-deen-YE-ra)   A clear soup served with squares of cheese-and-vegetable-flavoured custard.

Budino di pollo in brodo *(boo-DEE-nō dee PŌL-lō een BRŌ-dō)* (Bologna)   See p. 133.

Busecca *(boo-SEK-ka)*   (Milan) See p. 143.

Busecchina *(boo-sāk-KEE-na)*   (Milan) A soup of chestnuts, wine and milk.

Cacciucco *(kat CHOOK-kō)*   See under Fish, (p 61).

Ceci e tempia alla milanese *(CHĀ-chee ā TEM-pya al-la mee-la-NĀ-zā)*   See under Pork. p. 80.

Celestina *(chā-les-TEE-na)*   Clear soup with little stars of pasta.

Consommé caldo o freddo in tazza *(kōn-sōm-MĀ KAL-dō ō FRĀD-dŏ een TAT-tsa)*   Hot or cold consomme served in a cup.

Consommé all'uova *(kōn-sōm-MĀ al-WŌ-va)*   Thickened with egg yoke.

Crema *(KRĀ-ma)*   Cream soup, usually chicken or vegetable.

    Asparagi, d' *(das-PAR-a-jee)*   Cream of asparagus soup.
    Fagioli, di *(dee fa-JŌ-lee)*   Cream of haricot bean soup.
    Gallina, di *(dee gal-LEE-na)*   Cream of chicken soup.
    Orzo, di *(dee ORT-tsō)*   Cream of barley soup.
    Piselli, di *(dee pee-ZEL-lee)*   Cream of green pea soup.
    Pollo, di *(dee POL-lō)*   Cream of chicken soup.
    Pomodoro, di *(dee pō-mō-DO-rō)*   Cream of tomato soup.
    Porri, di *(dee POR-ree)*   Cream of leek soup.
    Riso con asparagi, di *(dee REE-zō kcn as-PAR-a-jee)*   Cream of rice and asparagus soup.
    Sedani, di *(dee SĀ-da-nee)*   Cream of celery soup.
    Spinaci, di *(dee spee-NA-chee)*   Cream of spinach soup.

Minestra *(mee-NES-tra)*   It is usually *minestra di* something-or-other, so you know roughly what the ingredients of this extremely filling dish are likely to be.

    Legumi, di *(dee lā-GOO-mee)*   Usually vegetables in general, but occasionally the Italians use the word *legumi* in its strict botanical sense meaning beans, peas, chick-peas, lentils and other members of the pulse family.
    Risō ē asparagi, di *(dee REE-zo a as-PAR-a-jee)* (Milan) Rice and asparagus tips; enough for most people's supper.

Verdure, di (*dee ver-DOO-rā*) This can contain any green stuff including or excluding the true legumi.

Minestrina (*mee-nās-TREE-na*) A broth with tiny bits of *pasta* in it.

Minestrone (*mee-nās-TRŌ-nā*) A 'big meal,' as we have already suggested. It consists of fresh vegetables diced – any sort that happens to be in season – dried vegetables such as beans of all kinds, and herbs, cooked together with either pasta or rice. To this there are sometimes added things like sausage, bacon, ham and chicken lights. Always served with grated cheese in it and on it.

    Fiorentina, alla (*al-la fyor-en-TEE-na*) With *soffritto* added – a flavouring made of chicken giblets, tomato, pork and chillies.

    Genovese, alla (*al-la jen-ō-VĀ-zā*) Beans, cabbage, aubergine, baby marrows, tomatoes, mushrooms, some sort of *pasta*, and served with *pesto* and cheese (for *pesto* see p. 51).

    Milanese, alla (*al-la mee-la-NĀ-zā*) Carrots, potatoes, baby marrows, French beans, dried beans, celery, cabbage, tomatoes, garlic, parsley and rice; served with grated cheese.

Nocciolini di vitello in brodo (*nōt-chyō-LEE-nee dee vee-TEL-lō een BRŌ-dō*) A broth with veal meat balls.

Pallottoline in brodo (*pal-lōt-tō-LEE-nā een BRŌ-dō*) Cheese-flavoured dumplings in broth.

Panata (*pa-NA-ta*) A bread soup, with grated cheese and egg.

Paparele e bisi (*pa-pa-REL-ā ā BEE-zee*) (Verona) Pea soup.

Paparele e fasoi (*pa-pa-REL-ā ā fa-ZΘY*) Bean soup.

Paparot (*pa-pa-ROT*) (Istria) A spinach soup thickened with maize flour and well flavoured with garlic.

Passatelli in brodo (*pas-sa-TEL-lee een BRŌ-dō*) (Modena, Bologna) A mixture of egg, breadcrumbs and cheese grated or chopped into a boiling broth, making a light *'pasta in brodo'*.

Passato di verdura *(pas-SA-tō dee ver-DOO-rā)*   A sieved vegetable soup, but not very thick.

Pasta e fasoi *(PAS-ta a fa-ZOY)*   (Veneto)   A soup of beans and pork rind, and pieces of *pasta*.

Pastina in brodo *(pas-TEE-na een BRŌ-dō)*   Small shapes of *pasta* in broth.

Risi e bisi *(REE-zee ā BEE-zee)*   (Veneto)   A soup of rice and peas flavoured with chopped celery, onion and ham; very thick.

Riso e latte *(REE-zō ā LAT-tā)*   (Piedmont)   A rice and milk soup, flavoured with cheese.

Riso e patate *(REE-zō ā pa-TA-tā)*   Rice and potato soup flavoured with pork, onions and herbs.

Riso e wurstel in brodo *(REE-zō ā VURS-tel een BRŌ-dō)*   Rice and sausage in broth (eaten in those parts of Italy which used to be Austria.

Soffioncini in brodo *(sōf-fyon-CHEE-nee een BRŌ-dō)*   Very light dumplings in broth.

Stracciatella *(strat-cha-TEL-la)*   (Rome)   Beaten egg, grated cheese and semolina, stirred into a chicken or beef broth.

Vellutata di carciofi *(vāl-loo-TA-ta dee kar-CHŌ-fee)*   Cream of artichoke thickened with egg yolk.

Vellutata di pollo *(vāl-loo-TA-ta dee PŌL-lō)*   Cream of chicken thickened with egg yolk.

Zuppa *(TSOOP-pa)*   Zuppa means soup unless it is *zuppa di pesce* when it is more of a fish stew than a soup (see p 67).

    Fagioli di Toscana, di *(dee fa-JŌ-lee dee tōs-KA-na)*   White bean soup flavoured with garlic.

    Montanara, di *(dee mōn-ta-NA-ra)*   The contents of this mountain-country soup are variable, but it is known to be a filling affair, with beans or lentils (sometimes both), as well as assorted vegetables, herbs and giblets.

    Pavese *(pa-VĀ-zā)*   Clear broth with an egg poached in it, served with fried bread spread with grated cheese and more cheese served separately.

    Pesce, di *(dee PESH-ā)*   See under Fish, p. 67.

    Verdura, di *(dee ver-DOO-ra)*   Vegetable soup.

PASTA ASCIUTTA AND FARINACEI

When it comes to the names of all the varieties of *paste asciutte* (*PAS-ta a-SHOOT-tā*) eaten in Italy we will admit frankly that though we have eaten platefuls of one kind or another in our time, there are hundreds which we have never seen, let alone eaten.

In the circumstances, we have thought it best to list the names of the pastas you are likely to meet on most menus. As for the numerous varieties we have omitted, it is safe as an almost general rule to presume that the more extravagantly named items found on a regional menu are some form or other of *pasta*.

If it turns out to be fish – well, that can happen to anybody – even the Italians, if they come from Piedmont and are eating in Basilicata.

Sauces for Pasta Asciutta   As many different sauces are served with almost all forms of *pasta*, we have added at the end of this section on *Pasta Asciutta and Farinacei* a list of sauces that you may come across (p. 47). The traveller who has reassured himself that *bigoli* is in fact another name for *spaghetti* in Venice can then refer to our list of *pasta* sauces and see what he is likely to get if they are offered on the menu *all'amatriciana*.

Agnolotti (*an-yō-LŌT-tee*) (Piedmont)   A variety of *ravioli*; cushions of *pasta* filled with a mixture of beef, spinach, egg, grated cheese, and flavoured with nutmeg.

Anelli (*a-NEL-lee*)   Small rings of pasta.

Anolini (*a-nō-LEE-nee*) (Parma)   A kind of small *ravioli*, filled with beef, pork, vegetable, breadcrumbs, egg, grated cheese and flavoured with nutmeg. Served either in broth or with butter and cheese.

Arancini (*a-ran-CHEE-nee*) (Sicily)   These are tomato-flavoured rice balls filled with *mozzarella* cheese, chopped meat, sausage or poultry and fried in deep oil. They were selling them on the platform at Messina once on our way to Palermo, but thinking they were oranges we didn't try them and have never seen them since.

Bigni (*BEEN-yee*)   Dialect name for *spaghetti*.

Bigoli (*BEE-gō-lee*)   Venetian for *spaghetti*.
  Bigoli con slasa (*kon SLA-sa*)   Wholemeal *spaghetti* with a sauce of onions and salted anchovies.

Bombardini rigati (*bōm-bar-DEE-nee ree-GA-tee*)   Literally 'striped baritone saxhorns'; in fact a *pasta* like *rigatoni* (*qv*).

Cannelli (*kan-NEL-lee*) Tubes of *pasta*.

Cannelloni (*kan-nāl-LŌ-nee*) Squares or tubes of *pasta* rolled and stuffed with cream cheese, spinach or meat or fish, and baked with butter and cheese, or a cream sauce and cheese.

Cappelletti (*kap-pāl-LET-tee*) 'Hats' of *pasta* filled with different ingredients in different districts of Italy, mainly northern. They are either served with butter and grated cheese, or in broth.

Casonsei (*ka-zōn-SĀY*) (Bergamo) Stuffed rings of *pasta*.

Ceci (*CHĀ-chee*) Chick-peas. They are cooked and mixed with *pasta*.

Chenelle di semolino (*kā-NEL-lā dee sā-mō-LEE-no*) Balls of semolina that have been cooked in broth.

Crochetti di riso (*kro-KET-tee dee REE-zō*) Rice croquettes.

Fagioli (*fa-JŌ-lee*) White beans cooked in many ways (see p. 26).

Farfalle (*far-FAL-lā*) Butterflies of *pasta*. *Farefallini* 'Pretty little butterflies'. Small bows of *pasta*.

Fettuccine (*fāt-toot-CHEE-nā*) (Rome) Ribbons of *pasta*; the Roman name for *tagliatelle*.

Fischietti (*fees-KYET-tee*) Thin *macaroni*, 'little whistles'.

Fusilli (*foo-ZEEL-lee*) Thin corkscrews of pasta.

Gnocchi (*NYŌK-kee*) These are little dumplings made of potato and flour, or semolina or *polenta* (maize flour).

    Genovese, alla (*al la jen ō VĀ-zā*) Potato dumplings served with *pesto* (see p 51).

    Parmigiana, alla (*al-la par-mee-JA-na*) Potato and flour dumplings with a tomato sauce and grated cheese.

    Patate, di (*dee pa-TA-tā*) Potato dumplings served with grated cheese and butter.

    Piemontese, alla (*al-la pyā-mōn-TĀ-zā*) Potato dumplings with gravy and grated cheese.

    Polenta, di (*dee pō-LEN-ta*) Made with maize flour and found mostly in the south of Italy; served with butter and cheese.

    Romana, alla (*al-la rō-MA-na*) Semolina dumplings with butter and cheese.

    Semolino, di (*dee sā-mō-LEE-nō*) Served with butter and grated cheese.

Gramigna (*gra-MEEN-ya*) 'Couch-grass' – a *pasta* said to look like it.

Incasciata *(een-ka-SHA-ta)* *Pasta.* Like a *timballo* (see p 46).

Lasagne *(la-SAN-ya)* Broad strips of *pasta*, first boiled, then served in a casserole with sauce between each layer.

COOKED IN SOUPS AND STEWS

Conchigliette

Semino di melo

Acina di pepe

Noccette

Anellini

BAKED WITH OTHER FOODS

Elbow macaroni

Spiedini

Cappelletti

Penne

Conchiglie

Occhi di lupo

Gramigna rigato

Pennini

Grosso rigato

Ruote

Farfalle

Tortiglioni

Lasagne

Curly lasagne

PASTA AT A GLANCE

Bolognese, alla *(al-la bō-lōn-YA-zā)* With a meat and creamy sauce.

Calabrese, alla *(al-la ka-la-BRĀ-zā)* With a sausage-meat and tomato sauce, *mozzarella* and *ricotta* cheese.

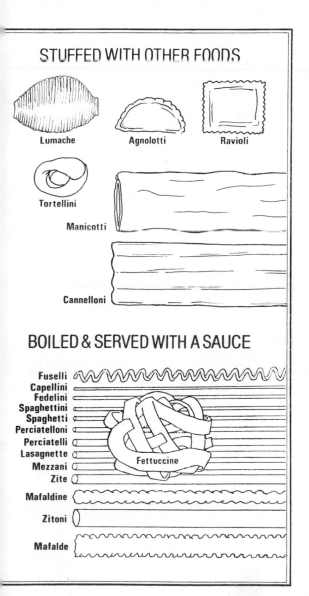

STUFFED WITH OTHER FOODS

Lumache

Agnolotti

Ravioli

Tortellini

Manicotti

Cannelloni

BOILED & SERVED WITH A SAUCE

Fuselli
Capellini
Fedelini
Spaghettini
Spaghetti
Perciatelloni
Perciatelli
Lasagnette
Mezzani
Zite

Fettuccine

Mafaldine

Zitoni

Mafalde

Genovese, alla *(al-la jen-ō-VĀ-zā)* With a *pesto* sauce (see p 51).

Marchigiana, alla *(al-la mar-kee-JA-na)* With a meat and giblet and truffle sauce.

Merluzzo, col *(kol mār-LOOT-tsō)* With cod.

Napoletana, alla *(al-la na-pō-lā-TA-na)* A meat and tomato sauce and cheese.

Verdi al forno *(VER-dee al FOR-nō)* Green *lasagne* baked with a rich meat and cream sauce.

Lenticchie *(len-TEEK-kyā)* Lentils.

Limoncini *(lee-moñ-CHEE-nee)* *Pasta* in the shape of lemon slices.

Linguini *(leen-GWEE-nee)* 'Little tongues' of *pasta*, often served with a clam sauce.

Maccheroncini *(mak-kā-rōn-CHEE-nee)* Very small macaroni.

Maccheroni *(mak-kā-RŌN-nee)* Tubes of *pasta*; also a generic name for *pasta* – as it was in England until fairly recently.

Maccheroni rigati *(mak-kā-RŌN-nee ree-GA-tee)* Ribbed maccheroni. *Rigati* means striped, or ribbed.

Paglia e fieno *(PAL-ya ā FYĀ-nō)* Literally 'straw and hay': green (spinach-flavoured) and ordinary *tagliatelle* mixed; usually eaten with a light sauce.

Panissa *(pa-NEES-sa)* (Piedmont) A rice and bean dish with bacon, onion and tomato.

Panzerotti *(pan-dzā-ROT-tee)* A kind of *ravioli*.

Pappardelle *(pap-par-DEL-lā)* Flat ribbons of *pasta* made with egg, and frequently served with a rich sauce of hare, duck or meat.

Pasta e piselli *(PAS-ta ā pee-ZEL-lee)* Chopped bacon and fresh peas served with pasta, cheese and butter.

Pasticciata *(past-teet-CHA-ta)* *Pasta* with a meat sauce, cheese and butter cooked in the oven.

Pasticciata alla milanese *(...al-la mee-la-NĀ-zā)* See *polenta pasticciata*.

Pasticcio di anolini *(pas-TEET-chō dee a-nō-LEE-nee)* (Parma) A pie of short crust pastry filled with *anolini* (qv).

Pasticcio di maccheroni *(...dee mak-kā-RŌ-nee)* A pie made of sweet pastry filled with *maccheroni*, a sauce and cheese; or can equally be our old friend Macaroni Cheese.

Pilau *(PEE-laō)* A pilaf.

Pizza *(PEET-tsa)* See under *Antipasti* (p. 22).

Polenta *(pō-LEN-ta)* Made from maize flour and eaten a great deal in northern Italy, particularly in Lombardy, Trentino and Alto Adige, and the Veneto. It is made by boiling the yellow flour in water; when it is cooked it is either left to go cold, cut into shapes and fried, baked or grilled, or eated plain boiled with butter and cheese. It is also served with game, birds, dried salt fish, *mozzarella* and *fontina* cheese, sausage, pigs' intestines and soup.

> **Fiur, in** *(een FYOOR)* (Lombardy) Polenta cooked in milk.
> **Lodigiana, alla** *(al-la lō-dee-JA-na)* (Lombardy) Rounds of *polenta* with a slice of cheese between dipped in egg and breadcrumbs and fried.
> **Nera** *(NĀ-ra)* Made with 'Saracen' grain and served with birds and game in Trentino.
> **Polenta e 'osei'** *(pō-LĒN-ta ā ō-ZĀY)* (Veneto, Trentino, Lombardy) Small roast birds served on slices of *polenta*.
> **Polenta pasticciata** *(…pas-teet-CHA-ta)* (Lombardy) Slices of *polenta* alternating with a cheese-flavoured sauce and meat mushroom sauce, baked in the oven. Sometimes, if you are lucky, white truffles are used.
> **Salvia, alla** *(al-la SAL-vya)* (Lombardy) Sage-flavoured *polenta*.
> **Valdostana alla** *(al-la val-dŏs-TA-na)* (Valle d'Aosta) Slices of plain boiled *polenta* with *fontina* cheese between them; baked until cheese is melted.

Ravioli *(rav-YŌ-lee)* This is the form of stuffed *pasta* we know best; it is a square or cushion of *pasta* made with egg and filled with different things in different parts of Italy – meat, cheese, vegetables, etc.

Rigatoni *(ree-ga-TŌ-nee)* Large ribbed *maccheroni* (rather like small drainpipes).

Riso *(REE-zō)* Rice.
> **Bianco, in** *(een BYAN-kō)* Boiled rice.
> **Bianco con tartufi bianchi, in** *(een BYAN-kō kon tar-TOO-fee BYAN-kee)* Boiled rice and white truffles, served with grated parmesan and butter.
> **Bomba di riso** *(BŌM-ba dee REE-zō)* (Parma) A rice dish with pigeons.
> **Cappuccina, alla** *(al-la kap-poot-CHEE-na)* (Lombardy) With anchovies, onion, butter and oil.

43

Coratella, riso e *(REE-zō ā kō-ra-TEL-la)* (Milan) Lung of veal cooked in meat broth and served with rice and chopped parsley. *Coratella* means lights, but in Milan it is applied to lung.

Quattro formaggi, a *(a KWAT-trō for-MAD-gee)* A rice dish with which four different cheeses are used.

Rognoncini trifolati, con *(kon rōn-yōn-CHEE-nee tree-fō-LA-tee)* Rice cooked in broth with butter and oil, chopped vegetables, kidneys and cheese.

Salsiccie, riso e *(REE-zō ā sal-SEET-chā)* Rice with sausage.

Salto, al *(al SAL-tō)* Cooked rice fried with mozzarella cheese.

Saracena, alla *(al-la sa-ra-CHĀ-na)* Rice with finely chopped shellfish.

Sartu di riso *(sar-TOO dee REE-zō)* (Naples) An elaborate rice dish with a variety of things in it – small meat rissoles, mushrooms, giblets of poultry, green peas, cheese and a tomato sauce; or even things like hard-boiled eggs, pieces of game, poultry or ham.

Uovo e limone, all' *(al-WŌ-vō ā lee-MŌ-nā)* Egg and lemon juice beaten up and mixed into the rice.

Verde *(VER-dā)* With sage and chopped spinach.

Zucca, riso e *(REE-zō ā ZOOK-ka)* Rice and pumpkin.

Risotto *(ree-ZOT-tō)* Nearly all *risottos* are made by slowly cooking the rice in butter or oil, or a mixture of both, until the rice has absorbed the fat, then adding beef, chicken or fish stock with, in some cases, a little wine and the chicken, duck, fish, meat and vegetable added. Butter and grated cheese are added before serving.

Bianco *(BYAN-kō)* A risotto cooked with water and white wine instead of broth.

Branzino or **branzin, di** *(dee bran-DZEE-no)* (Veneto) A fish *risotto* made with *branzino* or bass.

Cagnone, in *(een kan-YŌ-nā)* Flavoured with sage and garlic, butter and cheese.

Cape, risotto di *(ree-ZOT-tō dee KA-pā)* (Venice) With shellfish (usually clams).

Capro roman or **cavroman, risotto in** *(een KA-prō ro-MAN/KAV-rō-man)* A Venetian rice dish with mutton and tomatoes. '*Capro roman*' or '*Cavroman*' is dialect for a Roman goat and obviously Venetian slang for mutton, but we do not know its origin.

Carciofi, con *(kon kar-CHŌ-fee)* (Tuscany) With hearts of baby artichokes cut up and cooked with rice.

Certosina, alla *(al-la chār-tō-SEE-na)* With a sauce of peas, crayfish tails or prawns, and mushrooms.

Certosina con rane, alla (*...kən RA-nā*) As above, with frogs' legs.

Chioggiotta, alla (*al-la kōd-JŌT-ta*) (Venice) A fish risotto.

Fegatini, con (*kon fā-ga-TEE-nee*) (Padua) With poultry livers.

Finanziera, alla (*al-la fee-nan-TSYER-a*) Rice cooked in beef broth and beef marrow, with chickens' livers, onion, wine and cheese.

Fiorentina, alla (*al-la fyor-en-TEE-na*) With chickens giblets, cooked in butter, added to the rice.

Frutti di mare, risotto di (*ree-ZŌT-tō dee FROOT-tee dee MA-rā*) With shellfish.

Funghi con (*kon FOON-gee*) With mushrooms and chopped onion.

Gamberi, risotto di (*ree-ZOT-tō dee gam-BĀ-ree*) With prawns.

Gambolo, alla (*al-la gam-bō-LŌ*) (Lombardy) With butter, oil, tomatoes, basil and parsley.

Genovese, alla (*al-la jen-ō-VĀ-zā*) Served with a meat sauce which has wine, herbs and vegetables in it.

Lumache, con le (*kən lā loo-MA-kā*) With snails featured in a highly flavoured sauce.

Magro, risotto di (*ree ZOT-tō dee MA-grō*) With anything but meat.

Marinara, alla (*al-la ma-ree-NA-ra*) (Veneto) With sea food.

Milanese, alla (*al-la mee-la-NĀ-zā*) Cooked in chicken broth, flavoured with saffron and served with butter and grated parmesan cheese. it has the creamy consistency of a rich nursery rice pudding.

Monzese, alla (*al-la Mōn-TSĀ-zā*) (Lombardy) With sausage meat, tomato and Marsala.

Novarese, alla (*al-la nō-va-RĀ-zā*) Barbera wine and grated parmesan are added to the *risotto* when it is nearly cooked.

Paesana, alla (*al-la pa-ā-ZA-na*) Thick soup of rice with beans, cabbage, salami, bacon.

Parmigiana, alla (*al-la par-mee-JA-na*) Cooked in beef broth with chickens' livers, sausage, mushrooms, herbs, bacon and vegetables.

Peoci e di cape, risotto di (*ree-ZŌT-tō dee pā ō-CHYĀ-dee ka-pā*) (Venice) With shellfish, butter and cheese.

Pescatora, alla (*al-la pās-ka-TO-ra*) With fish.

Pesce, con (*kol PESH-ā*) With fish.

Piemontese, alla (*al-la pyā-mōn-TĀ-zā*) With butter, grated cheese, and sprinkled – when in season – with white truffles.

Pilota, alla (*al-la pee-LŌ-ta*) Dressed with an onion and butter sauce.

Pitocca, alla (*al-la pee-TŌK-ka*) (Lombardy) With chicken.

Primavera *(pree-ma-VE-ra)* (Parma) Saffron-flavoured *risotto* garnished with chickens' livers, fresh peas, rosemary and sage.

Quaglie, con *(kol KWAL-yā)* With quails cooked in white wine.

Risi e bisi *(Ree-zee ā BEE-zee)* (Venice) With ham and peas.

Sbirraglia, alla *(al-la sbeer-RAL-ya)* A chicken and rice dish, with herbs, vegetables, sausage, an wine in the sauce.

Scampi, risotto di *(ree-ZOT-tō dee SKAM-pee)* (Venice) With scampi (Dublin Bay prawns), butter and cheese.

Secole, risotto di *(...dee SĀ-kōl-lā)* (Venice) With small pieces of beef or veal added.

Tartufi, con *(køn tar-TOO-fee)* With truffles.

Telline, con le *(køn la tāl-LEE-nā)* (Viareggio) With clams and a tomato sauce with peppers.

Toscana, alla *(al-la tōs-KA-na)* In this *risotto* the rice is cooked in broth to which several spoonfulls of tomato sauce have been added. Diced *salame* and grated parmesan are mixed in before serving.

Valdostana, alla *(al-la val-dōs-TA-na)* With grated parmesan to which fontina cheese is added to make the whole thing into a thick cream.

Veronese, alla *(al-la ve-rō-NĀ-zā)* A ham *risotto* served with a mushroom sauce.

Vongole, risotto di *(ree-ZOT-tō dee VON-gō-lā)* With clams.

Zucca, risotto di *(...dee ZOOK-ka)* With small pieces of pumpkin in it.

Spaghetti *(spa-GET-tee)* Long strings of *pasta*.

Stacchiodde *(stak-KYŌD-dā)* (Brindisi) *Pasta* 'ears'.

Suppli al telefono *(soop-PLEE al tā-LĀ-fō-nō)* Rice croquettes filled with *mozzarella* cheese and ham, rolled in breadcrumbs and fried.

Tagliatelle *(tal-ya-TEL-lā)* Ribbons of *pasta* made with egg.

Taglioline *(tal-yō-LEE-nā)* (Florence) Thin strips of *pasta*.

Timballo *(teem-BAL-lō)* A buttered pie-dish lined with breadcrumbs, filled with *pasta* and many different savoury mixtures such as mushrooms, ham, chickens' livers, sweetbreads, etc, usually with a sauce and cheese, and baked in the oven.

Abruzzese *(a-broot-TSĀ-zā)* Sheets of *pasta*, chickens' livers and lights, *scamorza* cheese, small veal rissoles.

Riso, timballo di *(teem-BAL-lō dee REE-zō)* A rice mould filled or garnished with different things in different parts of Italy.

Tortelli alla parmigiana *(tor-TEL-lee al-la par-mee-JA-na)* Square cushions of *pasta* filled with cottage cheese, spinach and grated parmesan; flavoured with nutmeg and served with butter and more grated parmesan.

Tortellini alla bolognese *(tor-tāl-LEE-nee al-la bō-lōn-YĀ-za)* Stuffed rings of *pasta* filled with a mixture of veal, chicken and grated cheese, cooked in chick broth and served with butter and grated cheese.

Tortellini alla modenese *(...al-la mō-dān-Ā-zā)* Stuffed with a mixture of meat, ham, cheese and egg.

Tortelloni *(tor-tāl-LŌ-nee)* Larger than *tortelli* (qv).

Vermicelli *(ver-mee-CHEL-lee)* Fine *spaghetti.* But see also p 131.

Vincisgrassi *(veen-cheez-GRA-see)* (Umbria and the Marches) Sheets of *pasta* made with egg, laid in a dish in alternating layers in a rich sauce, made of such things as chickens' livers, sweetbreads, sausage, onions, truffles and Marsala. It is then browned in the oven in a baking dish with plenty of grated cheese. *Vincisgrassi,* like *pincigrassi* (p 124), is a highly corrupted form of *Windischgraetz,* the Austrian prince prince whose cook invented the dish when his master was campaigning in the Marches during the Napoleonic wars.

Ziti *(ZEE-tee)* 'Bachelors' – large *macaroni.*

Zitoni *(zee-TŌ-nee)* 'Large bachelors' – very long macaroni.

SAUCES FOR *PASTE ASCIUTTE*

Acciughe, all' *(al-lat-CHOO-gā)* Sauce of anchovies flavoured with garlic, oil and parsley.

Acciughe fresche, all' *(al-lat-CHOO-gā FRES-kā)* With fresh anchovies. This will be found only on the west coast and Riviera, never on the Adriatic.

Aglio e olio *(AL-yō ā ŌL-yō)* With garlic, olive oil and parsley.

Aglio e olio con peperone *(kon pā-pā-RŌ-nā)* (Abruzzi) Warning: when eaten in Campania the *peperoni* of this dish often turn out to be finely chopped and very hot chilli – acceptable no doubt to those who like curry, but to be avoided if you want to be able to enjoy any wine with your meal.

Aglio e olio con saettine *(kon sa-āt-TEE-na)* Garlic, oil and 'little arrows' (ground hot peppers).

Alfredo, all' *(al-lal-FRÅ-dō)* A sauce very popular in Rome where it is served with *fettucine* (buttercream and freshly grated cheese). It was invented by a man called Alfredo, who had a famous Roman restaurant.

Amatricana, all' *(al-lam-a-tree-CHYA-na)* This sauce of fresh tomatoes, chopped bacon, onion and garlic originally came from the small town of Amatrice in Lazio and is served with grated *pecorino romano* cheese instead of parmesan. For some reason half the menus in Italy call it incorrectly *alla matriciana*.

Anitra, con *(kən A-nee-tra)* With a duck sauce.

Aromatici *(a-rō-MA-tee-chee)* See spaghetti aromatici (p. 169).

Arrabbiata, alla *(al-la ar-rab-BYA-ta)* With tomatoes and peperoncini (hot peppers).

Bolognese, alla *(al-la bō-lō-NÅ-zā)* A rich meat sauce, flavoured with chickens' livers, wine, vegetables and nutmeg, served with butter and grated cheese; sometimes cream is added to the sauce.

Buranella, alla *(al-la boo-ra-NEL-la)* (Venice) A fish or shellfish sauce from the lagoon island of Burano.

Burro, al *(al BOOR-rō)* With plenty of butter and grated parmesan cheese. This is often a great relief after all the richer sauces one finds oneself eating in Italy.

Buttera, alla *(al-la boot-TÅ-ra)* (Tuscany) Tomato sauce with chopped salt bacon and celery, basil, oil, garlic and onion, mushrooms and hot peppers.

Cacciatora, alla *(al-la kat-cha-TO-ra)* (Tuscany) A meat and vegetable sauce flavoured with juniper.

Cacio e pepe *(KA-chō ā PÅ-pā)* (Lazio) With grated goat's cheese and pepper.

Calabrese, alla *(al-la ka-la-BRÅ-zā)* Tomato sauce flavoured with ginger.

Campagna, alla *(al-la kam-PAN-ya)* A sauce of minced beef and cottage cheese.

Campagnola, alla *(al-la kam-pan-YŌ-la)* Tomato sauce with mushrooms, wine, anchovies, garlic, and flavoured with red pimentos.

Carbonara, alla *(al-la kar-bō-NA-ra)* Finely chopped bacon, and eggs scambled into the *pasta,* and grated cheese.

Carne, sugo di *(SOO-gō dee KAR-nā)* Meat sauce, with vegetables, mushrooms and white wine, served with butter and grated cheese.

Carrettiera, alla *(al-la kar-rāt-TYÅ-ra)* (Basilicata) With tunny-fish and mushrooms.

Casalinga, alla *(al-la ka-za-LEEN-ga)* 'Home-made' – a tomato sauce well flavoured, with possibly chopped bacon in it.

Chitarra, alla *(al-la kee-TAR-ra)* (Abruzzi) The *abruzzese* method of cutting *pasta* on a 'chitarra' or 'guitar' – a wooden frame strung with fine wires; the *pasta* is served with a meat sauce. The meat is always lamb.

Ciociara, alla *(al-la chō-CHA-ra)* (Lazio) A sauce of fat bacon, ham and saugage.

Crema, alla *(al-la KRA-ma)* With buttercream and cheese.

Doppio formaggio, al *(al DŌP-pyō for-MAD-jō)* With more cheese than usual,

Fegatini, con salsa di *(kon SAL-sa dee fā-ga-TEE-nee)* Chicken liver sauce.

Filetti di sogliola, ai *(î fee-LET-tee dee SŌL-yō-la)* A sauce made with fillets of sole, often served with flat noodles, and a speciality of some coastal restaurants.

Filetto, al *(al fee-LET-tō)* (Campania) With whole fresh tomatoes.

Formaggi, ai tre *(i trāy for-MAD jee)* With three different cheeses, usually *parmesan*, *gruyère* and *fontina*.

Forno, al *(al FOR-nō)* The *pasta* is first boiled, then baked in the oven with a sauce or cheese and butter.

Frutti di mare, ai *(i FROO-tee dee MA-rā)* With a sea-food sauce, but you will never find crab, lobster or crayfish served with *pasta*.

Funghi e piselli, con *(kon FOON-gee ā pee-SEL-lee)* With a sauce of mushrooms, bacon and fresh green peas.

Gamberetti, con *(kon gam-bā-RET-tee)* With large shrimps (or small prawns) in a tomato sauce.

Ghiotta, alla *(al-la GYŌT-ta)* With fresh peas and truffles.

Girati *(jee-RA-tee)* 'Stirred around' – *rigatoni girati*, for instance, are rigatoni stirred around in a pan of tomato sauce instead of being served with a dollop of sauce on top of them in the plate put before you.

Graneresi, alla *(al-la gra-nā-RA-zee)* A sauce of pounded walnuts, cream cheese and garlic.

Gratinata, pasta *(PAS-ta gra-tee-NA-ta)* This is what we know as macaroni cheese.

Imbottiti *(eem-bōt-TEE-tee)* (Naples) Stuffed *pasta*. *Lasagne imbottite* are sheets of *pasta* stuffed with things like pork, ham, sausage, hard-boiled eggs and grated cheese, baked in the oven.

Lenticchie, pasta e *(PAS-ta ā len-TEEK-kyā)* Lentils and *pasta* cooked together.

Lepre, con la *(kən la LĀ-prā)* (Tuscany) A hare sauce flavoured with garlic, wine and herbs. Always served with *pappardelle*.

Livornese, alla *(al-la lee-vɔr-NĀ-zā)* (Livorno – Leghorn) Tomato sauce with mushrooms and grated cheese, baked in the oven with slices of *mozzarella* cheese.

Lucania, all'uso di *(al OO-zō dee loo-KAN-ya)* With black and green olives, pounded anchovies and olive oil and garlic. *(Lucania* is another name for *Basilicata).*

Mantovana, alla *(al-la man-tō-VA-na)* (Lombardy) With a meat ragu, white wine, cream, pounded walnuts and butter.

Marchigiana, alla *(al-la mar-kee-JA-na)* (The Marches) The *pasta* is made of bread dough and served with a meat or tomato sauce.

Marinara, alla *(al-la ma-ree-NA-ra)* (Naples) A sauce of fresh tomatoes, olive oil, garlic and basil. One might expect a fish sauce from its name, but *alla marinara* only means 'in the sailor's manner', and on this occasion the sailor is obviously on a vegetarian diet.

Matriciana, alla *(al-la ma-tree-CHA-na)* See *all'amatriciana.*

Melanzane con *(kən mā-lan-DZA-nā)* With a meat, tomato and aubergine sauce.

Molica, con la *(kon la mol-LEE-ka)* (Sicily) With breadcrumbs and anchovies fried in oil.

Napoletana, alla *(al-la na-pō-lā-TA-na)* Tomato sauce flavoured with herbs.

Neri, maccheroni *(mak-kā-RŌ-nee NĀ-ree)* (Abruzzi) With garlic, oil and hot red peppers.

Noci, alle *(al-lā NŌ-chee)* (Umbria) A sauce of pounded walnuts and pinenuts, with oil, garlic and chopped parsley.

Norcina, alla *(al-la nor-CHEE-na)* (Perugia) Black truffles from Norcina, olive oil, garlic, chopped parsley and anchovies.

Novelli, alla *(al-la nō-VEL-lee)* Tomato sauce with anchovies and herbs.

Olio, aglio e saettine, al *(al ŌL-yō, AL-yō ā sa-āt-TEE-nā)* Another way of listing *aglio, olio e saettine* (qv).

Olio e acciughe *(OL-yō ā at-CHOO-gā)*   With a sauce of olive oil, pounded anchovies and garlic.

Olive, con *(kən ō-LEE-vā)*   With a sauce of chopped olives usually with tomato.

Ostrica, all' *(al-LŌS-tree-kā)*   Ostrica means oyster, but all hopes that this has anything to do with oysters are ill-founded. It is a mushroom sauce.

Paesana, alla *(al-la pa-ā-ZA-na)*   A sauce of mushrooms, chopped fat bacon, tomatoes, herbs and cheese.

Panna, alla *(al-la PAN-na)*   With hot cream.

Papalina, alla *(al-la pa-pa-LEE-na)*   Chopped ham, mushrooms, cheese and butter.

Pesto, col *(kol PES-tō)*   (Genoa) A sauce of oil, grated cheese, walnuts, pine-nuts, basil and garlic pounded up together.

Pizzaiola, alla *(al-la peet-tsa-YŌ-la)*   A hot tomato sauce, flavoured with peppers and herbs.

Polpettine, con *(kən pōl-pāt-TEE-nā)*   With meat balls and a tomato sauce.

Pomodoro, al *(al pō-mō-DOR-ō)*   Tomato sauce.

Prosciutto, col *(kol prō-SHOOT-tō)*   (Bologna) Chopped ham, cheese and butter.

Puttanesca, alla *(al-la poot-ta-NES-ka)*   A sauce with tomatoes, black olives, oil, hot peppers, garlic and chopped parsley. The origin of all *puttanesca* – 'in a whorish manner' – is a little obscure. Sir William Walton, who first introduced us to it many years ago, is convinced that there is no question of the name being derived from anything but the Italian word *puttana*, a whore. Sir William, who has lived most of his life in the Bay of Naples, claims that the fierce smell of garlic in the sauce is proof in itself of its *puttanesca* origin. See also *Paillard di vitello* (p.74).

Quattro formaggi, ai *(i KWAT-trō fər-MAD-jee)*   With four cheeses – *parmesan, gruyère, provolone dolce* and *fontina*.

Ragu, al *(al ra-GOO)*   This is the same as *alla bolognese*, but is used on the menus of those cities which, like Modena, for instance, do not see much point in giving gastronomic publicity to Bologna, with whom they are in direct gastronomic competition.

Ricotta, con la *(kon la ree-KŌT-ta)*   Served with *ricotta*, a very mild cottage cheese, mixed into the *pasta*, and grated *parmesan*.

Rognoni, con salsa di *(kon SAL-sa dee rōn-YŌ-nee)* With chopped kidneys, herbs and spices in a tomato sauce.

Romana, alla *(al-la rō-MA-na)* Meat and chicken sauce with chopped mushrooms.

Salamini, con *(kon sa-la-MEE-nee)* With a sauce of tomatoes and fresh sausage.

Sarde, con le *(kon la SAR-dā)* (Sicily) Sauce containing sardines, fennel, pine-nuts, spices and olive oil.

Seppia, al sugo nero di *(al SOO-gō NĀ-ro dee SĀP-pya)* A cuttlefish sauce. 'Nero' means black.

Siciliana, alla *(al-la see-cheel-YA-na)* Tomato, baby marrow, black olives, pimentos, capers, garlic, anchovies and basil.

Siracusana, alla *(al-la see-ra-koo-ZA-na)* (Sicily) A tomato, aubergine and pimento sauce, with capers, olives, anchovies, well flavoured with garlic and wild marjoram *(origano)*.

Spoletina, alla *(al-la spō-lā-TEE-na)* Truffles and anchovies added to a tomato sauce.

Spuma, alla *(al-la SPOO-ma)* Home-made *pasta* is used for this dish; it is stirred into a sauce of hot cream and chopped ham.

Strascinate (-i) *(stra-shee-NA-tā(ee))* 'Strascinare' means to drag or trail, so the *pasta* is dragged through the sauce which clings to it.

Sugo di mare, con *(kən SOO-gō dee MA-rā)* Sea-food sauce.

Taormina, alla *(al-la ta-or-MEE-na)* With bacon, black olives, pounded anchovies, garlic and mushrooms.

Tartufata, alla *(al-la tar-too-FA-ta)* A truffle sauce.

Tartufi neri, a *(ī tar-TOO-fee NĀ-ree)* (Umbria) With black truffles added to the sauce of oil and garlic.

Tonno, col *(kōl TŌN-nō)* Tunny-fish sauce with olives, capers, tomatoes and anchovies.

Toscana, alla *(al-la tōs-KA-na)* For *pappardelle:* a sauce of chickens' livers, chopped ham, tomatoes, mushrooms, oil and butter and red wine.

Trainiera, alla *(al-la tra-een-YER-a)* (Basilicate) A sauce with olives, capers, garlic and ginger in it.

Trasteverina, alla *(al-la tras-tā-vā-REE-na)* A tomato sauce with white wine, chopped bacon and chickens' livers.

Tricolore, al *(al tree-kō-LO-rā)* Of three colours – green (Spinach), red (tomato), white (normal *pasta*).

How would the Italian have managed if their flag had included blue instead of green?

Triestina, alla (*al-la tree-es-TEE-na*) A meat sauce with chopped ham, butter and cream.

Umbria, all'uso di (*al OO-zō dee OOM-brya*) A sauce of pounded anchovies, oil and garlic flavoured with tomatoes and truffles.

Veneziana, alla (*al-la vū-net-TSYA-na*) A tomato sauce.

Vongole, alle (*al-la VON-go-lā*) A clam sauce with onions, tomatoes, olive oil and garlic.

Zucchini, con salsa di (*kon SAL-sa dee zook-KEE-nee*) A sauce of baby marrow, garlic, onion, tomato, pimento and little hot peppers.

UOVA (EGGS AND EGG DISHES)

In Italy there seems to be no traditional position on the menu which is occupied by Eggs and Egg Dishes as there is in France. Sometimes you may find a section headed *'Uova'* (WŌ-va), but it is as likely to be included after the Meat as before the Fish – if, indeed, it is included at all. At other times you may be able to find an omelette *(frittata)* under the *Piatti del giorno*, but more likely under the *Piatti da farsi*.

We must warn the foreigner who, when in doubt in France and obviously not very hungry anyway, is inclined to order an omelette and a salad and enjoy every mouthful of it, that in Italy he will find nothing like the variety of Egg Dishes that are to be found in France. The *frittata* indeed bears very little relation to the omelette as the French know it.

We have watched a *frittata* being produced in our own kitchen and it was a fascinating experience. First our Italian house-guest beat up her eggs in a bowl; she then added a stack of cold cooked and sliced potato and poured the whole lot into a pan of hot olive oil. The mixture was fried until it was cooked through – not an egg dish, but a vegetable dish held together by egg; then she tipped it out on to a plate, turned it upside down and put it back in the pan to fry the other side until it was brown and solid.

Ways of Cooking Eggs

Frittata *(freet-TA-ta)* Omelette.

Uova affogate *(WŌ-va af-fō-GA-tā)* Poached eggs.

Uova affrittellate *(Af-freet-tāl-LA-tā)* Fried eggs.

Uova al burro *(al BOOR-rō)* Cooked in butter in the oven.

Uova in camicia *(een ka-MEE-cha)* Poached eggs.

Uova fritte *(FREET-tā)* Fried in olive oil.

Uova impazzite *(eem-pat-TSEE-tā)* Scrambled eggs.

Uova mollette *(mōl-LET-tā)* Soft-boiled eggs.

Uova in padelea *(een pa-DĀL-ya)* Fried eggs.

Uova sode *(SŌ-dā)* Hard-boiled eggs.

Uova stracciate *(strat-CHYA-tā)* Scrambled eggs.

Uova strapazzate *(stra-pat-TSA-tā)* Scrambled eggs.

Uova al tegame *(al tā-GA-mā)* Cooked in butter in the oven.

Egg Dishes

Affogate in pomodoro *(af-fō-GA-tā een pō-mō-DOR-ō)* Poached in tomato sauce.

Affogate con punte di asparagi *(...kon POON-tā dee as-PAR-a-jee)* Poached with asparagus tips.

Affogate col riso *(...kol REE-zō)* Poached eggs served with cheese and rice.

Cacciatora, alla *(al-la kat-cha-TOR-a)* Poached in a tomato sauce, with herbs, onions, and chopped chickens' livers.

Divorziate *(dee-vort-TSYA-ta)* Mashed potato, garnished with hard-boiled egg yolks, and a purée of carrots garnished with the whites.

Fiorentina, alla *(al-la fyōr-en-TEE-na)* Poached eggs on spinach with a cheese sauce.

Frittata *(freet-TA-ta)* Omelette
  Basilico, con *(kon ba-ZEF-lee-kō)* Flavoured with basil.
  Carciofi, con *(kon kar-CHO-fee)* With artichoke hearts.
  Cipollo, di *(dee chee-POL-lō)* Onion omelette.
  Formaggio, al *(al fōr-MAD-jō)* Cheese omelette.
  Funghi, di *(dee FOON-gee)* Mushroom omelette.
  Genovese *(jen-ō-VĀ-zā)* Spinach omelette.
  Maccheroni, con *(kon mak-kā-RO-nee)* With some sort of cooked pasta mixed in with the eggs.
  Melanzane e zucchini, con *(kon mā-lan-DZA-nā ā zoo-KEE-nee)* With aubergine and baby marrow.
  Patate, di *(dee pa-TA-tā)* Potato omelette.
  Peperoni, con *(kon pā-pā-RO-nee)* Pimento omelette.
  Rane, di *(dee RA-nā)* Frogs' legs omelette.
  Spinaci, di *(dee spee-NA-chee)* Spinach omelette.
  Tartufo, al *(al tar-TOO-fō)* (Piedmont) An omelette of finely grated truffles.
  Trentina, alla *(al-la tren-TEE-na)* A fluffy omelette filled with either a sweet or savoury mixture.

Fritte al bacon *(FREET-tā al BĀ-kon)* Fried eggs and bacon. Streaky bacon is known as *pancetta*.

Fritte alla piemontese *(FREET-tā al-la pyā-mõn-TÃ-zā)* Fried eggs on a bed of rice with grated cheese, tomatoes and sliced truffles.

Insalata di uova *(een-sa-LA-ta dee WÕ-va)* Egg salad.

Mollette con funghi e formaggio *(mol-LET-tā kon FOON-gee ā for-MAD-jõ)* Soft-boiled eggs served with grated cheese and mushrooms that have been cooked in butter.

Mollette con tartufi *(mõl-LET-tā kən tar-TOO-fee)* (Piedmont) Soft-boiled eggs covered in slices of truffles and grated cheese.

Nella neve *(NEL-la NÃ-vā)* 'In the snow' – eggs baked in the oven on a bed of mashed potatoes and *mozzarella* cheese.

Omelette *(o-me-LET)* A plain omelette as we know it.

Panna, alla *(al-la PAN-na)* (Milan) Hard-boiled eggs with a cream sauce flavoured with nutmeg and parsley.

Parmigiana, alla *(al-la par-mee-JA-na)* Eggs baked in little dishes with ham and grated cheese.

Piatto con acciughi, al *(al PYAT-tõ kən at-CHOO-gee)* Eggs cooked in little dishes with anchovy and cheese.

Piatto all'emiliana, al *(al PYAT-tõ al-lā-meel-YA-na)* Baked eggs with a sauce of chickens' livers, butter and Marsala.

Piemontese, alla *(al-la pyā-mõn-TÃ-zā)* Eggs cooked in a dish with *gruyère* cheese, cream and grated cheese.

Piemontese tartufate, alla *(al-la pyā-mõn-TÃ-zā tar-too-FA-tā)* Fried eggs with a sauce of white truffles, garlic and parsley and Marsala or white wine.

Piselli, con *(kon pee-ZEL-lee)* A dish of bacon and peas with an egg on top.

Prosciutto e mozzarella, con *(kən prõ-SHOOT-tõ ā mõt-tsa-REL-la)* Baked eggs on a bed of ham and *mozzarella* cheese.

Pure di patate, con *(kon poo-RÃ dee pa-TA-tā)* Eggs on mashed potatoes.

Rapprese ai cardi *(rap-PRÃ-zā ī KAR-dee)* (Piedmont) Cheese-flavoured eggs, well beaten, poured over fried cardoons and baked.

Ripiene *(ree-PYEN-ā)* Stuffed eggs.

Sode con salsa maionese *(SÕ-dā kon SAL-sa ma-yõ-NÃ-zā)* Hard-boiled eggs with mayonnaise.

Stracciate al formaggio *(strat-CHA-tā al for-MAD-jō)* Scrambled eggs with cheese.

Strapazzate con la salsiccia *(stra-pat-TSA-tā kon la sal-SEET-cha)* Scrambled eggs with sausage.

PESCE – FISH

The Italians will eat anything they can fish out of the sea; which means, since they fish in the Mediterranean, that the greater part of what they catch has absolutely no counterpart elsewhere. In the lakes and rivers we find recognizable varieties like salmon, trout, pike, perch, carp and the like; but where the sea is concerned it is hard to believe that there are any stranger fish left in it than ever came out of it on to an Italian table.

Whatever the natives may say, Mediterranean fish cannot compare with what is caught in tidal waters of the Atlantic and the English Channel; they are gaudy, sometimes revolting, often alarming to look at, and most of all (perhaps because they do not get the healthy exercise or the ocean vitamins that make turbot a real fish) they just don't taste of very much.

And, of course, there is the added problem of how to translate their names into English. In trying to do this we have consulted the largest Italian-English dictionary we know of (the Cambridge Italian Dictionary of 1962) only to find that nine out of the ten Italian fish we wanted to know about are described there as 'a species of sea bream'. There follows the formal zoological name for the fish in every case, but that is more help to the ichthycologist than to the hungry traveller in search of fish and chips.

The number of different names for the same fish is naturally endless, and the student of dialect can have the time of his life collecting local variants; there are many more than a dozen names for eels, for a start. There is also an astonishing number of ways the Italians cook fish, so we have listed a selection of them below as a preface to the catalogue of the fish themselves. In some restaurants you may be asked to choose from a selection of raw fish and say how you would like it cooked; *ai ferri* or *al forno* as below (according to girth) will see you through most eventualities.

Ways of Cooking Fish

Affogato *(af-fō-GA-tō)* Poached

Agliata, all' *(al-lal-YA-ta)* Served in garlic sauce.

Arrostito e freddo *(ar-rōs-TEE-to ā FRĀD-dō)* Roasted and served cold.

Arrosto *(ar-RŌS-tō)* Large fish are roasted whole on the spit, basted with oil.

Baby, alla *(al-la BĀ-hee)* See *trota* (p 66).

Bianco, in *(een BYAN-kō)* Boiled, dressed with oil and lemon.

Bollito *(bol-LEE-tō)* Boiled.

Carpione, in *(een kar-PYŌ-nā)* Dipped in flour, fried in oil with onions, then marinated in vinegar and served cold.

Cartoccio, in *(een kar-TŌT-chō)* Cooked in a paper case.

Ferri, ai *(î FER-ree)* Grilled.

Forno, al *(al FOR-nō)* Baked

Fritelle *(free-TEL-lā)* Fritters of fish.

Fritto *(FREET-tō)* Fried.

Fritto dorato *(...dō-RA-tō)* Fried in deep oil to a golden colour.

Fritto misto mare *(...MEES-tō MA-rā)* Mixed fry of sea food.

Gratella, in *(een gra-TEL-la)* Grilled.

Gratinato *(gra-tee-NA-tō)* Cooked in the oven with oil, lemon juice, garlic, chopped parsley and bread-crumbs.

Griglia, alla *(al-la GREEL-ya)* Grilled.

Insalata, in *(een een-sa-LA-ta)* Cold cooked fish in a salad.

Lessato *(lās-SA-tō)* Boiled, stewed, poached.

Livornese, alla *(al-la lee-vor-NĀ-zā)* With a thick aromatic tomato sauce.

Mantecato *(man-tā-KA-tō)* (Venice) A puree of salt cod *(baccalà)*.

Marinara, alla *(al-la ma-ree-NA-ra)* Marinated and cooked in wine, herbs and vegetables.

Marinato *(ma-ree-NA-tō)* Marinated. See *in carpione*.

Mugnaia, alla *(al-la moon-YĪ-ya)* Meunière – butter, lemon juice and parsley.

Napoletana, alla *(al-la na-pō-lā-TA-na)* Tomato

sauce, capers, black olives, hot peppers, oil and garlic.

Oreganato *(ō-RĀ-ga-NA-tō)* Cooked with wild marjoram, oil and butter.

Parmigiana, alla *(al-la par-mee-JA-na)* With grated *parmesan* cheese.

Pizzaiola, alla *(al-la peet-tsa-YŌ-la)* With a tomato sauce flavoured with wild marjoram *(origano)* and garden marjoram.

Polpettine di ... *(pōl-pāt-TEE-nā dee)* Little fish cakes of ...

Purgatorio, in *(een poor-ga-TOR-yō)* In a very hot, highly flavoured tomato sauce.

Ripieno *(ree-PYEN-ō)* Stuffed.

Salvia, alla *(al-la SAL-vya)* Cooked in butter and sage.

Saor, in *(een sa-OR)* (Veneto) Same as in *carpione*.

Scapece, in *(een ska-PĀ-chā)* (Liguria, Campania, Puglia) Same as in *carpione*.

Siciliana, alla *(al-la see-cheel-YA-na)* With tomatoes, garlic, oil, wine.

Spuma di ... *(SPOO-ma dee)* Mousse of ...

Trancie di ... *(TRAN-chā dee)* Slices of ...

Umido, in *(een OO-mee-dō)* Stewed with vegetables and herbs.

Vicentina, alla *(al-la vee-chen-TEE-na)* When this is *baccalà* (qv) it is stewed in milk with olive oil and butter and onion.

Fish

Acciughe *(at-CHOO-gā)* Anchovies.

Acquadelle *(ak-kwa-DEL-lā)* Small Adriatic fish.

Agoni *(a-GŌ-nee)* Freshwater shad found in the Lombardy lakes *(Alosa lacustris)*.

Aguglia *(a-GOOL-ya)* Garfish.

Alici *(a-LEE-chee)* Anchovies.

Alosa *(a-LŌ-sa)* Shad.

Anguilla *(an-GWEEL-la)* Eel.

Aragosta/Arigusta *(ar-a-GŌS--ta/a-ree-GOOS-ta)* Langouste; popularly used for Lobster.

Aringhe *(a-REEN-gā)* Herrings.

Arselle *(ar-SEL-lā)* Clams.

Astaci *(as-TA-chee)* River crayfish; pop for Lobster.

Baccalà *(bak-ka-LA)* Dried salt cod.

Bisato *(bee-SA-tō)* 'Little snake' – Italian for eel.

Boga *(pl boghe)* *(BŌ-ga; BŌ-gā)* Various species of sea bream. *Boga comune* is the ox-eye; zoological name: *Box boops.*

Boldrò *(bōl-DRŌ)* Angler fish.

Bonito *(bō-NEE-tō)* Small tunny. The English name is *bonito.*

Branzino *(bran-DZEE-nō)* Pike, perch. In some dialects, sea bass.

Buttariga *(boot-ta-REE-ga)* Dried roe, served as antipasto.

Cacciucco *(kat-CHOOK-kō)* See under Fish Stews, p. 67.

Calamaretti *(ka-la-ma-RET-tee)* Small inkfish.

Calamari *(ka-la-MA-ree)* Inkfish.

Canestrelli di mare *(kan-ās-TREL-lee dee MA-rā)* Small clams, scallops *(Chlamys operculris).*

Canocchie *(ka-NΘK-yā)* Kind of shrimps *(Squilla mantis).*

Cannocie *(kan-NOCH-ā)* Venetian for *canocchie.*

Cantarella *(kan-ta-REL-la)* A kind of sea bream.

Caparozzoli/capperozzoli *(ka-pa-ROT-tso-lee/kap-pā-ROT-tso-lee)* Shellfish, similar to sea truffles, *tartufi di mare* and the various *cappe.*

Cape de deo/cape tonde *(KA-pā dā DĀ-yō/KA-pā TOÑ-dā)* (Venice) See *Cappe.*

Capitone *(ka-pee-TŌ-nā)* Large eel.

Capone *(ka-PŌ-nā)* Sea hen; gurnard.

Cappe *(KAP-pā)* A variety of edible bivalve molluscs, the best known of which are the *tartufi di mare* (qv). Others are *cappa chione* (...KYŌ-nā), *cappa lunga* (...LOON-ga) (razor shell), *cappa gallina* (...ga-LEE-na), *cappa verrucosa* (...vā-roo-KŌ-za) (see *Venere*).

Cappon magro *(KAP-pōn MA-grō)* Genoese fish salad.

Cardi *(KAR-dee)* Cockles.

Carpione *(kar-PYŌ-nā)* Carp. Also a kind of large trout found only in Lake Garda.

Cavedano *(ka-vā-DA-nō)* Chub.

Cée *(Chee)* Elvers (Pisa) Usually cooked and eaten like fish-flavoured spaghetti, with butter and a dusting of parmesan.

Cechine *(chā-KEE-nā)* Eels.

Cecoline *(chā-kō-LEE-nā)* Little eels, eel-fry.

Cèfalo *(CHĀ-fa-lō)* Grey mullet.

Cernia *(CHERN-ya)* Perch.

Cicale di mare *(chee-KA-lā dee MA-rā)* 'Sea grasshoppers' – another name for *canochie* (qv).

Ciechine *(chā-KEE-nā)* Eels.

Ciriole *(cheer-YŌ-lā)* Little eels.

Coregone *(kō-rā-GŌ-nā)* A lake whitefish, like the Irish pollan.

Corvi *(KOR-vee)* 'Crows' – black umber *(Johnius umbra)*.

Cozze *(KOT-tsā)* (S Italy) Mussels.

Cozze pelose *(KOT-tsā pa-LŌ-zā)* Mussels with hairy shells.

Cozzolo *(KOT-tsō-lō)* Star-gazer. See *lucerna*.

Crostacei *(krōs-TA-chāy)* Shellfish.

Datteri di mare *(DAT-tā-ree dee MA-rā)* 'Sea dates' – see under *Antipasti*.

Dentice *(DEN-tee-chā)* There is no English equivalent of this excellent but expensive fish. The Latin name is *Dentex dentex*, and the nearest the dictionary can get to it is – naturally – 'a kind of sea bream'.

Dorata *(dō-RA-ta)* Gilt-head, daurade; yet another 'kind of sea bream'.

Fragoline di mare *(fra-gō-LEE-nā dee MA-rā)* 'Sea strawberries' – small inkfish. Also called *moscardini* *(mos-kar-DEE-nee)* and *polipetti* *(po-lee-PET-tee)*.

Folpi *(FŌL-pee)* Venetian dialect for *polipi octopus*.

Gallinella *(gal-lee-NEL-la)* Sea-hen *(capone)*.

Gamberetti *(gam-bā-RET-tee)* Little prawns.

Gamberi *(GAM-bā-ree)* Big prawns.

Gamberi di fiume *(...dee FYOO-mā)* Freshwater crayfish.

Gamberoni *(gam-bā-RŌ-nee)* Giant prawns.

Gianchetti *(jan-KET-tee)* Tiny white boneless fish for Antipasti.

Granceole/grancevole *(gran-CHĀ-o-lā/gran-CHĀ-vo-lā)* Large Adriatic crabs.

Granchio *(GRAN-kyō)* Crab.

Grongo *(GRON-gō)* Conger eel.

Lacerto *(la-CHER-tō)* A name for mackerel. But see also under Veal, p 73, just in case.

Lampre *(LAM-prā)* Lamprey.

Lasca *(LAS-ka)* (Perugia) Roach.

Leccia *(LET-cha)* A fish resembling mackerel, 'darkie Charlie'.

Lucerna *(loo-CHER-na)* Moon-gazer. Another name for *pesce prete*.

Luccio *(LOOT-chō)* Pike.

Lumache *(loo-MA-kā)* Snails.

Lumache di mare *(...dee MA-rā)* 'Sea snails' – shellfish.

Maccarello *(mak-ka-REL-lō)* Unlikely, but in fact correct, name for mackerel.

Mansanete *(man-za-NET-ā)* Female crabs eaten in Venice.

Marsioni *(mar-SYŌ-nee)* Small Adriatic fish.

Mazzacuogni/mazzancolle *(mat-tsa-KWŌN-yee/mat-tsan-KŌL-lā)* Very large prawns.

Merlango *(mār-LAN-gō)* Hake.

Merlano *(mār-LA-nō)* A form of small cod; the nearest the Italians can get to whiting.

Merluzzo *(mār-LOOT-tsō)* Cod, hake.

Mitili *(MEE-tee-lee)* Mussels.

Molecche *(mō-LEK-kā)* (Venice) Soft-shell crabs.

Morena *(mō-RĀ-na)* Lamprey.

Moscardini *(mōs-kar-DEE-nee)* Very small octopus.

Muggine *(MOOD-jee-nā)* Grey mullet.

Murena *(moo-RĀ-a)* Lamprey.

Muscoli *(MOOS-kō-lee)* Mussels.

Melù *(mā-LOO)* A fish referred to by Ada Boni in her *Talismano della felicità;* we have never eaten it, but she describes it as having a brown back, silver sides and belly, and she finds it good eating.

Nasello *(na-ZEL-lō)* Hake; some say it is also whiting.

Nocchie *(NOK-kyā)* See *canonchie.*

Noci di mare *(NŌ-chee dee MA-rā)* 'Sea walnuts' – shellfish.

Ombrina *(ōm-BREE-na)* Black umber. See also *corvi.*

Orata *(ō-RA-ta)* Gilt-head, daurade; like sea bream. See *dorata.*

Ostreghe *(OS-trā-gā)* Venetian for oysters.

Ostriche *(ŌS-tree-kā)* Oysters.

Pagello *(pa-JEL-lō)* Various species of sea bream.

Palamita *(pa-la-MEE-ta)* Small tunny *(large mackerel);* bonito.

Palombo *(pa-LŌM-bō)* Species of dog fish.

Pannochia *(pan-NŌK-ya)* See *canochie.*

Peoci *(pā-YŌ-chee)* Venetian for mussels.

Pescatrice *(pās-ka-TREE-chā)* Frog fish. See also *rana pescatrice.*

Pesce passera *(PESH-ā PAS-sā-ra)* Flounder.

Pesce persico *(PER-see-kō)* Perch.

Pesce prete *(PRE-tā)* See *lucerna.*

Pesce San Pietro *(san PYĀ-trō)* John Dory.

Pesce spada *(SPA-da)* Swordfish.

Pesciolini *(pesh-yō-LEE-nee)* A substitute for whitebait.

Pidocchi *(pee-DŌK-kee)* 'Lice' – slang for mussels in the Marches *(see footnote on p 7).*

Polipetto/Polipo/Polpo/Poveracci *(pō-lee-PET-tō/PŌ-lee-pō/ POL-po/po-va-RAT-chee)* Inkfish.

Rana pescatrice *(RA-na pās-ka-TREE-chā)* Frog fish.

Rane *(RA-nā)* Frogs.

Razza *(RAT-tsa)* Skate.

Regina *(ra-JEE-na)* (Perugia) A large carp – about 20-30 lbs.

Reina *(rā-EE-na)* Bream.

Ricci *(REET-chee)* Sea-urchins.

Rombo liscio *(RŌM-bō LEESH-ō)* Brill.

Rombo maggiore/grande *(RŌM-bō mad-JOR-ā/GRAN-da)* Turbot.

Rosetto *(rō-ZET-tō)* Red sea bream.

Rospo *(RŌS-pō)* Angler fish. *'Rospo'* means toad, and *coda di rospo* is a familiar fish dish in Venice, where it was translated by one restaurant as 'toad's fish tail'.

Salmone *(sal-MŌ-nā)* Salmon.

Sampietro *(sam-PYĀ-trō)* John Dory.

Sarago *(sa-RA-gō)* (Naples) Like *orata* (qv).

Sarde *(SAR-dā)* Pilchards.

Sardelle *(sar-DEL-lā)* Sardines.

Sardelline *(sar-dāl-LEE-nā)* Young sardines.

Sargo *(SAR-gō)* (Naples) See *orata* above.

Scampi *(SKAM-pee)* Dublin Bay prawns – now known almost universally as 'scampi'.

Scaveccio *(ska-VET-chō)* Eel (Tuscany).

Scorfano *(skor-FA-nō)* Sea scorpion, used for fish stews. *'Scorfano'* is slang for an ugly person. If you've ever seen the fish you'll understand why.

Seppie *(SEP-pyā)* Inkfish, squids.

Sfirena *(sfee-RĀ-na)* Sea pike.

Sfogie *(SFŌ-ja)* (Venice) Sole.

Sgombro/Scombro *(ZGOM-brō/SKOM-BRŌ)* Mackerel.

Signorini *(seen-yō-REE-nee)* 'Little gentlemen' – small fry.

Sogliola *(SŌL-yō-la)* Sole.

Spannocchi *(span-NŌK-kee)* Large prawns.

Sparo *(SPA-rō)* Another Neapolitan version of *orata*.

Spigola *(SPEE-gō-la)* Sea bass.

Spinola *(spee-NŌ-la)* Dialect name for *spigola* – sea bass. See also *branzino*.

Squadro *(SKWA-drō)* Monk-fish.

65

Stoccafisso *(stōk-ka-FEES-sō)* Baccalà (qv). Stockfish. (Corruption of the German *Stockfisch*.)

Storione *(stor-YŌ-nā)* Sturgeon.

Tartufo di mare *(tar-TOO-fō dee MA-rā)* The *Venus verrucosa*, sea-truffle, Venus shell, which is best known to us as a cockle.

Telline *(tāl-LEE-nā)* The Tuscan name for cockles.

Temoli (pl) *(TĀ-mo-lee)* Grayling.

Tinca *(TEEN-ka)* Tench.

Tonnetto *(tōn-NET-tō)* Little tunny.

Tonno *(TŌN-nō)* Tunny.

Totani *(TO-ta-nee)* Squids.

Trachino dragone/tracina *(tra-KEE-nō dra-GŌ-nā/tra-CHEE-na)* The very picturesque weever fish. Beware of the dorsal spines; they are sharp and poisonous.

Triglie *(TREEL-yā)* Red mullet.

Trota *(TRŌ-ta)* Trout.
    Baby, alla *(al-la BA-bee)* Split open and sautéed in oil, flavoured with bayleaf and onion.

Trota salmonata *(TRŌ-ta sal-mō-NA-ta)* Salmon trout.

Venere *(VĀ-nā-rā)* Cockles – *tartufi di mare, Venus verrucosa*.

Ventresca di tonno *(vān-TRES-ka dee TŌN-nō)* Stomach of tunny, and the best part of the fish.

Vongole *(VON-gō-lā)* Clams.

Fish Stews

These cannot be called soups, in spite of their description on the menus as *Zuppa di* this, that or the other sort of fish. They are much too substantial and to the foreign and uninitiated palate they taste very much alike, although our Italian friends assure us that every seaside town produces a *zuppa* that is 'quite different' from the one cooked five miles up or down the coast.

Brodetto *(brō-DET-tō)* A stew in which many different kinds of fish are used, with oil, garlic, tomato, onion, chopped parsley and wine vinegar.

Broeto di pesce *(brō-E-tō dee PESH-ā)* The Venetian name for a *brodetto*.

Burridà *(boo-ree-DA)* A Genoese fish soup, first cousin to the *bourride* of Provence.

Burridà *(boo-ree-DA)* (Sardinia) The same sort of thing, but served cold.

Cacciucco *(kat-CHOOK-kō)* (Livorno) Tuscan speciality; fish soup with red wiñe and spices.

Cassola *(kas-SŌ-la)* (Sardinia) Fish stew.

Zimino *(DZEE-mee-nō)* Genoese fish stew.

Ziminu *(dzee-mee-NOO)* Sardinian fish stew.

Zuppa di cozze *(TSOO-pa dee KOT-tsā)* A mussel stew.

Zuppa alla marinara *(...al-la ma-ree-NA-ra)* A fish stew.

Zuppa di pesce *(...dee PESH-ā)* Nearly always more a stew of fish than a soup.

Zuppa di vongole *(...dee VON-gō-lā)* Clam stew.

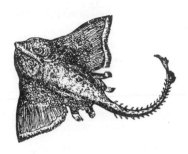

CARNE – MEAT

The Italians are great people for synonyms. To them the natives of Naples are not only Neopolitans; they are 'the devotees of San Gennaro', and 'the citizens of the Parthenopean capital'. So naturally when it comes to ways of cooking meat we find at least three different words that mean grilled, and none of them is dialect.

In the list we have made below of the ways meat is cooked and cut in Italy, we have included as many of these synonyms as we have encountered, though without being able to guarantee that the first meal you have in an Italian restaurant ·will not confront you with yet another series of synonyms which we haven't included.

Arrosto *(ar-RŌS-tō)*   Roast

Asce' *(a-SHĀ)*   Typewritten phonetic transcription of *haché* ·· minced.

Bollito *(bōl-LEE-to)*   Boiled (see *Bolliti* p 82).

Braciolette *(bra-chō-LET-tā)*   Chops.

Bracioline *(bra-chō-LEE-nā)*   Cutlets.

Braciuola *(bra-choo-WŌ-la)*   Chop.

Brasato *(bra-SA-tō)*   Braised.

Costata *(kō-STA-ta)*   Cutlet, chop, *entrecôte*.

Costolette *(kōs-tō-LET-tā)*   Cutlets.

Dorato *(dō-RA-tō)*   Dipped in flour and egg, fried golden.

Ferri, ai *(î FER-ree)*   Cooked on an iron griddle.

Fetta, una *(oo-na FET-ta)*   A slice.

Filetto *(fee-LET-tō)*   Fillet.

Forno, al *(al FOR-nō)*   Baked or roasted in the oven.

Fritto misto *(FREE-tō MEES-tō)*   A mixed fry (see p. 82).

Gratella, alla *(al-la gra-TEL-la)*   Grilled.

Graticola, alla *(al-la gra-TEE-kō-la)*   Grilled over charcoal (or should be).

Griglia, alla *(al-la GREEL-ya)*   Grilled.

Interiora *(een-tār-YOR-a)*   Offal.

Involtino *(een-vōl-tee-nō)*   Roulade.

Lesso *(LES-sō)*   Boiled.

Medaglioni *(mā-dal-YŌ-nee)*   Small round pieces of meat.

Misto di arrosti *(MEES-tō dee ar-RŌS-tee)* Mixed selection of roast meats.

Mix grillée *(meeks GREEL-lā)* Mixed grill – we think.

Spiedini *(spyā-DEE-nee)* Small pieces of meat, etc, cooked on a skewer.

Spiedo, allo *(al-lō SPYĀ-dō)* On the spit.

Soutte' *(soot-TĀ)* Typewritten phonetic transcription of sauté.

Turnedo' *(toor-nā-DO)* Typewritten phonetic transcription of tournedos. Small rounds of fillet steak.

Uccelli scappati *(oot-CHEL-lee skap-PA-tee)* See p. 79.

Bue, Manzo – Beef

To make sure your steak is:

'Blue' Ask for it *blu* *(bloo)* or *quasi cruda* *(KWA-zee KROO-du)*.

Rare Ask for it *al sangue* *(al SAN-gwā)*.

Medium Ask for it *cotta a puntino* *(KŌT-ta a poon-TEE-nō)*.

Well done Ask for it *ben cotta* *(ben KŌT-ta)*.

Arrosto *(ar-RŌS-tō)* This is nearly always down on the menu as *Roast-beef* or *Rosbif all'inglese*, and when eaten in the *autostrada* restaurants proves to be surprisingly tender and expertly cooked.

    Livornese, alla *(al-la lee-vor-NĀ-zā)* First marinated in wine with garlic, roasted with onions and basted with the marinade.

Asticciole alla calabrese *(as-teet-CHŌ-la al-la ka-la-BRĀ-zā)* Rolls of beef, mozzarella cheese and sausage, squares of bread and bayleaves alternating on a skewer, dipped in oil and grilled.

Bistecca *(bees-TEK-ka)* A large rib steak cut from a young animal, grilled over a charcoal fire.

Cacciatora, alla *(al-la kat-cha-TO-ra)* (Florence) With a wine and tomato sauce, flavoured with fennel, garlic and parsley.

Fiorentina, alla *(al-la fyor-en-TEE-na)* This is the pride of Tuscany. It is served 'straight' with half a lemon. It is often sold by weight in restaurants – so much an *etto*, or 100 grammes (3.527 ozs). It is expensive, but well worth the money when you are in or near Florence.

Pizzaiola, alla *(al-la peet-tsa-YŌ-la)* Campania) A thick tomato sauce (see p 00) is spread over your meat, which will probably be fairly tough.

Bistecchini asce' alla griglia *(bees-tāk-KEE-nee a-SHĀ al-la GREEL-ya)* Hamburgers.

Bocconcini asce' alla casalinga *(bōk-kŏn-CHEE-nee a-SHĀ al-la ka-za-LEEN-ga)* Small hamburgers (we presume) cooked by mamma.

Braciolette ripiene *(bra-chŏ-LET-tā ree-PYEN-ā)* Small rolls of beef and ham stuffed and cooked in butter and a little wine.

Brasato con lenticchie *(bra-SA-tō kon len-TEEK-kȳa)* Braised beef with lentils.

Carbonata *(kar-bŏ-NA-ta)* Slices of beef cooked in a casserole with herbs, onions, etc.

Carpaccio *(car-PAT-chō)* See *antipasti* (p 25).

Coda di bue *(KŌ-da dee BOO-wā)* Oxtail.

Coda di bue alla vaccinara *(… al-la vat-chee-NA-ra)* (Lazio) Braised oxtail with celery and tomato.

Costa di bue al barolo *(KŌS-ta dee BOO al ba-RŌ-lō)* (Piedmont) Sirloin of beef, braised with vegetables in Barolo wine.

Costata alla fiorentina *(kōs-TA-ta al-la fyor-en-TEE-na)* See *bistecca alla fiorentina*.

Cuore di bue *(KWO-rā dee BOO-wā)* Heart.

Farsumagru *(far-soo-MA-groo)* Although this dish is said to be Sicilian we ate it in a private house at Positano, cooked by a girl born and brought up there. It consists of breast of beef (or veal) stuffed with hard-boiled eggs, sausage, grated cheese and spices, rolled and stewed slowly in a tomato sauce.

Fegato *(FĀ-ga-tō)* Liver.

Garmugia alla lucchese *(gar-MOO-ja al-la look-KĀ-zā)* Braised beef with artichokes, peas, herbs, onions and garlic.

Garofolato *(ga-rō-fō-LA-tō)* (Rome) A stew flavoured with cloves, cooked with red wine and vegetables. The name is Roman dialect for *garofanato* – flavoured with cloves.

Granatina (*gra-na-TEE-na*)   Minced beef and bread shaped like a cutlet, egg-and-breadcrumbed and fried.

Lingua di bue (*LEEN-gwa dee BOO-wā*)   Tongue.

Lingua in agrodolce (*LEEN-gwa een ag-ro-DÓL-chā*)   Tongue in a sweet-sour sauce.

Muscolo alla fiorentina (*MOOS-cō-lō al-la fyor-en-TEE-na*)   A casserole of shin of beef, wine, vegetables and herbs, served with white beans.

Polpette (*pōl-PET-tā*)   Rissoles.

Polpettone (*pōl-pāt-TŌ-nā*)   A meat loaf. Diabetics must be warned that this dish, and *polpette* have a lot of breadcrumbs in them.

Rognone di bue (*rŏn-YŌ-na dee BOO-wā*)   Ox-kidney.

Rolè (*rō-LĀ*)   (Parma)   A beef roll filled with Parma ham and hard-boiled eggs, cooked slowly in white wine, butter and flavoured with a sage leaf.

Spezzato di muscolo (*spāt-TSA-tō dee MOOS-kō-lō*)   See muscolo alla fiorentina.

Stracotto (*stra-KŌT-tō*)   A beef stew with white or red wine, vegetables and herbs.

Stufato di manzo (*stoo-FA-tō dee MAN-dzō*)   A beef stew with white or red wine, vegetables and herbs.

Stufato alla romana (*stoo-FA-tō al-la rō-MA-na*)   Beef stew with red wine and tomatoes.

Trippa di bue (*TREEP-pa dee BOO-wā*)   For ways you will find tripe cooked, see *Trippa* in the veal section (p. 77).

Veal – Vitello

On the grounds that it is more urgent to know about veal when you're buying it, than when it has already been cooked and put on your plate in a restaurant, we have discussed the various qualities of veal encountered in Italy on page 177 of the SHOPPING GUIDE. We think some of the information will be useful to the eater-out.

Animelle di vitello alla ciociara (*a-nee-MEL-lā dee vee-TEL-lo al-la chō-CHA-ra*)   Sweetbreads in a white wine sauce with mushrooms and chopped ham.

Arrosto di vitello al forno (*ar-RŌS-tō dee vee-TEL-lō al FOR-no*)   Veal roast in the oven.

Arrosto di vitello ubriacato *(ar-RŌS-tō dee vee-TEL-lō oo-brya-KA-to)* Literally 'drunken veal' – a pot roast of veal with white wine, herbs and vegetables.

Assisiana, vitello all' *(vee-TEL-lō al-las-seez-YA-nā)* Larded with ham and cooked with vegetables, herbs, white wine and milk.

Bocconcini *(bōk-kōn-CHEE-nee)* Little mouthfuls of veal stewed in wine, or stuffed with ham and cheese cooked in butter or a sauce.

Braciolette ripiene *(bra-chō-LET-tā ree-PYEN-ā)* Small rolls of veal and ham stuffed.

Busecca *(boo-SEK-ka)* (Milan) A tripe stew with white beans, onions, carrots, celery and tomato, flavoured with nutmeg, sage and served with grated cheese.

Busecca alla panna *(... al-la PAN-na)* (Lombardy) Tripe and vegetables in cream sauce.

Cervello di vitello dorato *(cher-VEL-la dee vee-TEL-lo dō-RA-tō)* Brains dipped in egg and flour and fried.

Cima di vitello *(CHEE-ma dee vee-TEL-lō)* (Genoa) Breast of veal, stuffed, poached and served cold.

Costoletta *(kōs-tō-LET-ta)* Cutlet, escalope.
  Bolognese, alla *(al-la bō-lōn-YĀ-zā)* An escalope dipped in egg and breadcrumbs and fried in butter, served with ham and cheese.
  Castellana, alla *(al-la kas-tāl-LA-na)* Between two slices or cutlets of veal, a slice of ham and gruyère cheese and some white truffles. The whole thing is egg-and-breadcrumbed and fried in butter.
  Duchessa, alla *(al-la doo-KĀS-sa)* (Parma) The same as *alla castellana* but, patriotically grated *parmesan* is used instead of gruyère.
  Milanese, alla *(al-la mee-la-NĀ-zā)* Veal cutlet coated with egg and breadcrumbs and fried in butter. It is NOT served with *spaghetti* as a garnish; that is a *la milanaise*, a French invention.
  Modenese, alla *(al-la mō-dā-NĀ-zā)* The same as milanese, but with a tomato sauce.
  Valdostana, alla *(al-la val-dōs-TA-na)* A veal cutlet which, when you eat it, you find has a pocket filled with *fontina* cheese and white truffles.

Cuore di vitello bergamasca *(KWO-rā dee vee-TEL-lō ber-ga-MAS-ka)* Heart, chopped, fried in butter with basil, garlic and parsley.

Fegato di vitello *(FĀ-ga-tō dee vee-TEL-lō)* Calves' liver.
  Dorato *(do-RA-tō)* Dipped in batter and fried.
  Fiorentina, alla *(al-la fyor-en-TEE-na)* With a toma-

to sauce flavoured with sage.

Marsala, al *(al mar-SA-la)* Cooked in butter and Marsala.

Milanese, alla *(al-la mee-la-NĀ-zā)* Egg-and-bread-crumbed and fried.

Toscana, alla *(al-la tōs-KA-na)* Fried in oil with sage.

Veneziana, alla *(al-la vā-net-TSYA-na)* Sliced finely and fried slowly in oil and butter with onions.

Fesa primaverile *(FĀ-za pree-ma-vā-REE-lā)* (Parma) Leg of veal larded with ham, carrot, celery and bacon.

Focaccia di vitello *(fō-KAT-cha dee vee-TEL-lō)* Rissoles.

Foiolo in umido *(fō-YŌ-lō een OO-mee-dō)* (Milan) Tripe with garlic, onions, mushrooms, tomatoes and white wine.

Fricassea *(free-ku-SĀ-ya)* (Tuscany) A white veal stew with mushrooms; the sauce is thickened with egg yolks.

Garretto di vitello stufato *(gar-RET-tō dee vee-TEL-lō stoo-FA-tō)* Stewed hock of veal, vegetables and herbs.

Genovese, alla *(al-la jen-ō-VĀ-zā)* Slices of veal cooked in butter and white wine with artichoke hearts.

Involtini *(een-vōl-TEE-nee)* A thin slice of veal, another of ham, and a sage leaf, rolled and cooked in butter or oil on a skewer.

Laccett in agrodolce *(lat-CHET een a-grō-DŌL-chā)* (Lombardy) Sweetbreads in a sweet-sour sauce.

Lacerto al forno *(la-CHER-tō al FOR-nō)* This is something we have eaten only in Sicily. It was veal and in the shape of a roll and had an air about it of being preserved meat of some kind. But see Marro, p. 151.

Lingua in salsa verde *(LEEN-gwa een SAL-sa VER-dā)* Boiled tongue served with a green sauce (see p. 108).

Magro alla mormora *(MA-grō al-la mor-MOR-a)* Escalope cooked in butter with chopped parsley and lemon; simple and good. The name is misleading, for *mormora* is a fish, and, almost inevitably 'a kind of sea bream'.

Messicani *(mās-see-KA-nee)* 'Mexicans' – but in fact very much the same thing as *involtini*.

Nodini di vitello alla milanese *(nō-DEE-nee dee vee-TEL-lō al-la mee-la-NA-zā)* A loin chop dipped in flour and fried in butter with white wine and sage.

Olivette di vitello *(ō-lee-VET-tā dee vee-TEL-lō)* (Pesaro) Little rolls of veal filled with pounded anchovies and capers and fried.

Osso buco alla milanese *(ŌS-sō BOO-kō al-la mee-la-NA-zā)* Two-inch lengths of the shin bone of veal with the meat still on it and the marrow content intact, stewed with white wine and tomato, and served with risotto alla milanese (see p 45).

Pagliata di vitello *(pal-YA-ta dee vee-TEL-lō)* Intestines of veal.

Paillard di vitello *(PĪ-yar dee vee-TEL-lō)* Minute veal steak. This one took an immense amount of sorting out. All that any Italians could tell us was that *paillard* was not Italian. We knew that; but knowing the French word was not very helpful either, for it was scarcely one which was encountered in the kitchen or, come to that, in any polite society.

Paillard as an adjective means wanton, lewd; as a noun, a rake and frequenter of brothels. This last meaning raised our hopes for a moment; perhaps it had some connection with *spaghetti alla puttanesca* (see p.51). It hadn't.

It was not until we read a book by Vernon Jarratt, our fellow-contributor to *Wheeler's Review* and the owner of George's in Rome, that we discovered that *paillard* was a cut of veal named after M Paillard, a Frenchman who invented what was originally a very thin beef steak. In Italy it is always veal.

Perla, vitello alla *(vee-TEL-lō al-la PER-la)* (Emilia-Romagna) Braised veal with diced ham, flavoured with spices and herbs and onions.

Petto di vitello ripieno *(PET-tō dee vee-TEL-lō ree-PYEN-ō)* Stuffed breast of veal.

Piccata al marsala (peek-KA-ta al mar-SA-la) Thin slice of veal cooked in butter and Marsala.

Piccatina partenopea *(peek-ka-TEE-na par-tā-no-PĀ-ya)* *Escalopes* of veal with *mozzarella* cheese.

Polmone di vitello *(pōl-MŌ-nā dee vee-TEL-lo)* Calves' lung.

Polpette *(pōl-PET-tā)* Rissoles.

Polpettone *(pōl-pāt-TŌ-nē)* Minced veal roll stuffed with hard-boiled eggs, ham and cheese. See under Beef (p.71).

Punta di vitello alla genovese *(POON-ta dee vee-TEL-lō al-la jen-o-VĀ-zā)* Virtually the same thing as *cima di vitello*, but roast.

Quagliette di vitello *(kwal-YET-tā dee vee-TEL-lō)* Little rolls of veal and ham on skewers alternating with onion, sage leaves and bread, served with rice. Literally 'little quails' of veal. What is the recurrent association in Italy of veal on skewers with birds? There must be some deep psychological significance. See *uccelli scappati* below, and *Tordi matti* (p 98).

Rognoncini di vitello trifolati *(rōn-yōn-CHEE-nee dee vee-TEL-lo tree-fo-LA-tee)* Finely sliced kidneys.

Rognoni trifolati *(rōn-YŌ-nee tree-fō-LA-tee)* Calves' kidneys sliced and cooked in butter with lemon juice and chopped parsley.

Rognoni di vitello *(rōn-YŌ-nee dee vee-TEL-lō)* Calves' kidneys.

Rognoni di vitello al marsala *(... al mar-SA-la)* Sautée'd in butter with Marsala.

Rognoni di vitello alla panna *(... al-la PAN-na)* Sautée'd in butter with onions or mushrooms and cream and a little brandy.

Rolè di vitello *(rō-LÀ dee vee-TEL-lō)* A veal roll stuffed with a mixture of eggs, mortadella sausage and grated chese.

Rollatini di vitello *(rōl-la-TEE-nee dee vee-TEL-lō)* Little stuffed veal rolls.

Romagna, vitello all'uso di *(vee-TEl-lō al-LOO-zō dee rō-MAN-ya)* (Emilia-Romagna) Roast veal flavoured with rosemary and garlic and tomato, served with peas.

Saltimbocca alla romana *(sal-teem-BŌK-ka al-la rō-MA-na)* Little rolls of veal, ham and sage leaves cooked in butter and Marsala. The dish, 'jump-in-the-mouth', originally came from Brescia, but is now considered typically Roman.

Sanato *(sa-NA-tō)* Veal from a very young animal.

Scaloppa farcita *(ska-LŌP-pa far-CHEE-ta)* A veal 'sandwich' filled with ham, cheese and truffles.

Scaloppa alla milanese *(... al-la mee-la-NĀ-zā)* Escalope of veal coated in egg and breadcrumbs and fried in butter.

Scaloppine alla bolognese *(ska-lō-PEEN-nā al-la bō-lōn-YĀ-zā)* Finely chopped veal and ham, potato and grated cheese.

Scaloppine di vitello *(ska-lō-PEEN-nā dee vee-TEL-lō)* Small thin slices of veal.

  Buongustaia, alla *(al-la bwōn-goos-TA-ya)* With a tomato sauce flavoured with sage and chickens' livers.

  Cacciatora, alla *(al-la kat-cha-TO-ra)* Thin slices of veal cooked in butter with a sauce of tomato, onion, mushrooms, herbs and red wine.

  Limone, al *(al lee-MŌ-nā)* A thin slice of veal cooked in butter and a squeeze of lemon juice.

  Perugina, alla *(al-la pā-roo-JEE-na)* Small slices of veal cooked in butter and served with chopped chickens' livers.

  Tartufi alla modenese, coi *(koy tar-TOO-fee al-la mo-da-NA-zā)* Veal cutlets egg-and-breadcrumbed, cooked with grated cheese and truffles.

Sformato di vitello e zucchini *(sfor-MA-tō dee vee-TEL-lō-ā zook-KEE-nee)* Thin slices of veal and baby marrow baked with cheese and butter.

Spezzatino di vitello *(spāt-tsa-TEE-nō dee vee-TEL-lō)*
  Napoletana, alla *(al-la na-pō-lā-TA-na)* Small pieces of veal *sautéed* in oil with pimentos, mushrooms and tomatoes.

  Romana, alla *(al-la rō-MA-na)* Small pieces of veal sautée'd in oil with beaten egg and lemon juice.

  Toscana, alla *(al-la tōs-KA-na)* Pieces of veal stewed in a tomato sauce with black olives and onion sauce.

Spiedini alla milanese, gli *(lyee spyā-DEE-nee al-la mee-la-NA-za)* Veal, chipolata sausages, sage and bacon cooked on skewers and served with rice or *polenta*.

Spuma di fegato *(SPOO-ma dee FĀ-ga-tō)* Mousse of calves' liver, flavoured with bayleaf and Marsala.

Stecchini alla petroniana *(stak-KEE-nee al-la pā-trōn-YA-na)* Squares of veal, bread, *mortadella* sausage and gruyère cheese on a skewer, egg-and-breadcrumbed and fried.

Stracotto di vitello *(stra-KŌT-tō dee vee-TEL-lō)* (Florence) A veal stew (see p. 177 in SHOPPING GUIDE for more about *vitello*).

Stufatino *(stoo-fa-TEE-nō)* (Florence) A veal stew with white wine.

Tenerumi di vitello alla paesana *(tā-nā-ROO-mee dee vee-TEL-lo al-la pa-ā-ZA-na)* (The Marches) Breast of veal braised with vegetables and served with peas and carrots.

Testa/testina di vitello (TES-ta/tās-TEE-na dee vee-TEL-lō) Calves' head.

Trippa *(TREE-pa)* Tripe. If you like tripe, the Italian ways of cooking it are all worth tasting. Although nothing like English tripe and onions, they are very good indeed.

    Bolognese, dorata alla *(dō-RA-ta al-la bō-lōn-YĀ-zā)* Cooked in oil with onion, garlic and parsley, and served coated with lightly cooked egg yolks and grated cheese.

    Fiorentina, alla *(al-la fyor-en-TEE-na)* Cooked in a meat and tomato sauce, flavoured with marjoram and served with grated cheese.

    Genovese, alla *(al-la jen-ō-VĀ-zā)* With onion, herbs, garlic and white wine and tomato.

    Lucchese, alla *(al-la look-KĀ-zā)* With onion, butter, cheese and cinnamon.

    Marchigiana, alla *(al-la mar-kee-JA-na)* With herbs, vegetables and bacon.

    Ostriche, con *(kon OS-tree-kā)* An unexpected combination which seems to us the best of the lot – tripe and oysters in a white wine sauce.

    Parmigiana, alla *(al-la par-mee-JA-na)* Cooked with herbs and vegetables and a tomato sauce, served with plenty of parmesan cheese.

    Romana, alla *(al-la rō-MA-na)* In a tomato sauce flavoured with mint; served with grated *pecorino* cheese.

    Senese, alla *(al-la sā-NĀ-zā)* With a local sausage and flavoured with saffron.

Uccelli scappati *(oot-CHEL-lee skap-PA-tee)* This is one of those 'joke' dishes. Like toad-in-the-hole, which offers neither toad nor hole, the 'escaped birds' of *uccelli scappati* have nothing to do with birds at all, but are pieces of veal, sometimes calves' liver, bacon and sage leaves alternating on a skewer and fried.

At a pinch the joke might be that as *uccelli* are often cooked on a skewer the fact that there aren't any on this one must mean that they are *scappati*. That they are *uccelli* and not any of the dozens of different fish that are cooked on skewers, is obviously due to the veal-bird obsession we mentioned on p. 75.

Vitello tonnato *(vee-TEL-lo ton-NA-to)* Cold veal with tunny-fish sauce.

Vitello alla villeroy *(... al-la vee-lā-ROY)* The veal is dipped in a *béchamel* sauce thickened with egg yolks, grated cheese, chopped ham and tongue, then bread-crumbed and fried.

Agnello – Lamb
Montone, Castrato – Mutton
Capretto – Kid

Lamb and mutton were at one time seldom found on Italian menus. Now, however, mutton-eating is on the increase, particularly in the south where meat is scarce, and recently New Zealand signed an agreement with the Italians to supply a large quantity of lamb and mutton every year. Lambs tend to get killed younger in Italy and joints may be smaller than you expect. Young roast kid, incidentally, is very good.

Abbacchio *(ab-BAK-yō)* Spring lamb.

Agnello *(an-YEL-lō)* Lamb.
 Aretina, all' *(al-lar-ā-TEE-na)* Roast with rosemary, basted with oil and vinegar.
 Arrabbiata, all' *(al-lar-rab-BYA-ta)* (Umbria) Cooked over a hot fire, basted with oil and sprinkled with vinegar.
 Cacciatora, alla *(al-la kat-chya-TO-ra)* Braised with herbs, wine, garlic, vinegar and anchovy added to the sauce.
 Ciociara, alla *(al-la chō-CHA-ra)* Braised with ham, flavoured with rosemary and garlic.
 Villeroy, alla *(al-la veel-lā-ROY)* Cutlet dipped in Villeroy sauce (see p.108) breadcrumbed and fried.

Brodettato alla romana *(brō-dāt-TA-tō al-la rō-MA-na)* A stew with herbs and vegetables, the sauce thickened with eggs and flavoured with lemon.

Capretto al forno *(ka-PRĀT-tō al FOR-nō)* Roast kid.

Capretto ripieno *(... ree-PYEN-ō)* (Puglia) Stuffed roast kid.

Capretto allo spiedo *(... al-lō SPYA-dō)* (The Marches) Kid cooked on the spit, with a little garlic and rosemary.

Capretto al vino bianco *(... al VEE-nō BYAN-kō)* Kid cooked in white wine.

Castradina *(kas-tra-DEE-na)* (Veneto) Roast mutton.

Castrato *(kas-TRA-tō)* Mutton.

Coratella d'agnello *(kō-ra-TEL-la dan-YEL-lō)* The insides, lungs, heart, etc. They are usually cut up small and fried with vegetables.

Coratella di capretto *(... dee ka-PRĀ-tō)* Lung and intestines of kid.

Cosciotto d'agnello allo spiedo *(kō-SHYŌT-tō dan-YEL-lō al-lō SPYA-do)* (Umbria) Leg of lamb roasted on a spit.

Costoletta *(kōs-tō-LET-ta)* Cutlet.

Cutturiddi *(koot-too-REED-dee)* A lamb stew flavoured with rosemary.

Gnummarielli *(nyoom-mar-YEL-lee)* Entrails of baby lamb, roasted on a spit.

Scottadito *(skōt-ta-DEE-tō)* Grilled cutlets. **Scottadito** means something you burn your fingers on.

Sovè di lepre *(sō-VĀ dee LEP-rā)* Kid stewed in red wine.

Spezzatini d'agnello *(spāt-tsa-TEE-nee dan-YEL-lō)* Cut-up pieces of lamb, usually cooked *alla cacciatora* (see above).

Spezzatini di capretto alla trentina *(... dee ka-PRĀT-tō al-la tren-TEE-na)* Pieces of kid, egg-and-breadcrumbed, fried in oil and then cooked slowly with a little milk and lemon rind added to the oil.

Testarelle d'agnello *(tās-ta-REL-lā dan-YEl-lō)* Roast lambs' heads. Flavoured with rosemary.

Villeroy d'agnello con carciofi *(veel-lā-ROY dan-YEL-lō kon kar-CHO-fee)* Lamb cutlets dipped in Villeroy sauce (p 00) breadcrumbed and fried; served with artichokes.

Maiale – Pork

Aceto, all' *(al-la-CHĀ-to)* Cooked in butter with white wine, vinegar, sauce flavoured with anchovies.

Àrista *(A-rees-ta)* Loin or saddle of pork.
  Fiorentina, alla *(al-la fyor-en-TEE-na)* Saddle of pork roast in water, not in fat, with garlic, rosemary and cloves.
  Perugina, alla *(al-la pā-roo-JEE-na)* Roast in the same way as *alla fiorentina* but with fennel instead of rosemary and cloves.

Braciola di maiale *(bra-CHŌ-la dee ma-YA-lā)* Pork chop.

Budelli di maiale *(boo-DEL-lee dee ma-YA-lā)* The entrails of pork.

Cazzoeula alla milanese *(kat-tsō-wā-OO-la al-la mee-la-NĀ-zā)* A stew of pigs' trotters, onion, sausage, carrots, celery and tomatoes, with cabbage added shortly before serving.

Cazzoeula alla novarese *(… al-la nō-va-RĀ-zā)* The same as *alla milanese* but with the addition of meat from the pig's stomach and goose.

Ceci con la tempia di maiale *(CHĀ-chee kon la TEM-pya dee ma-YA-lā)* A stew of chick-peas and pig's face, cooked long and slowly.

Cervella di maiale *(chār-VEL-la dee ma-YA-lā)* Pigs' brains.

Ciccioli *(cheet-CHŌ-lee)* (Genoa) A pork-meat sausage which is fried.

Coratella *(kō-ra-TEL-la)* The insides of pork. Heart, lungs, liver, etc.

Costa di maiale *(KŌS-ta dee ma-YA-lā)* Pork chop.

Costolette di maiale *(kōs-tō-LET-tā dee ma-YA-lā)* Pork chops.
   Marinate *(ma-ree-NA-tā)* Marinated in oil and lemon juice and grilled.
   Milanese *(mee-la-NĀ-zā)* Rolled in grated cheese and breadcrumbs, fried, then cooked in a tomato sauce.
   Modenese *(mō-dā-NĀ-zē)* Cooked with herbs and white wine.
   Panate *(pa-NA-ta)* Egg-and-breadcrumbed and fried.
   Toscana *(tos-KA-na)* Cooked in oil flavoured with fennel and garlic.

Cotechino *(kō-tā-KEE-nō)* (Modena) A large pork sausage which is boiled and served hot with vegetables. Rather like *zampone* (see below), but not so good.

Fegatini *(fā-ga-TEE-nee)* Small pieces of liver.
    Aretina, all' *(al-la-ren-tee-na)* Wrapped in bay leaves and fried.
    Fiorentina, alla *(al-la fyor-en-TEE-na)* With fennel, bay, garlic and breadcrumbs.
    Romana, alla *(al-la rō-MA-na)* With bread, ham, and bayleaf, cooked on a spit.
    Toscana, alla *(al-la tōs-KA-na)* With bread and bay leaves, cooked on a spit.
Fegato *(FĀ-ga-to)* Liver.

Filetto di maiale alla salvia *(fee-LET-tō dee ma-YA-la al-lā SAL-vya)* Small slices of fillet of pork on a skewer, alternating with ham, sage and bread.

Lombato di maiale *(lōm-BA-tō dee ma-YA-lā)* Loin of pork.
    Con castagne *(kon kas-TAN-ya)* With chestnuts.
    Ubriaco *(oo-BRYA-ko)* Cooked in wine, oil, parsley, garlic. *'Ubriaco'* means drunk.

Lombo di maiale *(LŌM-bō dee ma-YA-lā)* Loin of pork.

Luganica *(loo-GA-nee-ka)* (Friuli-Veneto Giulia) A pork sausage fried or grilled, or dried and eaten raw. (See *Frulli*, p 137).

Maiale al latte *(ma-YA-lā al LAT-tā)* Stewed in milk with herbs.

Maiale marinato *(... ma-ree-NA-tō)* Pork marinated in wine and herbs and cooked slowly in the marinade.

Mazzafegati *(MAT-sa-FĀ-ga-tee)* A highly flavoured pigs'-liver sausage, fried. (See *Umbria*, p. 168).

Osso di prosciutto con fagioli *(ŌS-sō dee prō-SHOOT-tō kon fa-JO-lee)* Ham bone with white bones.

Piedini di maiale *(pya-DEE-nee dee ma-YA-lā)* Pigs' trotters.

Porceddu *(por-CHAD-doo)* (Sardinia) Sucking pig flavoured with myrtle and roasted whole.

Porchetta *(por-KET-ta)* (Abruzzo, The Marches) Sucking pig flavoured with rosemary and garlic and roasted whole.

Salsiccia *(sal-SEET-cha)* Sausage (for smoked, dried sausage, see under Antipasti, p. 32).
    Romana, alla *(al-la rō-MA-na)* Cooked in tomato sauce flavoured with sage.
    Torinese, alla *(al-la to-ree-NĀ-zā)* Found in Piedmont generally; hot sausage cooked in butter and tomato with chickens' liver and snails. This seems worth returning home via Mont Blanc or Mont

Cenis for; it's a much better sausage dish than toad-in-the-hole at any time.

Sanguinaccio *(san-gwee-NAT-chō)* Blood pudding, fried.

Stufato di maiale alla padovana *(stoo-FA-tō dee ma-YA-lā al-la pa-do-VA-na)* Braised leg of pork flavoured with cinnamon.

Testa di maiale *(TES-ta dee ma-YA-lā)* Pig's face.

Testa di 'puorco' *(... PWOR-kō)* (Sicily) Jellied pig's head.

Zampone *(tsam-PŌ-nā)* (Modena) A world-famous speciality from Modena. Pork meat stuffed into the skin of a pig's trotter, boiled, served with lentils.

Bolliti – Boiled Meats

Bolliti misti *(bōl-LEE-tee MEES-tee)* Boiled 'meats' of every description – beef, chicken, calves' heads and feet, and sausage. It is served with *salsa verde* or *salsa pizzaiola* (see p.107), white beans, lentils, cabbage, spinach and potatoes. Although it is a speciality of northern Italy we have eaten it in most parts of Italy, and once on a train going from Reggio di Calabria to Rome on a boiling hot day; there was no alternative. In spite of this last experience it is a very good dish, well worth eating for the *salsa verde* alone.

Fritto Misto – Mixed Fry

The basis of the classic *fritto misto (FREET-tō-MEES-tō)* is small pieces of veal offal and vegetables dipped in batter and deep-fried. There are several variants of this dish, four of which we list below.

Alla campagnia *(al-la kam-pan-YEE-a)* Fish, cheese, potato, sweetbreads and cauliflower.

Alla fiorentina *(al-la fyor-en-TEE-na)* Calves' brains, sweetbreads, chicken, artichoke hearts and *mozzarella* cheese.

Milanese *(mee-la-NĀ-zā)* Calves' liver, brains, thin slices of veal, cockscombs, artichokes, baby marrow (zucchini), egg-and-breadcrumbed and fried.

Alla romana *(al-la rō-MA-na)* Calves' brains, sweetbreads, artichoke, liver and fried bread.

Piatti Freddi – Cold Dishes

This is a section of the Italian menu which is found far too seldom in our experience – in so many words on the *carta*, that is. But that isn't to say that *piatti freddi*

(PYAT-tee FRĀD-dee) are not available even in the menu-less *trattoria*; it is then only a matter of asking.

Where no *piatti freddi* are listed we suggest that the following catalogue of items be read from right to left – that is, to look first at the English descriptions of the normally encountered cold dishes and then ask for the Italian dish.

Where *piatti freddi* are shown on a menu then, of course, we hope they will include the dishes we have selected. But as it is unlikely that they will include all of them it is still worth while asking for what you don't see on the menu.

Cappon magro *(kap-PŌN MA-grō)* (Genoa) 'Lean capon' – another 'joke' dish, for the only connection with chickens in this case is the hard-boiled eggs which are an ingredient of this salad of vegetables, cold fish and shellfish, a garlic-flavoured sauce made with oil, vinegar, anchovy and parsley.

Cima alla genovese *(CHEE-ma al-la jenō-VĀ-zū)* Cold rolled breast of veal stuffed with minced veal, brains, sweetbreads, peas, egg, artichoke hearts and herbs.

Coppa romana/Coppa di testa *(KŌP-pa rō-MA-na/ KŌP-pa dee TES-ta)* Brawn. See also under *Antipasti* (p.25).

Filetto alla tartara *(fee-LET-tō al-la TAR-ta-ra)* Steak tartare. Raw beef finely ground and dressed with raw egg yolk, capers, onion and parsley. This is not an Italian dish, of course, but it is nevertheless found on Italian menus.

Insalata di riso e pollo *(een-sa-LA-ta dee REE-sō ā PŌL-lō)* Rice and chicken salad.

Lesso carpionato *(LES-sō kar-pyō-NA-tō)* Cold boiled meat in oil, vinegar and chopped herbs.

Lingua in gelatina (LEEN-gwa een jā-la-TEE-na) Tongue in aspic.

Lingua salmistrata (... sal-mee-STRA-ta) Cold tongue.

Misto carne fredda con pollo *(MEES-tō KAR-nā FRAD-da kon POL-lo)* Cold meats including chicken.

Noce di vitello glassata *(NO-cha dee vee-TEl-lō glas-SAT-ta)* Fillet of veal in aspic.

Piatto misto in gelatina *(PYA-tō MEES-tō een jā-la-TEE-na)* Cold meats in aspic.

Pollo in gelatina *(PŌl-lō een jā-la-TEE-na)* Cold chicken in aspic.

Pollo tonnato *(PŌL-lō tōn-NA-tō)* Cold chicken with a tunny-fish mayonnaise.

Rollata fredda *(rōl-LA-ta FRĀD-da)*   Cold rolled stuffed veal.

Rosbif freddo *(RŌZ-beef FRĀD-dō)*   Cold roast beef.

Vitello tonnato *(vee-TEL-lō ton-NA-tō)*   Cold veal with a tunny-fish mayonnaise.

POLLAME – POULTRY
Pollo – Chicken

Cappone *(kap-PŌ-nā)* Capon.

Gallina *(gal-LEE-na)* Boiling fowl.

Pulcino *(pool-CHEE-nō)* Spring chicken, petit poussin.

Cappone con ripieno di noci *(kap-PŌ-nū kon ree-PYEN-ō dee NO-chee)* Capon stuffed with walnuts and breadcrumbs.

Cappone ripieno *(… ree-PYEN-ō)* Stuffed and roast capon.

Costoletta di pollo *(kōs-tō-LET-ta dee PŌL-lō)* Breast of chicken.

Crochette di pollo *(krō-KET-ta dee PŌL-lō)* Chicken croquettes.

Crochette di pollo dorate *(… dō-RA-tā)* Croquettes of chicken dipped in egg and breadcrumbs and fried.

Fegatini di pollo alla salvia *(fā-ga-TEE-nee dee PŌL-lō al-la SAL-vya)* Chicken' livers, chopped ham and sage cooked in butter with Marsala and served on fried bread.

Fegatini di pollo con carciofi *(… kon kar-CHŌ-fee)* Chickens' livers, slices of globe artichoke, chopped ham, cooked in butter with chopped parsley and lemon juice.

Filetti di pollo alla modenese *(fee-LET-tee dee PŌL-lō al-la mod-da-NA-za)* Breasts of chicken 'egg-and-breadcrumbed and fried, then cooked with slices of ham and cheese.

Finanziera di pollo *(fee-nan-TSYER-a dee POL-lo)* (Valle d'Aosta) A chicken giblet stew with sweetbreads, mushrooms, truffles and a rich sauce.

Gallina bollita *(ga-LEE-na bōl-LEE-ta)* Boiled fowl.

Gallina del ghiottone *(... del gyōt-TŌ-na)* Fowl stuffed with *maccheroni* in a white sauce, with a white sauce poured over it, sprinkled with cheese and browned in the oven.

Panetti di pollo *(pa-NET-tee dee PŌL-lo)* Cold minced chicken made into rissoles and reheated.

Petti di pollo *(PET-tee dee PŌL-lō)* Breast of chicken.
    Bolognese, alla *(al-la bo-lōn-YĀ-za)* Cooked with a slice of ham and a slice of cheese over each breast and some finely sliced white truffles.
    Cavour, alla *(al-la ka-VOOR)* Sautée'd in butter with a slice of ham and and a slice of cheese, and served with a truffle sauce.
    Crema e funghi *(KRĀ-ma ā FOON-gee)* Cream and mushrooms. For some reason instead of using the usual word *panna* for cream here the Italians talk about *crema*, which strictly speaking is sweet egg-custard. If you happen to know that *crema* is custard, don't be put off when you see this dish on a menu.
    Fiorentina, alla *(al-la fyor-en-TEE-na)* Breasts of chicken fried in butter.
    Griglia, alla *(al-la GREEL-ya)* Grilled breast of chicken.
    Marsala, al *(al mar-SA-la)* Breast of chicken fried in butter, flavoured with Marsala and grated parmesan.
    Milanese *(mee-la-NĀ-zā)* Breast of chicken egg-and-breadcrumbed and fried.
    Sorpresa *(scr-PRES-a)* The breast is stuffed with a 'surprise' filling – whatever the chef feels like.
    Sovrana *(sōv-RĀ-na)* With artichokes and a cream sauce.
    Valdostana, alla *(al-la val-dōs-TA-na)* Breast of chicken cooked with slices of cheese, white truffles, white wine and brandy.

Pollo *(PŌL-lō)* Chicken, size unspecified.
    Arrostito alla genovese *(ar-rōs-TEE-tō al-la jen-ō-VĀ-zā)* Stuffed with its giblets, onion, celery, herbs, breadcrumbs and butter, and roasted.
    Arrostito alla romana *(... rō-MA-na)* Stuffed with chestnuts, breadcrumbs, celery, onion, parsley and grated cheese, roasted.
    Arrosto alla bolognese *(ar-RŌS-tō al-la bō-lōn-YĀ-zā)* Roasted in butter and oil, with chopped ham and tomato and flavoured with garlic and rosemary.
    Baby, alla *(al-la BĀ-bee)* Cooked in the same way as alla Nerone (below), but without the cognac and firework display.

Bianco, in *(een BYAN-kō)* (Campania)   Pieces of chicken sautée'd with onion, celery and herbs (parsley, basil).

Cacciatora, alla *(al-la kat-cha-TŌ-ra)* (Florence)   Chicken cooked in garlic, onion, mushrooms, tomatoes and herbs.

Casseruola, in *(een kas-sā-roo-Ō-la)*   Cooked in a casserole.

Castellana, alla *(al-la kas-tāl-LA-na)*   Two slices from the breast of chicken with a slice of *gruyère* cheese and a slice of ham and some white truffles between them. Egg-and-breadcrumbed and fried in butter.

Coccio, al *(al KŌT-chō)*   Baked in a clay case.

Contadina, alla *(al-la kōn-ta-DEE-na)*   Cooked whole with ham, tomatoes, rosemary and garlic.

Diavola, alla *(al-la DYA-vō-la)*   Grilled chicken.

Dorato *(dō-RA-tō)*   Pieces of chicken coated with flour and egg and fried in deep oil.

Duchessa, alla *(al-la doo-KĀS-sa)* (Parma)   The same as alla *castellana* above but with grated parmesan – naturally – in place of a slice of gruyère.

Forno, al *(al FOR-nō)*   Baked in the oven.

Fracasse, alla *(al-lu fru-KA-sā)* (Parma) see *fricassea* below.

Fricassea *(free-KAS-SĀ-a)*   Pieces of chicken poached in a cream sauce with onions and rosemary, the sauce is thickened with egg yolks and flavoured with lemon.

Fritto alla fiorentina *(FREET-tō al-la fyor-en-TEE-na)*   Pieces of chicken are marinated in oil and lemon juice before being coated with flour and egg and fried in deep oil.

Fritto alla toscana *(… tōs-KA-na)*   See *alla fiorentina* above.

Fritto alla viennese *(… vyen-NĀ-zā)*   Coated in egg and breadcrumbs and fried in butter.

Funghi, ai *(ī FOON-gee)*   Pieces of chicken *sautéed* in butter with mushrooms and a tomato sauce.

Ghiottona, alla *(al-la gyōt-TŌ-na)*   In butter with white wine, milk and tomatoes.

Giudecchina, alla *(al-la joo-dāk-KEE-na)* (Veneto)   Stuffed with breadcrumbs, the bird's livers and lights, onion, ham and grated cheese, and roasted.

Grillettato all'aretina *(greel-lat-TA-tō al-lar-ā-TEE-na)*   Grillettato means sizzling hot. The chicken is cooked with onions, peas, rice and a little white wine.

Gris, alla *(al-la grees)* (Parma)   Pieces of chicken fried in oil, flavoured with salt, pepper and squeeze of lemon.

Imbottito *(eem-bōt-TEE-tō)*   Stuffed and roast chicken.

Latte, al *(al LAT-tā)* Chicken cooked in milk.

Lesso *(LES-so)* Boiled chicken.

Limone, al *(al-lee-MŌ-na)* (Parma) Roast chicken served with a creamy sauce thickened with flour and egg yolk, parsley and lemon juice.

Livornese, alla *(al-la lee-vor-NĀ-zā)* A very nice way of eating chicken if you don't want anything either elaborate or rich. The chicken is poached in a casserole with a little broth, butter, parsley and the juice of a lemon – very Greek.

Maceratese, alla *(al-la ma-chā-ra-TA-za)* (The Marches) Poached chicken with a sauce thickened with egg yolks and flavoured with lemon.

Mantovana, alla *(al-la man-tō-VA-na)* (Lombardy) *Sautéed* in butter with vegetables and garnished with olives.

Marcugo, alla *(al-la mar-KOO-gō)* (Piedmont) Fried in oil and butter with rich tomato-flavoured sauce and mushrooms.

Montagnuola, alla *(al-la mōn-tan-yoo-WŌ-la)* Pieces of chicken rolled in egg and breadcrumbs and baked.

Napoletana, alla *(al-la na-pō-lā-TA-na)* Jointed and cooked for a long time with mushrooms, onions, garlic, tomato and wine.

Nerone, alla *(al-la nā-RŌ-na)* Half a chicken *sautéed* in oil, with onion and bayleaf, covered with cognac and set alight to burn like Nero's Rome.

Olive, alle *(al-la ō-LEE-vā)* Chicken *sautéed* with vegetables and olives.

Oreganato *(ō-RA-gā-NA-tō)* Chicken cooked in oil and lemon juice and flavoured with wild marjoram.

Padovana, alla *(al-la pa-dō-VA-na)* Highly spiced and spit-roast.

Panna, alla *(al-la PAN-na)* Cooked in a casserole in cream and butter with a little onion and parsley. Frequently the chef will add a little wine to the sauce, or spirit such as whisky or brandy.

Peperoni, coi *(koy pā-pā-RŌ-nee)* Cooked with pimentos, tomatoes, white wine, herbs and onions.

Porchetta, in *(een por-KET-ta)* (Tuscany) Chicken stuffed with ham, garlic and fennel.

Potenzese, alla *(al-la pō-ten-TSĀ-zā)* (Basilicata) Pieces of chicken roast with sliced potatoes, garlic, parsley and grated cheese.

Ripieno *(ree-PYEN-ō)* Stuffed and roast chicken.

Romana, alla *(al-la ro-MA-na)* Pieces of chicken cooked in a pan with onion, ham, pimento, tomatoes, rosemary, oil and butter.

Rosmarino, con *(kon rōz-ma-REE-nō)* *Sautéed* in oil and butter with garlic and rosemary.

Salsa piccante, in *(een SAL-sa peek-KAN-tā)* Pieces

of chicken cooked with oil, garlic, white wine, vinegar, black olives and chopped anchovy.

Salsa d'uovo *(SAL-sa DWŌ-vō)* Poached chicken served with a cream sauce flavoured with lemon juice and thickened with egg (see also *alla Maceratese*).

Salvia, alla *(al-la SAL-vya)* Pieces *sautéed* in a mixture of oil and butter with chopped ham and sage, and white wine.

Siciliana, alla *(al-la see-cheel-YA-na)* *Sautéed* in oil and butter with vegetables and Marsala.

Tartufato *(tar-too-FA-tō)* Chicken which has been stuffed with white truffles and had thin slices of truffle inserted under the skin of the breast, roast in the oven in butter and Marsala.

Tecia, in *(een TĀ-cha)* Baked in a shallow earthenware pan *(teglia)*. 'Tecia' is Venetian dialect for 'teglia'.

Tetrazzini, alla *(al-la tā-trat-TSEE-nee)* Small pieces of chicken and mushrooms in a sauce in a casserole with alternate layers of some sort of *pasta*, topped with grated cheese. No wonder Luisa Tetrazzini was a plump little lady, even for a singer.

Umido, in *(een OO-mee-dō)* Pieces of chicken cooked with vegetables and herbs in a covered pan.

Valdarno, di, arrosto girato *(ar-ROS-tō jee-RA-tō dee val-DAR-no)* Roast on a spit.

Villeroy, alla *(al-la veel-lā-ROY)* Pieces of cooked chicken coated with Villeroy sauce (see p 108), then egg-and-breadcrumbed and fried in deep fat.

Vino bianco, al *(al VEE-nō BYAN-kō)* Pieces of chicken cooked slowly in a white wine sauce, thickened with flour.

Zingara, alla *(al-la DZEEN-ga-ra)* Baked in a clay case.

Puddinghinos a pienu *(pood-deen-GEE-nōs a PYĀ-noo)* (Sardinia) Young chickens *(pulcini* in Italian) filled with a stuffing of giblets, breadcrumbs, eggs, milk and tomatoes and baked.

Rigaglie acciugate *(ree-GAL-yā at-choo-GA-tā)* Chicken giblets with an anchovy sauce.

Rottami di pollo in padella *(rŏt-TA-mee dee PŎL-lō een pa-DEL-la)* Chicken cut up and *sautéed*.

Sformato di pollo *(sfor-MA-tō dee PŎL-lō)* A mousse of chicken.

Spezzatino di pollo *(spăt-tsa-TEE-nō dee PŎL-lō)* (Campania) Small pieces of chicken *sautéed* in oil with pimentos, onion, mushrooms and tomatoes.

Stecchini alla bolognese *(stăk-KEE-nee al-la bō-lōn-YĀ-zā)* Chickens' livers, truffles, cheese, sweetbread, tongue on skewers *(stecchini)*, coated with a white wine sauce, egg and breadcrumbs and fried in butter.

Anitra – Duck
Anatroccolo – Duckling

Anitra *(A-nee-tra)*
Agrodolce, in *(een a-grō-DŌL-cha)* Duck with a sweet-sour sauce.
Arrosto *(ar-RŌS-tō)* Roasted, sometimes with a flavouring of sage.
Arrosto alla genovese *(... al-la jen-ō-VĀ-zā)* Roasted in olive oil with herbs, and fresh lemon juice added to the gravy.
Arrostita alla siciliana *(ar-rōs-TEE-ta al-la see-cheel-YA-na)* Stuffed with pork, herbs, peppers and black olives with Marsala and roasted.
Cognac, al *(al KŌN-yak)* Duck cooked with brandy, juniper berries and rosemary.
Muta alla novarese *(MOO-ta al-la nō-va-RĀ-zā)* (Piedmont) Stuffed with rice and meats, herbs and spices, and roasted.
Nizzarda, alla *(al-la neet-TSAR-da)* Duck cooked with tomatoes, herbs, olives, mushrooms and brandy.
Olive, all' *(al-lō-LEE-vā)* Casserole of duck with olives.
Salmí, in *(een sal-MEE)* (Umbria) Marinated in red wine with onion, herbs, garlic and anchovies, fried and then cooked in its marinade.
Salmí alla romana, in *(een sal-MEE al-la rō-MA-na)* Salmis of duck in a peculiarly Roman manner; it is slowly cooked with herbs, an onion and a mixture of oil and wine vinegar.

Salsa arancio, con *(kon SAL-sa a-RAN-chō)* Roast duck with orange sauce.

Salsa di capperi, in *(een SAL-sa dee KAP-pā-ree)* (Piedmont) Cooked in the oven with a sauce of Marsala, capers and white truffles.

Selvatica *(sel-VA-tee-ka)* Wild duck. The most usual method of serving wild duck is roast, with garlic and parsley, the juice of an orange and a glass of Marsala.

ppardelle all'arentina (Arezzo) or **coll'anitra** (Flornce) *(pa-par-DELL-ā al-lar-ān-TEE-na/kol-LA-nee-tra)* uck cooked with red wine, tomatoes, and herbs, rved with wide ribbon *pasta*.

etto di anitra *(PET-tō dee A-nee-tra)* Breast of duck.

ca *(Ō-ka)* **Goose**

Arrosto in forno *(ar-RŌS-tō een FŌR-nō)* Stuffed with sausage, herbs, chestnuts and breadcrumbs and roasted in the oven.

Arrostita con ripieno di salvia e cipolla *(ar-rōs-TEE-ta kon ree-PYEN-ō dee SAL-vya a chee-POL-la)* Roast and stuffed with – you'll never guess – sage and onion.

Onto, in *(een ŌN-to)* (Venice) Preserved goose.

Salmi, in *(een sal-MEE)* Cooked with wine, herbs, vegetables, mushrooms and truffles.

Faraona *(fa-ra-Ō-na)* **Guinea fowl**

Arrosto *(ar-RŌS-to)* Plain roast.

Coccio, al *(al KOT-chō)* Baked in a clay case.

Creta, alla *(al-la KRĀ-ta)* Baked in clay case.

Incrostata *(een-krōs-TA-ta)* Pie.

Panna, alla *(al-la PAN-na)* (Parma) Baked in the oven in a paper case with sage, juniper and rosemary and served with hot cream.

Piemontese, alla *(al-la pyā-mōn-TĀ-zā)* Stuffed with herbs, juniper berries, breadcrumbs, its liver and lights, and cooked in the oven with vegetables and white wine.

Ripiena *(ree-PYEN-a)* Stuffed.

Salmì, in *(een sal-MEE)* Cooked in a rich wine and vegetable sauce.

Salsa di capperi, in *(een SAL-sa dee KAP-pā-ree)* With a caper sauce.

Spiedo, allo *(al-lō SPYĀ-dō)* Roasted on a spit.

Tecia, in *(een TA-chya)* Cooked in an open earthenware pan *(teglia)*. See under *Pollo*.

Tacchino (N Italy, Dindo) – Turkey

Filetti di tacchino *(fee-LET-tee dee tak-KEE-nō)* Slices of turkey breast.

Bolognese *(bō-lōn-YĀ-zā)* Cooked with ham, cheese and white truffles; in some places it is served with tomato sauce and no truffles. Such establishments should be avoided – or their *filetti di tacchino bolognese* should.

Burro, al *(al BOOR-rō)* Cooked in butter.

Cardinale, alla *(al-la kar-dee-NA-lā)* Sautéed in butter. On each piece of turkey is a slice of tongue or ham, white truffles and *parmesan* cheese.

Castellana, alla *(al-la kas-tā-LA-na)* Cooked like *pollo alla castellana* (see p. 87).

Duchessa, alla *(al-la doo-KAS-sa)* See *pollo alla duchessa* on p. 87.

Funghi, ai *(ī FOON-gee)* Egg-and-breadcrumbed, fried in butter and served with a Marsala sauce and mushrooms.

Margaret Rose *(MAR-gar-et rōz)* With ham, truffles and cheese in a flaky pastry case.

Marsala, al *(al mar-SA-la)* Cooked in butter and Marsala.

Modenese, alla *(al-la mō-da-NÃ-zā)* Egg-and-breadcrumbed, fried in butter; with slices of gruyère or *fontina* cheese and ham.

Pasta sfoglia *(PAS-ta SFŌL-ya)* In flakey pastry.

Prosciutto, al *(al prŏ-SHOOT-tō)* Egg-and-breadcrumbed and fried. A slice of ham and some grated cheese are placed on each *filetto* and served with a tomato sauce.

Gallinaccio brodettato *(gąl-lee-NAT-chō bro-dāt-TA-tō)* (Rome) Turkey-cock stewed with wine, vegetables and herbs, and served with a cream sauce thickened with egg yolks.

Petto di tacchino *(PET-tō dee tak-KEE-nō)* Breast of turkey. See *filetti* above.

Rotolo di tacchino *(RŌ-tŏ-lō dee tak-KEE-nō)* Turkey meat boned and rolled.

Tacchino *(tak-KEE nō)* Turkey pure and simple.

Arrosto *(ar-ROS-to)* Roast turkey.

Arrosto ripieno *(... ree-PYEN-ō)* Roast, stuffed turkey.

Arrosto ripieno con castagne *(... KON kas-TAN-ya)* Filled with a chestnut stuffing and roasted.

Arrosto tartufato *(... tar-too-FA-tō)* Roast with truffles, Marsala and butter.

Bollito *(bŏl-LEE-tō)* Boiled with vegetables; usually served cold.

Carpione, in *(een kar-PYŌ-nā)* Cooked, then marinated in a sauce of wine, herbs, oil and vinegar.

Maionese, in *(een ma-yō-NA-zā)* Cold sliced turkey served with mayonnaise.

Pasticcio, in *(een pas-TEET-chō)* In pastry with a cream sauce.

Ripieno *(ree-PYEN ō)* Stuffed turkey.

Ripieno alla lombarda *(... al-la lōm-BAR-da)* A turkey stuffed with sausage, minced veal and beef, herbs, apple and prunes, chestnuts and cheese.

Stufato al vino bianco *(stoo-FA-tō al VEE-nō BYAN-kō)* Stewed turkey with white wine, herbs, vegetables and mushrooms.

Tetrazzini, alla *(al-la tā-tra-TSEE-nee)* Pieces of turkey, a creamy mushroom sauce and *pasta*, covered with grated cheese and breadcrumbs, baked in the oven.

CACCIAGIONE, SELVAGGINA – GAME

Allodole *(al-LŌ-dō-lā)*   Larks.

Alzavola/Arzavola *(al-dza-VŌ-la/ar-dza-VŌ-la)*   Teal.

Beccaccia *(bāk-KAT-cha)*   Woodcock.
Farcita *(far-CHEE-ta)*   Stuffed and roasted.
Salmí, in *(een sal-MEE)*   Sautéed in oil and butter, a sauce made with their intestines, and a little onion.
Romagnola, alla *(al-la rō-man-YŌ-la)*   Stuffed and roasted.

Beccaccino *(bāk-kat-CHEE-nō)*   Snipe

Beccafichi *(bāk-ka-FEE-kee)*   'Fig-peckers' or garden warblers *(Sylvia borin)* but the word is used to describe any small bird for the table.
Marsala, al *(al mar-SA-la)*   Cooked in oil, tomato, anchovies, garlic, black olives and Marsala, served on fried bread and the sauce in which it has been cooked.

Camoscio *(ka-MŌ-shō)*   Chamoix
Polenta, con *(kən pō-LEN-ta)*   Served with *polenta* (see p. 41).

Salmì, in *(een sal-MEE)*   First marinated and then stewed in wine, herbs, anchovies, garlic and olive oil.

Capriolo *(ka-pree-YŌ-lō)*   Roe-buck.
Salmì, in *(een sal-MEE)*   Cooked in wine, herbs and vegetables.

Cervo, Selvaggina *(CHER-vō, sāl-vad-JEE-na)*   Venison.
Arrosto di selvaggina *(ar-ROS-tō dee sāl-vad-jee-na)* (Sardinia)   Well flavoured with garlic and roasted with many different herbs sprinkled over it.
Mario, alla *(al-la MAR-yō)*   Marinated, then roasted with a wine-flavoured sauce. Named after the great tenor, Giovanni Mario (1810-1883).
Salsa di ciliege, con *(kon SAL-sa dee cheel-YĀ-jā)*   Venison cooked in a casserole with wine, herbs, spices, mushrooms and vegetables, and served with a cherry sauce.

Cinghiale *(cheen-GYA-lā)* Wild boar.

Agrodolce alla romana, in *(een a-grō-DŌL-chā al-la rō-MA-na)* Marinated with herbs, wine and spices and cooked in a sweet-sour sauce.

Arrosto *(ar-RŌS-tō)* Roast wild boar.

Cacciatora, alla *(al-la kat-cha-TO-ra)* Cooked with wine and vegetables.

Coniglio *(kō-NEEL-yō)* Rabbit (never wild; wild rabbit is *coniglio selvaggio*)

Agostino, alla *(al-la a-gōs-TEE-nō)* Pieces of rabbit cooked in oil and red wine, with sultanas and pine-nuts and a little lemon peel.

Agrodolce, in *(een a-grō-DŌL-chā)* Stewed rabbit served with a sweet-sour sauce.

Borghese, alla *(al-la bor-GĀ-zā)* *Sautéed* in white wine, herbs, onions and mushrooms.

Buongustaio, del *(del bwōn-goos-TĪ-yō)* Cooked with herbs, vegetables and Marsala.

Cacciatora, alla *(al-la kat-cha-TO-ra)* With oil and vegetables, herbs and wine with plenty of garlic.

Campagnola, alla *(al-la kam-pan-YŌ-la)* Cooked in oil with garlic, rosemary and white wine.

Capperi, ai *(ī KAP-pā-ree)* Marinated in red wine, vinegar, celery and carrot, then cooked in a casserole with oil and the marinade, and served with a sauce of anchovies and capers.

Fricassea, in *(een free-kas-SĀ-ya)* Pieces of rabbit stewed in a white-wine sauce which is then thickened with egg yolks and flavoured with lemon.

Fritto *(FREET-tō)* Fried in bacon fat and oil and flavoured with sage and garlic.

Fritto alla lombarda *(... al-la lōm-BAR-da)* Lombardy speciality of pieces of rabbit dipped into egg and chopped herbs before it is breadcrumbed and fried.

Livornese, alla *(al-la lee-vor-NA-za)* Casserole of rabbit with tomatoes and anchovies.

Marsala, al *(al mar-SA-la)* Cooked in Marsala with onions, pimentos, tomatoes and aubergine, and flavoured with herbs and garlic.

Padella, in *(een pa-DEL-la)* *Sautéed* in oil with bacon, tomatoes, garlic, white wine and chopped parsley; usually served with rice.

Peperonata, in *(een pā-pā-rō-NA-ta)* Cooked in a pimento and tomato sauce highly flavoured with garlic.

Ripieno al forno *(ree-PYEN-ō al FOR-nō)* Stuffed and roasted.

Salmì, in *(een sal-MEE)* Marinated in wine with herbs, and then cooked with finely chopped vegetables, olive oil and the wine and herbs it has been soaking in.

Salsa piccante, in *(een SAL-sa peek-KAN-tā)*   Rabbit in a piquant sauce cooked with vegetables, herbs, spices, wine, capers and anchovies.

Salsa d'uova, in *(een SAL-sa DWŌ-va)*   Poached rabbit with gammon and onion and parsley, in a sauce thickened with eggs and flavoured with lemon juice.

Salsicce, con *(kon sal-SEET-chā)*   Boned, flattened, seasoned with herbs and rolled. Cooked in the oven with sausages.

Umido, in *(een OO-mee-dō)*   Stewed slowly in wine with onions, tomatoes and potatoes.

Umido di Bergamo, in *(een OO-mee-dō dee BER-ga-mō)*   Stewed and flavoured with basil, parsley, onion and little vermouth.

Fagiano *(fa-JYA-no)*   Pheasant (**Fagianella** *(fa-jya-NEL-la)* Young pheasant).

Arrosto tartufato *(ar-RŌS-tō tar-TOO-fō)*   Stuffed with truffles and roasted.

Casseruola, in *(een kas-sār-WŌ-la)*   Cooked in butter with cognac.

Crema, alla *(al-la KRĀ-ma)*   Cooked in butter and cream with lemon juice.

Diavola, alla *(al-la DYA-vō-la)*   Cut in half, brushed with oil and lemon juice and grilled.

Norcese, alla *(al-la nor-CHĀ-zā)*   Stuffed with truffles, herbs and chopped onion, roast in the oven or on a spit, with a glass of *grappa* – a white fiery liquid distilled from the pips of grapes – added to the gravy.

Salmí, in *(een sal-MEE)*   Cooked and served in a rich vegetable, brandy and mushroom sauce.

Folaga *(fo-LA-ga)*   Coot.

Germano *(jer-MA-nō)*   Mallard.

Gallinella d'acqua *(gal-lee-NEL-la DAK-kwa)* Moorhen.

Lepre *(LĀ-prā)*   Hare.

Agrodolce, in *(een a-grō-DŌL-chā)*   Cooked with Marsala, ham, herbs, and served with a sweet-sour sauce.

Barolo, con *(kon ba-RŌ-lō)*   Hare in a stew or red wine (Barolo) and vegetables.

Cacciatora, alla *(al-la kat-cha-TO-ra)*   Cooked with wine, herbs and vegetables.

Campagnola, alla *(al-la kam-pan-YŌ-la)*   Marinated in wine and herbs, then cooked in a casserole with red wine.

Dolce-forte *(DŌL-chā FUR-tā)*   (Tuscany)   Marinated in red wine, onions, spices and herbs; when the hare has been cooked in the marinade a sauce of bitter chocolate, candied fruits, raisins and nuts are added.

Salmì, in *(een sal-MEE)* Marinated in wine, herbs and vegetables; cooked in the marinade and served with the sauce it has been cooked in, with garlic, anchovies and more wine added.

Sant'Uberto, alla *(al-la san-too-BER-tō)* Cooked like *lepre in salmi* (above) but with juniper berries and grated orange rind added.

Toscana, pappardelle con la lepre alla *(pap-par-DEL-lā kon la LĀ-prā al-la tōs-CA-na)* Casserole of hare with herbs, gammon, tomatoes, vegetables and Marsala served with a wide ribbon pasta.

Trentina, alla *(al-la tren-TEE-na)* Sometimes cooked with herbs, juniper berries and white wine; at others stewed in wine with raisins, pine-nuts and a little sugar.

Umido, in *(een OO-mee-dō)* Casserole of hare, with mushrooms, gammon, vegetables, tomato, garlic and Marsala.

Merli *(MER-lee)* Blackbirds.

Ortolani *(or-tō-LA-nee)* Ortolans.

Palombacci alla perugina *(pa-lōm-BAT-chee al-la pā-roo-JEE-na) Palombacci* is a dialect word for wood-pigeons, otherwise called piccioni selvatici. This dish from Umbria consists of roast wood-pigeons, served with a sauce made from their intestines, red wine, olives, juniper berries and sage.

Pernice *(per-NEE-chā)* Partridge.

Arrosto *(ar-RŌS-tō)* (Lombardy) Roast partridge stuffed with bacon, juniper berries and mushrooms and served on fried bread.

Crema, alla *(al-la KRĀ-ma)* Cooked in a casserole with cream, butter, onion and a little lemon juice.

Forno, al *(al FOR-nō)* Roast.

Salmì, in *(een sal-MEE)* Cooked in a rich vegetable and brandy sauce.

Sarda, alla *(al-la SAR-da)* (Sardinia) Cold boiled partridge in a dressing of oil and vinegar, capers and chopped parsley.

Zabaione, allo *(al-lo dza-ba-YŌ-nā)* (Piedmont) Roast partridge served with a covering sauce of *zabaione* or (*zabaglione* – see p. 113).

Piccioni *(peet-CHŌ-nee)* Pigeons (Always tame)

Piccioncini arrostiti *(peet-chōn-CHEE-nee ar-rōs-TEE-tee)* Roast baby pigeons.

Gratella, in *(een grā-TEL-la)* Grilled, with a thin coating of mustard and breadcrumbs, and served with a piquant sauce.

Salmì, in *(een sal-MEE)* Marinated and cooked in wine, herbs, garlic, anchovies, capers, oil and vinegar, with a little onion.

Piccioni selvatici *(peet-CHŌ-nee sāl-VA-tee-chee)* Wood-pigeons.

Aceto, all' *(al-la-CHĀ-tō)* Cooked with oil and vinegar, herbs, cinnamon and cloves.

Cacciatora, alla *(al-la kat-cha-TO-ra)* Cooked long and slowly with white wine, herbs and oil.

Romana, alla *(al-la rō-MA-na)* Cooked with herbs and vegetables in red wine and vinegar; pounded garlic and anchovies and chopped parsley are added to the sauce just before serving.

Spiedo, allo *(al-lō SPYĀ-dō)* On the spit.

Quaglie *(KWAL-yā)* Quails.

Arrosto con polenta *(ar-RŌS-tō kon pō-LEN-ta)* Roast quails on fried polenta (see p 41).

Griglia, alla *(al-la GREEL-ya)* Wrapped in bacon and grilled.

Piemontese, alla *(al-la pyā-mōn-TĀ-zā)* Roast and served with rice and truffles and a cream sauce flavoured with Marsala and chopped truffles.

Puré di piselli, alla *(al-la poo-RA dee pee-SEL-lee)* Cooked in a casserole and served with a puree of peas and ham and bacon.

Riso, col *(kol REE-zō)* (Parma) Cooked in a pan with rice, ham, onion, bacon and covered with grated parmesan.

Risotto, al *(al ree-ZŌT-to)* Quails cooked with herbs, vegetables and wine and served with rice.

Salmì, in *(een sal-MEE)* First roasted, then cooked with wine, herbs, vegetables, juniper and chopped ham.

Spiedo, allo *(al-lō SPYĀ-dō)* On the spit.

Vino bianco, al *(al VEE-nō BYAN-kō)* Quails stuffed with pine-nuts and raisins, cooked in a white wine with herbs and spices, cream, garlic and onion.

Selvaggina *(sēl-vad-JEE-na)* Where *salvaggina* appears on the menu as an item instead of a category it is a synonym of *cervo* (venison).

Starna *(STAR-na)* Grey partridge. Cooked like *pernice* (above).

Tordi *(TOR-dee)* Thrushes.

Tordi matti *(... MAT-tee)* This is another of those culinary jokes and has nothing to do with thrushes; as you might guess by now it is veal cut into pieces and cooked on a skewer.

Torresani farciti *(tōr-rā-SA-nee far-CHEE-tee)* Stuffed doves or tame pigeons from Torreglia near Padua.

Uccelletti *(oot-chāl-LET-tee)* Small birds.

Maremmana, alla *(al-la ma-rām-MA-na)* (Southern Tuscany, Grosseto) Small wild birds – 'field fare' – cooked in oil, with tomatoes, garlic, anchovy and olives. They are cooked undrawn, heads left on, and served on fried bread.

Uccelletti scappati *(oot-chāl-LET-tee skap-PA-tee)* See under Vitello, p. 69.

CONTORNI, LEGUMI*, VERDURE – VEGETABLES

Although we have grouped a great many of the vegetables you find in Italy under this heading, they are seldom served on the same plate as your main dish. They are nearly all eaten as an *antipasto* or as a separate dish, or cold as a salad. Potatoes are generally very well cooked, but the Italians sometimes serve them cold – even roast potatoes.

Asparagi *(as-PA-ra-jee)* Asparagus. Usually eaten as an *antipasto*.

    Aglio, all' *(al-LAL-yō)* Boiled and served with a dressing of hot oil flavoured with garlic and grated cheese.

    Agro, all' *(al-LA-grō)* Boiled and served with a dressing of oil and lemon or vinegar.

    Burro, al *(al BOOR-rō)* Boiled and served with butter.

    Burro e formaggio, con *(kon BOOR-rō ā for-MAD-jō)* Boiled, served with butter and grated cheese.

    Campo, del *(del KAM-pō)* This is wild, uncultivated asparagus and very good indeed; it is very much the sort of thing we grow in our garden at home, and which, because of all the sweat and tears it involves, we naturally regard as highly cultivated.

    Coltivati *(kōl-tee-VA-tee)* 'Cultivated' – large fat white asparagus, rather flavourless and often served with cheese.

    Fiorentina, alla *(al-la fyor-en-TEE-na)* Boiled, served with butter and grated cheese and garnished with fried eggs. This is a dish we have met on the menus many times all over Italy, but nearly always listed under the *piatti del giorno (PYAT-tee del JYOR-nō)* or 'Today's Specials'.

---

* The term, *legumi,* is rarely used to describe vegetables in Italy unless they are in fact legumes – peas, beans, lentils. But there are a great many proprietors who are not such purists and use it nevertheless – influenced perhaps by the French.

Genovese, alla *(al-la jen-ō-VĀ-zā)* Boiled and served with oil.

Lombarda, alla *(al-la lōm-BAR-da)* With two fried eggs.

Milanese alla *(al-la mee-la-NA-zā)* Also with eggs like *alla lombarda,* but the eggs can also be baked or poached.

Panna, alla *(al-la PAN-na)* Boiled and served with cream.

Parmigiana, alla *(al-la par-mee-JA-na)* Boiled, then covered in butter and cheese, and browned.

Piacere, a *(a pya-CHER-ā)* Cooked and dressed as you like.

Prosciutto, al *(al prō-SHOO-tō)* Asparagus tips rolled in ham and baked with butter and grated cheese.

Sformato di asparagi *(sfor-MA-tō dee as-PA-ra-jee)* An asparagus mould.

Asparagi, punte di *(POON-tā dee as-PAR-a-jee)* Asparagus tips.

Barbabietola *(bar-ba-BYĀ-tō-la)* Beetroot.

Bietole *(BYĀ-tō-la)* Spinach beet.

Broccoletti di rape *(brōk-kō-LET-tee dee RA-pā)* Turnip tops. See also *cima di rape* below.

Broccoli *(BRŌK-kō-lee)* Broccoli, cauliflower.

Carciofi *(kar-CHŌ-fee)* Artichokes. See under *Antipasti* (p. 24).

Cardi *(KAR-dee)* Cardoons
  Bagna caoda, con *(kon BAN-ya ka-Ō-da)* (Piedmont). See under *Antipasti* (p. 23).
  Besciamella, alla *(al-la bā-sha-MEL-la)* Cardoons with a white *(béchamel)* sauce flavoured with cheese.

Carote *(ka-RŌ-tā)* Carrots

Castagne *(kas-TAN-yā)* Chestnuts

Cavoletti *(ka-vō-LET-tee)* Another name for *cavoli di Brusselle* or Brussels sprouts.

Cavolfiore *(ka-vōl-FYOR-ā)* Cauliflower.

Cavoli di Brusselle *(KA-vō-lee dee broos-SEL-lā)* Brussels sprouts.

Cavolo *(KA-vō-lō)* Cabbage.

Cavolo marino *(… ma-REE-nō)* Sea-kale.

Cavolo romano *(… rō-MA-nō)* Broccoli.

Ceci *(CHĀ-chee)* Chick-peas.

Cetrioli *(chā-tree-YŌ-lee)* Cucumbers

Cicorea/cicoria *(chee-KO-rā-ya/chee-KO-rya)* Chicory.
Romana, alla *(al-la rō-MA-na)* Cooked with tomatoes, garlic, anchovy fillet, butter and broth.

Cicorina *(chee-kō-REE-na)* Young chicory.

Cima di rape *(CHEE-ma dee RA-pā)* Turnip tops.

Cipolle *(chee-PŌL-la)* Onions.

Cipolline in agrodolce *(chee-pōl-LEE-nā een a-grō-DŌL-chā)* Young onions cooked in a sweet-sour sauce.

Cornetti *(kɔr-NET-tee)* A name for French beans *(fagiolini)*.

Coste *(KŌS-tā)* When you are served spinach-beet instead of real spinach in Italy you will find on the menu *'spinaci e coste'*; the *spinaci* are the leaf of the beet and the *coste* are the ribs cooked and served separately.

Crescione *(krā-SHŌ-nā)* Watercress.

Fagioli *(fa-JŌ-lee)* White haricot beans.
Assoluti *(as-sō-LOO-tee)* First boiled, then cooked in oil with garlic, chopped parsley, and chilli peppers.
Con le cotiche *(kon lā KŌ-tee-kā)* See alla romana below.
Fiasco, al *(al FYAS-kō)* Cooked in the familiar Tuscan wine flask, or *fiasco*, without its straw covering, although nowadays it tends to mean any sort of closed container. The beans are cooked slowly in the oven with oil, salt, pepper and tomatoes.
Fiorentina, alla *(al-la fyor-en-TEE-na)* Boiled and served with a lot of oil, salt and pepper, lemon juice.
Romana, alla *(al-la rō-MA-na)* Cooked long and slowly in a tomato sauce with pork crackling.
Toscana, alla *(al-la tōs-KA-na)* Cooked in oil with garlic and sage, traditionally in a *fiasco* (see *al fiasco* above), but this is no longer general. This was a favourite dish of Puccini, who was a Tuscan.
Uccelletto, all' *(al-loot-chāl-LET-tō)* (Tuscany) First boiled and then cooked in oil with garlic, sage and a tomato sauce.

Fagiolini *(fa-jō-LEE-nee)* French beans.

Fave *(FA-vā)* Broad beans. In some parts of Italy – Genoa particularly – they are eaten raw, when very young, as an *antipasto*.

Finocchi *(fee-NŌK-kee)* Fennel.
Forno, al *(al FOR-no)* First boiled, then cooked in the oven with grated cheese and butter.
Fritti *(FREET-tee)* (Sicily) Slices of fennel dipped in egg and breadcrumbs and fried.

Gratin, al *(al gra-TEEN)* First boiled, then served in a sauce with breadcrumbs on top and browned.

Tegame, in *(een tā-GA-me)* Fennel *sautéed* slowly in oil and garlic.

Fungi *(FOON-gee)* Mushrooms.

Acciugati al forno *(at-choo-GA-tee al FOR-nō)* Stuffed with anchovy and breadcrumbs and baked.

Affogati *(af-fō-GA-tee)* Cooked in garlic-flavoured olive oil.

Aglio, all' *(al-LAL-yō)* Cooked in a tomato sauce with a lot of garlic.

Crostini di funghi *(krōs-TEE-nee dee FOON-gee)* Mushrooms on toast – but not quite as we are used to them. They are chopped and served in a cream sauce.

Fritti *(FREET-tee)* Fried mushrooms.

Funghetto alla genovese, funghi al *(FOON-gee al foon-GET-tō al-la jen-ō-VA-zā)* Mushrooms cooked in oil with garlic and parsley.

Graticola, alla *(al-la gra-TEE-kō-la)* Grilled mushrooms.

Imbottiti *(eem-bōt-TEE-tee)* Stuffed.

Marsala, al *(al mar-SA-la)* In a Marsala-flavoured sauce.

Napoletana, alla *(al-la na-pō-lā-TA-na)* Sauteéed in oil with garlic and slices of tomato.

Olio, all' *(al-LŌL-yō)* In oil.

Panna, alla *(al-la PAN-na)* Cooked in butter and cream.

Parmigiana, alla *(al-la par-mee-JA-na)* (Emilia-Romagna) Baked with a stuffing of breadcrumbs, grated Parmesan, garlic, parsley and wild marjoram.

Pignoli, con *(kən peen-YŌ-lee)* Cooked in butter with pine-nuts and garlic.

Polpettoni di funghi alla genovese *(pōl-pāt-TŌ-nee dee FOON-gee al-la jen-ō-VA-zā)* Large mushrooms covered with a mixture of sweetbreads and brains, grated cheese and yolk of egg, and baked.

Ripieni *(ree-PYEN-ee)* Stuffed.

Ripieni alla piemontese *(... al-la pyā-mōn-TA-zā)* Stuffed with a mixture of breadcrumbs, chopped anchovies, onion and parsley, bound together with egg and olive oil, and baked.

Stufato di funghi *(stoo-FA-tō dee FOON-gee)* A mushroom stew.

Toscana, alla *(al-la tōs-KA-na)* Cooked in a tomato sauce flavoured with garlic and marjoram.

Trifolati *(tree-fō-LA-tee)* Finely sliced mushrooms fried in garlic-flavoured oil, to which chopped anchovies, parsley and butter are added and a good squeeze of lemon.

Indivia/indivia di Belgio *(een-DEE-vya/een-DEE-vya dee BEL-jyō)* Chicory. See *cicorea* above.

Lenticchie *(lān-TEEK-kyā)* Lentils. These are not the orange lentils we are used to; they are green and much larger.

Melanzane *(mā-lan-DZA-nā)* Eggplant, aubergine. See under *Antipasti* (p. 28).

Patane *(pa-TA-nā)* Sweet potatoes.

Patate *(pa-TA-tā)* Potatoes.
   Arrostite *(ar-rōs-TEE-ta)* Roast potatoes, very often served cold.
   Burro, al *(al BOOR-rō)* Boiled and served with butter.
   Crochette di patate *(krō-KET-tā dee pa-TA-ta)* Potato croquettes.
   Duchessa *(doo-KĀS-sa)* Boiled and mashed with butter, egg yolk, salt and pepper.
   Fritte *(FREET-tā)* Fried in oil.
   Fritte alla bolognese *(FREET-tā al-la bōl-ōn-ȲA-ža)* Dipped in egg and flour and fried in olive oil.
   Fritte alla casalinga *(... al-la ka-za-LEEN-ga)* As done at home – usually with a little rosemary added.
   Fritelle di patate *(free-TEL-lā dee pa-TA-tā)* Potato cakes.
   Latte, al *(al LAT-tā)* Cooked in milk.
   Lesse *(LES-sa)* Boiled. Always served cold with a dressing. If you want them plain ask for them *'non condite'* *(nōn kōn-DEE-tā)*.
   Panna, alla *(al-la PAN-na)* With cream.
   Puré di patate *(poo-RĀ dee pa-TA-ta)* Mashed potatoes to which the Italians sometimes add cheese or onion or both. You will find them much better done than in the average restaurant at home; they really are beaten up into a purée.
   Saltate *(sal-TĀ-tā)* Sautéed.
   Veste da camera, in *(een VES-tā da KA-mā-ra)* Potatoes in their nightshirts – baked in the oven in their skins.

Patatine novelle *(pa-ta-TEE-nā nō-VEL-lā)* New potatoes.

Peperonata *(pā-pā-rō-NA-ta)* See under *Antipasti* (p. 29).

Peperoncini *(pā-pā-rōn-CHEE-nee)* Small hot peppers, chillis.

Peperoni *(pā-pā-RŌ-nee)* Sweet peppers, pimentos.

Piselli *(pee-ZEL-lee)* Peas.
   Finocchio, al *(al fee-NŌK-kyo)* Green peas cooked with fennel.

Funghi, ai *(ī FOON-gee)* Cooked in butter with a shredded lettuce, herbs and mushrooms.

Parigina, alla *(al-la pa-ree-JEE-na)* 'A la parisienne' – with lettuce, onion and butter.

Prosciutto, al *(al prō-SHOOT-tō)* Cooked with ham, a little onion and butter.

Romana, alla *(al-la rō-MA-na)* Same as al *prosciutto* above.

Rapanelli *(ra-pa-NEL-lee)* A kind of radish.

Rape *(RA-pā)* Turnips.

Scariola/scarola *(skar-YŌ-la/ska-RŌ-la)* Batavia, endive, curly lettice.

Sciule piene *(SHOO-lā PYEN-ā)* Stuffed onions (Piedmont).

Sedano *(SĀ-da-nō)* Celery.

Fagioli, sedani e *(sā-DA-nee ū fa-JYŌ-lee)* (Basilicata) Celery and beans cooked with tomatoes, oil and garlic.

Forno, al *(al FOR-nō)* Baked celery.

Milanese, alla *(al-la mee-la-NĀ-zā)* Served with a green sauce and grated cheese.

Parmigiana, alla *(al-la par-mee-JA-na)* Cooked in broth with onion and a little chopped ham, and served with grated parmesan cheese.

Spinaci *(spee-NA-chee)* Spinach.

Acciughe, all' *(al-lat-CHOO-gā)* With chopped anchovies and butter.

Affogati *(af-fō-GA-tee)* With oil and garlic.

Aglio, all' *(al-LAL-yō)* Same as *affogati*.

Borghese, alla *(al-la bor-GĀ-zā)* Same as all'*acciughe*.

Crochette di spinaci *(krō KET-tā dee spee-NA-chee)* Spinach croquettes with parmesan.

Lessi *(LES-see)* Boiled spinach; it is usually tossed in oil when it is cooked, or in some places in butter.

Parmigiana, alla *(al-la par-mee-JA-na)* With butter and grated cheese.

Piemontese, alla *(al-la pyā-mōn-TĀ-zā)* With brown butter, garlic and chopped anchovies, and served with croutons of fried bread.

Polpettine con ricotta, in *(een pol-pāt-TEE-na kōn ree-KŌT-ta)* Little balls of spinach and cottage cheese, fried in oil, and served with butter and grated cheese.

Prosciutto, col *(kol prō-SHOOT-tō)* Cooked in the oven with ham and beaten eggs.

Romana, alla *(al-la rō-MA-na)* Cooked with garlic, sultanas, pine-nuts, oil and butter.

Uvette, con *(kon oo-VET-tā)* Same as alla romana, above.

Spinaci e coste *(spee-NA-chee ā KŌS-tā)* See under *Coste* (p 102).

Topinamburi *(tō-pee-nam-BOO-ree)* Jerusalem artichokes.

Verze *(VERT-tsā)* Green cabbage.

Zucca *(TSOOK-ka)* Pumpkin, gourd.

Zucchini *(tsook-KEE-nee)* Baby marrows, courgettes. See *Antipasti* (p 33).

INSALATA – SALAD

In the better-class Italian hotel and restaurant they will bring oil and vinegar with your salad and make your dressing as you like it. In more modest places they will bring it to you already dressed and it will be full of vinegar. If you want to dress it yourself you must ask for 'insalata non condita'*(een-sa-LA-ta non kon-DEE-ta)* and they will bring the oil and vinegar for you to do it with.

Insalata *(een-sa-LA-ta)* Salad.
  Belga *(BEL-ga)* Chicory salad (also cicoria).
  Bietole rosse, di *(dee BYĀ-tō-lā RŌS-sā)* Beetroot salad.
  Cetrioli, di *(dee chā-tree-YŌ-lee)* Cucumber salad.
  Cicoria, di *(dee chee-KO-rya)* Chicory salad.
  Cipolle cotte, di *(dee chee-PŌ-lā KOT-tā)* Cooked onion salad.
  Composta *(kōm-PŌS-ta)* Mixed salad.
  Cotta *(KŌT-tā)* Salad of cold cooked vegetables.
  Finocchi, di *(dee fee-NŌK-kee)* Fennel salad.
  Mista *(MEES-ta)* Mixed salad.
  Patate, di *(dee pa-TA-ta)* Potato salad.
  Pomodoro, di *(dee pō-mō-DOR-ō)* Tomato salad.
  Radicchio rosso, di *(dee ra-DEEK-kyō RŌS-sō)* A red chicory or endive salad (from the Veneto).
  Stagione, di *(dee sta-JŌ-nā)* The salad in season.

SALSE – SAUCES

Every now and again you will find a section on an Italian menu headed Salse *(SAL-sā)* (Sauces), which includes some reassuring items as 'HP', 'Wooster' and 'Colman's Mustard'. It will also include what one might call *sauces du jour* – the sauces which are 'on' for that day. Many of these are already to be found in our section on Sauces for *pasta asciutta* (p. 38). A selection of the remainder is listed below.

Acciughe, con *(kən at-CHYOO-ğa)* An anchovy sauce which you will be relieved to know doesn't come out of a bottle.

Acetosa *(a-chā-TŌ-za)* Vinaigrette.

Agliata, l' *(lal-YA-ta)* (Liguria) A garlic sauce made from the pounded crumb of bread and garlic, thinned with wine vinegar.

Agrodolce *(u-grō-DŌL-chā)* Sweet-and-sour sauce.

Aurora *(aoo-RŌ-ra)* A cream sauce coloured with tomato to suggest the rosy dawn.

Balsamella/Besciamella *(bal-sa-MEL-la/bā-sha-MEL-la)* *Béchamel:* a white sauce.

Bianca *(BYAN-ka)* White sauce – and like most Italian white sauce likely to taste of cheese.

Capperi, con *(kən KAP-pā-ree)* Caper sauce.

Cipolla, alla *(al-la chee-PŌL-la)* Onion sauce.

Funghi alla veronese, di *(dee FOON-gee al-la vā-rō-NĀ-zā)* Mushroom sauce, speciality of Verona.

Genovese *(jen-ō-VĀ-zā)* Chopped veal, vegetables, mushrooms, tomatoes and white wine.

Maionese *(ma-yō-NĀ-zā)* Mayonnaise.

Maionese all'aglio *(… al-LAL-yō)* Garlic-flavoured, rather like the French *aioli.*

Maionese verde *(… VER-dā)* A mayonnaise coloured green with spinach and containing capers and gherkins.

Olandese *(ō-lan-DĀ-zā)* Hollandaise.

Peperoni, di *(dee pā-pā-RŌ-nee)* Sweet peppers, tomato, garlic.

Pesto *(PES-tō)* See p 51.

Piccante *(peek-KAN-tā)* Piquant sauce made with ham, onion, celery, clove, bay, garlic, vinegar, *mostarda* (see p. 19), capers and gherkins.

Pizzaiola *(peet-tsa-YŌ-la)* (Naples) Fresh tomato sauce, flavoured with wild marjoram (origano) or basil, and garlic. The original *pizza* sauce.

Rafano, di *(dee RA-fa-nō)*   Horseradish sauce.

San Bernardo, di *(dee san ber-NAR-dō)* (Sicily) Sweet-and-sour sauce of pounded almonds and breadcrumbs, anchovies, orange juice, grated chocolate and vinegar.

Tartufata *(tar-too-FA-ta)*   Meat sauce flavoured with Marsala or white wine and garlic, with sliced truffles added.

Tocco *(TŌK-kō)* (Genoa)   Meat sauce.

Uvette e pinoli, con *(kon oo-VET-tā ā pee-NŌ-lee)* (Sicily)   Tomato sauce with raisins and pine-nuts.

Verde *(VER-dā)*   Chopped parsley, onion, basil, marjoram, capers, anchovy and hard-boiled egg mixed with oil and vinegar or lemon juice. Served with boiled meats (see *Bolliti* p. 82).

Villeroy *(veel-lā-ROY)*   White sauce thickened with egg yolk and flavoured with such things as grated parmesan, truffles, tongue, pieces of cooked ham.

DOLCI – DESSERTS AND SWEETS

Ananas liquore *(A-na-nas lee-KWO-rā)* Pineapple served with a liqueur.

Arancia affettata *(a-RAN-chya af-fā-TA-ta)* Slices of orange poached in liqueur.

Bongo Bonga *(BŌN-go BŌN-ga)* Profiteroles (Florence).

Budino *(boo-DEE-no)* Pudding.

Budino di mandorle *(boo-DEE-nō dee MAN-dorR-lā)* Almond pudding.

Budino di ricotta *(... dee ree-KŌT-ta)* Sweetened ewe's milk cheese cooked with nuts, lemon peel and egg whites.

Cannoli *(kan-NŌ-lee)* Pastry horns filled with cream, flavoured with lemon, vanilla, chocolate and candied peel.

Cassata alla siciliana (dolce) *(kas-SA-ta al-la see-cheel-YA-na) (DOL-cha))* A rich mould of ricotta cheese, candied fruit, chocolate, flavoured with vanilla and maraschino and supported by sponge fingers.

Cassata alla siciliana (gelato) *(... jā-LA-tō))* This is what most of us hope to get when we ask for a *cassata;* a hunk of ice-cream made in several different coloured layers with candied fruit and almonds.

Crema *(KRĀ-ma)* Custard.

Crema caramella *(... ka-ra-MEL-lā)* Caramel custard *(crème caramel)*.

Fragole al vino *(FRA-gō-lā al VEE-nō)* Strawberries soaked in wine.

Fragoline *(fra-gō-LEE-nā)* Wild strawberries.

Frutta cotta *(FROOT-ta KŌT-ta)* Stewed fruit.

Frutta fresca *(... FRES-ka)* Fresh fruit.

Frutta sciroppata *(... shee-rōp-PA-ta)* Fruit in syrup – but likely to be out a tin.

Gelati *(jā-LA-tee)* Ice-creams.

Gelato di tutti frutti *(jā-LA-tō dee TOOT-tee FROOT-tee)* Ice-cream full of different fruits and chopped candied peel.

Granita di caffe *(gra-NEE-ta dee kaf-FĀ)* Cold coffee poured over crushed ice.

Granite *(gra-NEE-tā)* General term to describe sweets like the *granita* above. There are many different flavours.

Macedonia di frutta *(ma-chā-DŌN-ya dee FROOT-ta)* Fresh fruit salad, sometimes with vermouth or wine added.

Macedonia di stagione o secca *(... dee sta-JŌ-nā o SEK-ko)* Fruit salad of fruit in season or dried fruit.

Marroni canditi/glassati/glacés *(mar-RŌ-nee kan-DEE-tee/glas-SA-tee/gla-SĀ)* Marrons glacés: candied chestnuts.

Mascarpone *(mas-kar-PŌ-na)* A sweetened cream cheese often eaten with strawberries or mixed into a pudding with chocolate, liqueurs etc.

Monte Bianco *(MŌN-tā BYAN-kō)* 'Mont-Blanc' – a purée of chestnuts and sugar, covered with brandy-flavoured whipped cream.

Omelette alla fiamma *(ō-mā-LET-tā al-la FYAM-ma)* A fluffy, sweet omelette with jam, set alight at the table with brandy.

Panettone *(pā-nāt-Tōnā)* Spiced brioche of any size or shape containing sultanas and candied fruit. Invariably eaten at Christmas.

Panforte *(pan-FOR-tā)* (Siena) A famous hard cake of nuts, cocoa, spices, candied orange and lemon peel, melon and honey.

Panna montata con cialdoni *(PAN-na mōn-TA-ta kοn chal-DO-nee)* (Tuscany) Whipped cream served with wafers.

Pera al forno *(PE-ra al FOR-nō)* Pears baked as we bake apples. Very good.

Pere caramellate *(PE-rā ka-ra-mal-LA-ta)* Pears dipped in boiling sugar.

Pere cotte bianche/rosse *(PE-rā KOT-ta BYAN-kā/RŌS-sa)* Pears baked in white or red wine.

Pesche ripiene *(PES-kā ree-PYEN-nā)* Stuffed baked peaches.

Profiteroles *(prō-FEE-tā-rōl)* Cream buns covered with hot chocolate sauce.

Semifreddo *(sā-mee-FRĀD-dō)* Ice-cream cake.

Sorbetti *(sor-BET-tee)* Sorbets – water ices.

Spumone *(spoo-MŌ-nā)* An ice-cream with nuts and strawberries or raspberries.

Tirami Su *(TEE-ra-mee-SOO)* Literally 'pick-me-up': a famous variation on the *mascarpone* theme. Not to be missed.

Torrone gelato *(tōr-RŌ-nā jā-LĀ-tō)* Iced nougat pudding.

Torta di frutta *(TOR-ta dee FROOT-tā)*   Fruit flan.

Torta di frutta alla panna *(... al-la PAN-na)*   Fruit flan with cream.

Trancia di torta farcita *(TRAN-cha dee TOR-ta far-CHEE-ta)*   Slice of fruit tart.

Zabaglione/Zabaione *(dza-ba-LYŌ-nā/dza-ba-YŌ-nā)*   Beaten eggs, sugar and Marsala.

Zuppá inglese *(TSOOP-pa een-GLĀ-za)*   Trifle.

FRUTTA – FRUIT ON THE MENU

One of the great joys of eating in Italy is the abundance of fresh fruit to choose from – from May to September, that is. If one spends February, March and April there one may soon tire of the sight of oranges, apples and bananas at every meal; it is too much like being at home. But once the summer starts it is another matter, from the cherries and wild strawberries in May to the peaches, figs and grapes of August and September.

Frutta di stagione *(FROOT-ta dee sta-JŌ-nā)*   Fruit of the season.

Albicocca *(al-bee-KŌK-ka)*   Apricot.

Ananas *(A-na-nas)*   Pineapple.

Arancia *(a-RAN-cha)*   Orange.

Banana *(ba-NA-na)*   Banana

Cachi *(KA-kee)*   Persimmon.

Ciliegie *(cheel-YA-jā)*   Cherries.

Cocomero *(kō-KŌ-mă-rō)*   Water melon.

Datteri *(DAT-tā-ree)*   Dates.

Fico/fichi *(FEE-kō/FEE-kee)*   Figs.

Fragole *(FRA-gō-lā)*   Strawberries.

Fragole/fragoline di bosco *(FRA-gō-lā/fra-gō-LEE-nā dee BOS-kō)*   Wild strawberries.

Lamponi *(lam-PO-nee)*   Raspberries.

Mandarino *(man-da-REE-nō)* Tangerine.

Mela *(MEL-a)* Apple.

Melagranata *(mā-la-gra-NA-ta)* Pomegranate.

Melone *(mā-LŌ-nā)* Melon.

Nespole di Giappone *(NES-pō-lā dee jap-PŌ-nā)* Loquat, Japanese medlar.

Pera *(PE-ra)* Pear.

Pesca *(PES-ka)* Peach.

Pescanoce *(pās-ka-NŌ-chā)* Nectarine.

Susine *(soo-ZEE-nā)* Plums.

Susine verdi *(soo-ZEE-nā VER-dee)* Greengages.

Uva *(OO-va)* Grapes

FORMAGGI – CHEESES

The list below is designed as a selection of the less parochial cheeses, some of which (and only some) are likely to be found on menus in the average good-class Italian restaurant regardless of what region it is in.

Formaggi assortiti al carrello *(fŏr-MAD-jee as-sŏr-TEE al kar-RĔL-lō)* Assorted cheese on the trolley.

Asiago *(as-YA-gō)* Cow's milk from the province of Vicenza.

Bel paese *(bel pa-Ā-zā)* What has been so well described as a 'bland' cheese – mild, soft, harmless, made of cow's milk and thoroughly 'safe' for those who are suspicious of foreign cheese. *Bel paese* is a brand name, made in Lombardy by the firm of Galbani – the Kraft of Italy.

Caciocavallo *(ka-chō-ka-VAL-lō)* Made from buffalo or cow's milk, firm (not hard) but with a spicy flavour. Rather like *provolone* (see below).

Caciocavallo is short for *cacio a cavallo* – cheese on horseback – which comes from the way the cheese are ripened in pairs astride a horizontal pole. It does not, as so many writers will keep telling us, derive from the cheese having originally been made with mare's milk. It is a picturesque idea, but unfortunately you don't get milk from a *cavallo*; the Italian for mare is *cavalla*.

The Neapolitans, characteristically suspicious of other Italians, do not subscribe wholeheartedly to the idea of *cacio a cavallo*. They think it might come from *cacio col cavallo* – cheese 'stamped with the effigy of the wild horse shown in the coat of arms of the city of Naples'. Could be…

Caciotta *(ka-CHŌT-ta)* A soft cheese made from ewe's milk in Tuscany, cow's milk in Umbria, a mixture of both in the Marches, and a goat's milk in Capri.

Crescenza *(krā-SHEN-dza)* Cow's milk cheese from Lombardy, with a texture that has been described as like eating cheese, butter and cream in one mouthful.

Dolcelatte *(dōl-chā-LAT-tā)* A mild veined cheese which has been poetically called 'parsley in cream'.

Fior di latte *(fyor dee LAT-tā)* 'Flower of the milk' – a fresh, as distinct from salted, *mozzarella* (qv), and which when really fresh is terribly good; it squeaks in the mouth as you eat it.

Fontina *(fōn-TEE-na)* A famous 'bland' cheese which gets into everything in Piedmont. It is fat, made from full cow's milk from one milking.

Gorgonzola *(gor-gōn-ZŌ-la)* This is one cheese which is best eaten in Italy where they are better judges of the right moment to eat it. There is also a white variety – *gorgonzola bianca* – which is worth asking for.

Grana *(GRA-na)* The generic name for the finely grained cheese of Emilia. A table as well as a cooking and grating cheese. See *Parmigiano* below.

Groviera *(grō-VYER-a)* The Italian spelling of *gruyère;* which is a Swiss cheese, but appears on menus all over Italy as *groviera*.

Mozzarella *(mōt-tsa-REL-la)* This famous soft Neapolitan cheese is as much a part of the Naples landscape as Vesuvius. It should be made of buffalo milk and eaten really fresh; once the buttermilk has drained from it, they say, it is only fit for cooking with. Like the *pizza napoletana* it decorates, *mozzarella* is now made in many foreign parts of Italy – but with cow's milk.

Parmigiano *(par-mee-JA-nō)* The most famous of all grating cheeses is also eaten at the table when it is young and bears no resemblance to the unyielding grey brick so often sold as parmesan.

Table *parmigiano* has a slightly sweet taste and is an excellent cheese to finish your wine with.

Pastorella *(pas-tō-REL-la)* 'Bland' cheese; it is indistinguishable from *Bel paese* by most people.

Pecorino *(pā-kō-REE-nō)* Ewe's milk cheese made in every province of Italy with many variations – some distinctly better than others.

Provola *(PRŌ-vō-la)* A fresh cheese made with buffalo milk – or should be. A speciality of Campania, but not so famous as . . .

Provolone *(prō-vō-LŌ-nā)* Which is made with buffalo or cow's milk and comes in all shapes and sizes – spherical, pear-shaped, sausage-shaped, marrow-shaped.

Ricotta *(ree-KŌT-ta)* A cottage cheese made from the whey of ewe's milk and found in every region of the peninsula except three – we forget which.

Robiola *(rō-BYŌ-la)* A creamy cheese from Lombardy and absolutely delicious eaten *all'olio*.

Sardo *(SAR-dō)* More fully *pecorino sardo* – the ewe's milk cheese from Sardinia used by the Genoese in the making of pesto (see p. 53) but also eaten as an excellent table cheese.

Scamorza/Scamozza *(ska-MOR-tsa/ska-MŌT-tsa)* The same kind of cheese as *mozzarella* (qv) but made only with cow's milk.

Stracchino *(strak-KEE-nō)* Soft creamy cheese with a name used to describe many other Lombardy cheeses of the same nature.

Svizzero *(ZVEET-tsā-rō)* 'Swiss'. Likely to be *gruyère* or *emmenthaler*.

Taleggio *(ta-LED-jō)* Italy's answer to *camembert*. A soft, creamy cheese from Bergamo; pongy but delicious in an advanced state.

LA LISTA DEI VINI – THE WINE LIST

In terms of sheer volume Italy produces more wine than any other country, and vast quantities of it are exported: mostly the cheaper kinds of what is politely called 'table wine', and for many years the very idea of Italian wine conjured up visions of endless rows of screw-topped bottles of *Valpolicella* and *Soave*. But every region of Italy produces its own wines – there are literally thousands of them – and some are very good indeed. The last twenty years have seen an astonishing leap in the overall quality, yet long-established prejudice against the notion that the Italians can produce fine wines makes it very hard for the better producers to get a fair price for their vintages. Which means that now is a very good time from the consumer's point of view, with excellent Italian wine obtainable in and outside the country relatively cheaply (certainly much more cheaply than comparable French wines), although this state of affairs will not last for ever; indeed the situation is already changing, with 'class' labels such as *Venegazzu* and *Carmagnino* beginning to appear in the chain-stores – and prices rising.

Such has been the pace of change that even experts struggle to keep up, but it is possible to do some homework, and the standard guide is still Burton Anderson's *Vino* (Little, Brown, 1980) or, if you find that too bulky, Nicolas Belfrage's *Life Beyond Lombrusco* (Sidgwick and Jackson, 1985). In the next section of the book, THE REGIONS OF ITALY, we have done our best to indicate the best wines to try in each area that you might visit, but this is in no way meant to put you off the *vino della casa* (house wine) – a much safer bet in Italy than in France. But that will still be on the table next year, when the currently-underpriced 'stars' have moved beyond our reach.

The DOC system, and beyond

Before embarking on our survey, however, we had better have a quick look at the way in which wine is produced, classified and sold in Italy, and try to make some sense of what is unquestionably a fairly chaotic situation. When writing on the same subject in 1971 we said:'The idea of the principle of *appellation contrôlée* in Italy is still very much in its infancy; only a handful of wine districts are affected by the Government's move in 1965 to make fake labels and general Passing-Off illegal. In Piedmont they are strict about appellation, and in Tuscany the *Chianti classico* – which is more often found in ordinary bottles than in straw-covered flasks – can be recognised by the small label on the neck showing the *gallo nero sul campo d'oro* – in heraldic terms; or, a cockerel rampant sable.

Wines made just outside the central region of Chianti may call themselves *Chianti,* but not *Chianti classico.*

'Even with the introduction of compulsory classification of this kind, however, one rarely has to bother about vintage dates. Italian wine is drunk very young as a rule, as soon as it is fit to drink – about six months old. Some growers keep their wine longer, and we once drank a bottle of *Chianti* from the late Sir Osbert Sitwell's estate at Montegufoni *(Proprietà del Sir Barone Osbert Sitwell,* the label said), which bore a notice informing the consumer that "as a result of long maturing, the contents of this bottle may produce a certain sediment". The wine was less than three years old – an age when even a precocious claret has scarcely got its eyes open.'

Since then the system of controls has advanced considerably, although it is still nowhere near the French standard, and vintage dates are – as we shall see – now much more relevant. The DOC system (DOC stands for *Denominazione di Origine Controlata)* corresponds to the French AOC system, and there are three types of DOC. In the first, just the geographical name appears on the label, and this can be the name of a village, a valley or an entire zone (e.g. *Chianti).* In the second, the geographical name appears in conjunction with the type of grape from which the wine is made (e.g. *Moscato d'Asti).* In the third, the name is simply invented, appearing alongside the geographical name, or on its own *(Est! Est!! Est!!!).* Purely imaginary names are rare, however, and the main purpose of the DOC classification is to guarantee the origin of the wine. It is not, though, a guarantee of *quality,* and while it is true that some DOC wines are poor, it is also the case that many quality producers refuse to toe the DOC line (politics, general cussedness), so that some very fine wines are classified in what is in theory the lowest category of Italian wine, *vino da tavola* (table wine).

Other excellent wines win Italy's highest appellation, the recently-introduced DOCG (DOC 'and guaranteed', with a paper seal over the cork). This means that not only does the wine come from a designated area, but that some of the vintage has also been tested and approved by an official, Rome-based tasting panel. There are only five DOCG wines: *Barbarescu, Barolo, Brunello di Montalcino, Chianti* and *Vino Nobile di Montepulciano,* some of which are better than others, to put it tactfully: politics again?

At the bottom end of the scale is the aforementioned *vino da tavola,* which may come either with or without a geographical label. Because of the peculiarities of the DOC system a great deal of very respectable wine goes out into the world as *vino da tavola,* as well as some more than respectable wines (see above) – and of course a lot of fairly rough stuff too. Some of the better wines in this seemingly catch-all category may soon earn a classification called *vino tipico* (roughly the same as the French *vin de pays),* but meanwhile you do need to know your way around. We hope that Section III of this book will help.

The DOC system therefore has some way to go before it gains full credibility and, after some years of political intrigue and general confusion, progress was not helped by the recent scandal in which certain producers were discovered to have been boosting their wine with methyl alcohol – a more serious, though less widely reported, matter even than the Austrian anti-freeze horror of 1985. The wines concerned were all at the very bottom end of the price and quality scale, however, and no suspicion attached itself to the quality producers. It is something about which they are philosophical – and we can be too, for here is a justification (as if one were needed) to explore those superb and often under-priced wines of which we spoke earlier. In our regional survey, we therefore concentrate on *producers* rather than just names, and these are given as NAMES TO TRUST, with a selection of reliable wines listed in a summary at the end of each regional section.

What to ask for

A bottle *Una bottiglia.*

Half a bottle *Una mezza bottiglia.*

A flask (about a litre) *Un fiasco.*

A small flask *Un fiaschino.*

Red wine *Vino rosso* (or *vino nero* in Sicily and Sardinia).

White wine *Vino bianco.*

Rosé *Rosato* (but often listed as *rosé).*

Dry wine *Vino secco.*

Sweet, sweetish *Abboccato.*

Really sweet *Dolce.*

Sparkling *Spumante.*

Pétillant *Frizzante.*

Local wine *Vino Locale* (or *vino del paese).*

A glass *Un bicchiere.*

In a carafe *In caraffa.*

A litre *Un litro* (approx 1.75 pints).

Half a litre   *Un mezzo litro* (approx 0.88 pints).

Quarter of a litre   *Un quartino* (approx. 0.44 pints).

Deciphering the label

Abbocato   A light, fresh sweetness, but not cloying.

Amabile   Slightly sweeter than *abbocato*.

Annata   The vintage.

Asciutto   Dry.

Azienda agricola   Farm estate.

Bianco, vino   White wine.

Brut   Means dry in relation to sparkling wines.

Cantina   Cellar.

Cantina sociale   A co-operative of growers.

Casa vinicola   Winery.

Cerasuolo   A dark rosé wine.

Chiaretto   A medium rosé wine.

Classico   Denotes a wine grown in the heart of the region where the wines were traditionally grown (e.g. *Valpolicella Classico*).

Consorzio   A voluntary organisation set up to regulate style and promote the wines.

DOC   *Denominazione di Origine Controllata:* the national wine law controlling the origin of a wine, the grape varieties that can be used, and a host of other details.

DOCG   As DOC, but with a *garantito* added. Only applies to a handful of wines, and involves adherence to a much more rigid set of regulations.

Fattoria   Farm.

Frizzante   Lightly sparkling, frothing.

Imbottigliato all'origine   Bottled on the spot: a term that can only be used by estates which bottle their own wines.

Imbottigliato da   Bottled by . . . (i.e. bottled by someone other than the grower).

Imbottigliato dal viticoltore   Bottled by the grower.

Imbottigliato nella zona di produzione   Bottled in the region where the wine is produced (but not on the estate).

Passito   A sweet wine made from grapes that have been partially or wholly dried.

Produttore   Producer.

Riserva   Means that the wine has been aged for a specified period, as controlled by law, which varies from wine to wine.

Riserva speciale   Aged a little more than a *riserva*.

Rosato, vino   Rosé wine.

Rosso, vino   Red wine.

Secco   Dry.

Spumante   Sparkling.

Superiore   A DOC wine made to (usually) higher standards, such as a higher degree of alcohol.

Vendemmia   Harvest.

VIDE   Denotes that the producer of the wine belongs to an association of quality producers, which means that the wine itself has passed certain rigorous tests.

Vigna/vigneto   Vineyard; on labels, the term can only be used when the grapes from which the wine is made are grown in the same place.

Vino della casa   House wine.

Vino da tavola   Table wine; applied to wine made without regard to DOC regulations, the term encompasses some of the greatest, as well as the least, of Italian wines.

Vino tipico   A new category for middle-of-the-range wines, corresponding roughly to the French *vin de pays:* table wine assigned to a specific geographical area, and usually better than *vino de tavola*.

Vino novello   New wine, as with *vin nouveau* in France. The term is applied to a wine meant for drinking as soon as possible after the vintage.

VQPRD   *Vini di Qualita' Prodotti in Regioni Delimitate:* a quality wine produced in a delimited area. Embraces all DOC wines.

VSQPRD   As above, for sparkling wine.

SECTION TWO

The Regions of Italy

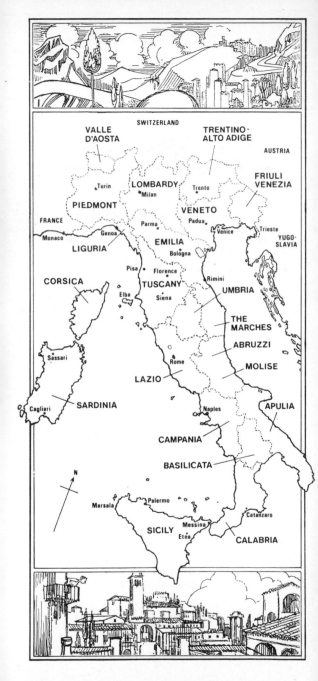

THE REGIONS

Our own first experience of the fascination of the
Italian regions was during a long winter's journey
from Venice to Palermo and Catania to Turin. Our
journey was frequently interrupted (its purpose was
a study of the great opera houses of Italy) and at each
stop our hosts made a point of introducing us to the
food and drink of their own area. In this way we
enjoyed an enormously satisfying, and almost comprehensive, initiation into the pleasures of regional
eating and drinking.

Our tour took us to Venice, Milan, Parma, Florence, Rome, Naples, Palermo, Catania, Genoa and
Turin (in that order), which meant that we not only
visited, and lingered in, at least six of the most interesting gastronomic centres of Italy, but ate on the
shores of the peninsula's four seas as well – the
Adriatic, the Ionian, the Tyrrhenian and Ligurian.
We also encountered some typical regional dishes
from time to time in the railway restaurant cars,
though on the whole these are best avoided nowadays.

Since then we have always made a point of dawd-
ling on our way through Italy, not only for the food
and drink to be enjoyed on overnight stops, but because there are so many other obvious attractions to
be found, in unfamiliar places which too many tourists dash through too fast, without ever giving so
much as a look in their direction.

What so many people do not realize is how accessible these just-off-the-*autostrada* places are. It occurs to
few travellers on their way along the Autostrada del
Sole to turn off at Chiusi to spend the night in Perugia
only 30 miles away and so have their first sight of the
peculiarly lovely Umbrian countryside on their way
to one of the most fascinating towns in Italy. And of
the thousands of visitors who drive to and from Rimini and the Adriatic coast every year, few ever think to
spend a few hours in Parma, a city of great character,
with magnificent food, a superb collection of pic-
tures, and understandably proud of its unique association with the Empress Marie-Louise, Verdi and
Toscanini.

Indeed, if the traveller uses no other routes to get
him to his holiday destination and back, he could not
choose an easier jumping-off ground than the *auto-
stradas* for spontaneous and enjoyable excursions into
the hearts of the regions.

If you leave via the Mont Blanc tunnel, your way
takes you through the lush pastures of Piedmont and
the spectacular scenery of the Aosta valley, two districts which offer some of the best food in the country. The *autostrada* from Venice to Milan has exits

along it for Padua and Verona, Vicenza and Bergamo, towns full of individuality and the most pleasant surroundings to eat good food in. Vicenza in particular is a town to return to, and for those staying in Venice scarcely an hour's *autostrada* drive away.

While the best food in Italy – to our personal taste anyway – is to be eaten north of Rome, much of what appears on the menus of the southern regions is better than one has been told – providing one sticks to fish, *pasta*, local hams, sausages and vegetable dishes; cheese and fruit, of course, are always excellent. Curiosity may well encourage you to try some of the odder dishes found in Sicily and Calabria, and we will not dissuade you; it is the principal purpose of this section to try and let the ambitious, the cautious or the merely inquisitive eater know what he is in for and leave him to it.

ABRUZZI – MOLISE

Towns: Abruzzi – L'Aquila, Chieti, Pescara; Molise – Campobasso

Regional Specialities

Brodetto See p.66.

Capocollo See p.24.

Cif Cin Pork dish flavoured with garlic and rosemary.

Maccheroni alla chitarra See p.49.

Mazzarella Dish of lamb's or kid's intestines, with egg, flavoured with spices.

Mortadella di campotosto More highly spiced than Bologna *mortadella* and strongly flavoured with garlic.

Mulette Smoke salt pork.

Orecchie di preti 'Priests' ears' – *pasta*.

Panarda, la Traditional epic feast involving many of the listed specialities.

Papicci al pomodoro A kind of *pasta* with tomatoes.

Pincigrassi See *vincisgrassi* (p.47).

Polpi in purgatorio Inkfish in a highly spiced tomato sauce.

Porchetta As in the Marches (see p.168).

Riso e fagioli Highly spiced stew of rice and white beans, flavoured with tomato.

Salsicce di fegato Pig's liver sausage, flavoured with garlic and orange peel.

Scapece Pickled fried fish, flavoured with saffron.

Scripelle imbussi Pancakes filled with cheese and chopped ham.

Scrippelle in brodo Very thin fritters in broth, with chickens' livers, cheese and meat.

Sopporessate Salami.

Tacchino alla canzanese Boned turkey in aspic.

Timballo abruzzese See p.46.

Trippa alla paesana Tripe cooked with fresh tomatoes, small hot peppers, mint and served with *pecorino* cheese or parmesan.

Ventricina, la A sausage made of pig's stomach cooked with pimentos, fennel and orange rind.

Virtu, le Minestrone of pork sausage, veal rissoles, *pasta* and fresh vegetables.

Cheeses

Caciocavallo (cow)
Caciofiore (cow)
Mozzarella (see p.114)
Pecorino (ewe)
Provola, provolone (see p.115)
Ricotta (cottage cheese of ewe's milk whey)
Ricottina (small ricotta cheese)
Scamorza (cow)

Wine

Most vines are grown on a narrow coastal plain which gives way to a mountainous , rugged interior, where only several favoured valleys are suitable for cultivation. The two major grape varieties; the red *Montepulciano* and the white *Trebbiano* lend their names to the local DOC's.

Montepulciano d'Abruzzo A DOC for both red and *rosé* wines made fron the *Montepulciano* grape. The *Cerasuolo (rosé)* version is a pleasantly pink, dry *rosé* which is usually fresh if unexciting but can, from some producers *(Valentini)*, be amongst the best in Europe.
 The red is a rich, smooth and full-bodied wine, which can be one of Italy's finest. Some producers *(Sant'Agnese)* make a lighter, fresher style, best drunk young, while others *(Valentini, Pepe)* make a fuller wine which will age well for up to 15 years. Good recent vintages include '85, '83 and '82.

Trebbiano d'Abruzzo A pale, dry wine which is made from the localized clone of the *Trebbiano* grape.

Usually neutral and pleasant from most producers, it is rich, complex and flavoursome when made by *Valentini* or *Pepe*.

Names to trust:

Cantina Sociale di Tollo	Sant' Agnese
Illuminati	Pepe
Casal Thaulero	Valentini

Molise Independent since 1963, this tiny region is still thought of as nothing more than a southern appendage of the Abruzzi, and has only just been granted its first two DOC's, which closely resemble those of its northern neighbours. Both *Pentro* and *Biferno* are made in red and rosé versions from the Montepulciano grape, and in a white from the Trebbiano.

RED	WHITE
Montepulciano d'Abruzzo	Trebbiano d'Abruzzo
Rosso del Molise	Peligno Bianco
Cerasuolo d'Abruzzo (rosé)	Bianco del Molise

BASILICATA (LUCANIA)

Towns: Matera, Potenza

Regional Specialities

Warning: there is ginger with almost everything.

Anguille del Lago Monticchio Eels roasted, or in *carpione* – that is, fried and then marinated in wine, oil, onion, etc.

Cazmarr Stew of lamb's guts, cheese and *prosciutto*.

Cutturieddu Lamb and tomato stew.

Gnommerielli di animelle Sweetbreads cooked on skewers.

Lann Home-made macaroni served with beans or lentils.

Lepre alla cacciatora Hare with tomatoes, sage, garlic, olive oil, rosemary.

Maccheroni alla carrettiera See p.48.

Maccheroni alla trainiera See p.52.

Minestra di cavoli Cabbage soup with bacon and hot red peppers.

Pollo alla lucana Chicken stuffed with *pecorino* cheese, chopped chickens' livers and egg.

Pollo alla potentina Pieces of young chicken cooked in oil with onion and ground red peppers, white wine, fresh tomatoes and flavoured with basil.

Soppressate Sausage flavoured with garlic.

Cheese

Burrini Cheese with a butter filling
Casiddi Little hard cheese
Caciocavallo (cow)
Mozzarella (see p.114)
Scamorza (cow)

Wine

This stark, southern region has only one wine of note, made from the *Aglianico* (of Hellenic origin) grape grown on the slopes of the extinct volcano Vulture. *Aglianico del Vulture* is one of the great red wines of Italy. Rich, smooth and well-balanced, it is an ideal partner to the rich meat stews of the region. Good recent vintages are '81, '79 and '77. Names to trust are *Fratelli D'Angelo* and *Paternoster*.

The white wines of the region are made primarily from the *Malvasia* and *Moscato* grapes, and are mostly sweet and often sparkling. A drier version of *Malvasia* is produced, and is best drunk young.

A local curiosity is *Asprino;* a dry, frothing white. Best left to the curious.

RED

Aglianico del Vulture
Montepulciano

WHITE DRY

Asprino

WHITE SWEET AND SPARKLING
DESSERT WINES

Malvasia del Vulture
Moscato del Vulture

CALABRIA

Towns: Reggio di Calabria, Catanzaro, Cosenza

Regional Specialities

Note: In Calabria *pasta* is made into curious and elaborate shapes – it is thought to make up for the fact that it is only flour and water without fillings. We include in the list below some of the peculiar names given to *pasta* in the region, in order to identify them for the reader who may want to eat *pasta* – or, more important, may not.

Capiddi d'angilu 'Angel's hair' – *pasta*.

Filatelli *Pasta*.

Fusilli *Pasta.*

Lasagne imbottite *Lasagne* (see p.40) with meat sauce, cheese and meat balls.

Licurdia A broth in which there are *croutons* of bread with lots of hot red peppers.

Maccheroni con la ricotta See p.51.

Melanzane farcite Aubergines stuffed with anchovy, tomato, and flavoured with garlic and parsley.

Melanzane in agrodolce Aubergines in a sweet-and-sour sauce.

Melanzane ai funghetti See p.28.

Millescosedde A very thick soup made of two sorts of dried beans, chick-peas, lentils, cabbage, onion, mushrooms, celery.

Morseddu Pork and veal offal in tomato sauce, flavoured with cayenne pepper, and served with *pitta* – a kind of crustless bread.

Nocchetedde *Pasta.*

Pasta alla calabrese With a ginger-flavoured tomato sauce.

Paternostri *Pasta.*

Pesce spada Swordfish; cooked in many ways.

Recchietelle 'Little ears' – *pasta.*

Ricchie 'i prieviti 'Priests' ears' – *pasta.*

Ricci di donna 'Ladies' curls' – *pasta.*

Sagne *Pasta.*

Schiaffetoni A local version of *cannelloni* (with a meat and cheese filling).

Sopressata Sausage.

Spaghetti al filetto di pomodoro With whole fresh tomatoes.

Stivaletti *Pasta* in the form of 'little boats'.

Stranugugliapreviti 'Strangle-priests' – *gnocchi* of semolina.

Trota arrostita Trout roasted over an open fire, served with mayonnaise or lemon and oil. Other Calabrian ways of cooking trout are baking and steaming.

Turridu You will probably not see this on a menu, but if you hear of it in Calabria you may well wonder what it has to do with the hero of *Cavalleria rusticana*. The answer is nothing that we can discover. It is an almond biscuit with icing sugar.

Ziti alla reggiana   Very large *spaghetti* cooked in the oven with aubergines, *mozzarella* cheese, a thick meat sauce, and grated *pecorino* cheese.

Cheese

Burielli/butirri   With butter filling.
Caciocavallo   (see p.113)
Mozzarella   (see p.114)
Pecorino piccante   Piquant ewe's milk cheese.
Provola   (see p.115)
Ricotta fresca   Fresh cottage cheese
Ricotta salata e affumicata   Salted and smoked.

Wine

Calabria is the toe of Italy, and is a region of great antiquity, with Greek ruins scattered about the coast. *Ciro*, the most famous of the region's eight DOC's, is said to have been given to those returning triumphantly from early Olympics.

Ciro   A DOC for red, white and *rosato* wines made on the Ionian coast around the town of Ciro. The red and *rosato* are made from the *Gaglioppo* grape; with the latter being fresh and light while the former is big and robust and an ideal accompaniment to the rich pork dishes of the region.
  The white, made from the *Greco Bianco* grape, has improved dramatically in recent years as modern vinification techniques have filtered into the region.

Good vintages: '85, '81, '79 and '78.

Names to trust: *Librandi, Caruso, Ippolito*.

Donnici   A DOC from the western part of the region, it is lighter than *Ciro* and best drunk young.

Greco di Bianco   This is undoubtedly one of Italy's greatest sweet wines, and from one producer, Ceratti, it ranks with the greatest of France and Germany. Made from semi-dried grapes (and, in the case of Ceratti, without any sulphur, the universal tool of winemakers that is used to prevent re-fermentation and bacterial spoilage, and often the cause of whopping headaches the morning-after) it is delicate, rich and perfumed. It matches perfectly the sweet delicacies for which the region is renowned.

Lacryma di Castrovillari   These 'tears' are rich, red and full of flavour, and come in either dry *(secco)* or sweet *(amabile)* versions.

Melissa   This new DOC is similar to *Ciro*, with a full red made from the *Gaglioppo* grape and the white from *Greco Bianco*.

Pellaro A very strong wine of 16% that will improve in bottle, and is a suitable match for roast hare.

Savuto After *Ciro*, probably the best red of the region, medium-bodied and fragrant. There is also a *rosato* version.

Other noted reds from the *Gaglioppo* grape include *Lamezi*, *Mocastro*, *Pollino* and *Sant'Anna di Isola Capo Rizzuto*. Whites that will partner the tuna and swordfish caught off the Calabrian coast include *Aquillace*, *Villa Santelia* and *Lamentino*.

CAMPANIA

Towns: Naples, Avellino, Benevento, Caserta, Salerno, Capri, Ischia

Regional Specialities

Bistecca alla pizzaiola A piece of steak served with *pizzaiola* sauce (see p.51).

Calzoni alla napoletana Stuffed *cannelloni* (see p.39).

Canelloni ripieni (Amalfi) Stuffed *cannelloni* (see p.39).

Fritto misto In Naples this is likely to be a fry of fish, cheese, vegetables and sweetbreads.

Fritto di pesce Mixed fish fry.

Lasagne imbottite Large sheets of *pasta* with *ricotta* cheese, meat sauce, pork rissoles, ham, hard-boiled eggs, sausage. Said to have been invented by Rossini.

Linguine aglio e olio Thin tongue of *pasta* with garlic and oil.

Melanzane alla parmigiana See p.28.

Mozzarella in carrozza See p.29.

Mpepatella di cozzeche Mussels and red peppers.

Olivette sautées Olives sautéed in butter.

Parmigiana di melanzane Aubergine baked with tomato and cheese.

Pastiera Pastry filled with *ricotta* cheese and candied peel.

Peperoni gratinati Stuffed pimentos, rolled in breadcrumbs and cooked in the oven.

Peperoni imbottiti Pimentos stuffed with breadcrumbs, garlic, anchovies, black olives and capers.

Pizza alla napoletana See p.30.

Polpi affogati Baby octopus stewed in their own

juice in a closed pan with tomatoes and chopped parsley.

Polpi alla luciana   Octopus in a sauce of oil, parsley and ginger.

Sartu   See p.44. This is the only Neapolitan rice dish; very little rice is eaten in Naples by the natives anyway.

Sfogliatella   Very like *pastiera* (see above), but made with flaky pastry.

Spaghetti al filetto di pomodoro   With whole fresh tomatoes.

Spaghetti al pomodoro   With characteristically watery tomato sauce served in Naples and miles around.

Spaghetti alle vongole   See p.53.

Strangoloprevete   'Strangle-priests' – *gnocchi* made of semolina.

Vermicelli con vongole   *Vermicelli* is the Neapolitan word for *spaghetti*. It is served with a clam and tomato sauce.

Zuppa alla marinara   Fish stew.

Zuppa di carciofi   Artichoke soup.

Zuppa di soffrito   Soup of pig's entrails cooked in a hot sauce.

Zuppa di vongole   See p.67.

Cheese

Burrini   Cheese with butter filling.
Caciocallo   (see p.113).
Mozzarella   (see p.114).
Provola   Sometimes buffalo milk, usually cow.
Provola di pecora   Made with ewe's milk instead of buffalo's.
Provolone   Buffalo or cow.
Ricotta   Cottage cheese of whey.
Ricotella   Smaller *ricotta*.
Scamorza   Cow.
Provolini   Little *provole*.

Wine

North of Calabria lies Campania, home of Mount Vesuvius and Naples, *pizza* and *spaghetti* and some of the finest and most individual of Italy's wines. The best is produced around Avellino, west of Vesuvius, from *Fiano* and *Aglianico* grapes.

Capri   A DOC for the tiny amount of red and white wine made on this beautiful island. Little, if any, is exported (thankfully) as it is used to slake the thirst of the tourist hordes who annually invade the island.

Falerno While the white is seldom of interest, the red, made from the *Aglianico* grape, can, after five years, develop a fine fragrance and full-bodied smoothness. *Falernum* was a favourite of the ancient Romans, but *Villa Matilde* is the best of the modern producers. Good recent vintages include '83, '81 and '80.

Fiano di Avellino One of the best and most distinct of Italy's white wines, made from the *Fiano* grape grown in the hills above Avellino. Dry and rich, it has an intriguing and complex character that defies description. *Mastroberardino's* version, especially their single vineyard *Vignadora*, is a must for any connoisseur. Recent vintages of note include '84, '83 and '82.

Greco di Tufo Another speciality of *Mastroberardino*, this fine dry white is made from the *Greco* grape north of Avellino. The single vineyard *Vignodangelo* has a nutty richness but can only aspire to the heights reached by *Fiano*.

Lacrima Christi del Vesuvio Although the white is light and fresh and the red warm and generous, neither is as distinguished as the superb name of this new DOC. Grown on the slopes of Mount Vesuvius, *Mastroberardino* (again) and Savriano are names to trust.

Taurasi When made by Campanian wizards *Mastroberardino*, this wine can be awkward and unpleasant in youth but, after 8-10 years, unfolds into a rich, smooth wine of great character. It is best bought young and left to mature, and will accompany roasts perfectly. Good vintages: '83, '81, '77, '75, '73 and '71.

Other lesser wines of Campania include *Biancolella, Ischia* (red and white), *Ravello* and *Solopaca* (red and white). These are best drunk in the region.

RED	WHITE
Ischia rosso	*Ischia Bianco*
Taurasi	*Fiano di Avellino*
Solopaca	*Greco di Tufo*
Lacryma Christi rosso	*Lacryma Christi Bianco*
(also *rosato*)	(also *amabile* – sweet)
Episcopio	*Gran Caruso*

EMILIA-ROMAGNA

Towns: Bologna, Ferrara, Forlí, Modena, Parma, Piacenza, Ravenna, Reggio Emilia, Rimini

Regional Specialities

Anolini *Pasta,* (see p.38).

Anitra in creta Duck baked in a clay case.

Bomba di riso (Parma) See p.43.

Brodetto Fish stew *zuppa di pesce* on Adriatic coast.

Budino di pollo in brodo (Bologna) A chicken broth served with a chicken cream made from a *pureé* of chicken, eggs and grated cheese.

Canestrelli di pollo (Bologna) Fillet of chicken stuffed with smoked ham and onion, served on a pureé of spinach.

Cappellacci di zucca (Ferrara) *Ravioli* filled with pumpkin and grated cheese.

Cappelletti *Pasta* (see p.39).

Chizza Crisp, flaky pastry eaten with plenty of butter and cheese.

Cima ripiena Stuffed veal.

Coppa Sausage from the Val d'Arda.

Cotechino (Modena) See p.80.

Culatello di Soragna/di Zibello Loin of pork cured and eaten like ham.

Eggs on chips Speciality of Rimini (summer only).

Erbazzone (Reggio Emilia) Vegetable soup with spinach, cheese and butter, which was known to Virgil (born 37 miles away) as *moretum.*

Faraone in creta See p.91.

Fogliate *Pasta.*

Gnocchi alla parmigiana See p.39.

Lasagne al forno Baked *lasagne* (see p.40).

Melanzane alla parmigiana Slices of aubergine fried with ham and tomatoes and cooked diced ham added. Peeled tomatoes can be added according to taste. This dish, eaten in Parma itself, differs considerably from that on page .28.

Padellete A *cassoulet* of pork ribs and white beans.

Porcini bianchi White mushrooms.

Prosciutto Ham. The best comes from Felino, Langhirano and Parma.

Risotto al sugo (Reggio Emilia) *Risotto* with cheese and minced chicken.

Risotto alle vongole *Risotto* with clams.

Spalla di San Secondo Shoulder of pork cured like ham. There are several references to it in the letters of Verdi, one of whose favourite dishes this was.

Stracotto In Parma this is topside stewed whole, with wine, pork sausage, vegetables, spices – including cinnamon – and herbs, garnished with mushrooms or truffles.

Taitadei Tagliatelle (ribbon *pasta*) in Piacenza.

Tortelli d'erbette Small cushions of *pasta* filled with cheese and spinach.

Tortellini *Pasta* (see p.47).

Turtei *Tortelli* in Piacenza – filled with cheese and spinach.

Zampone (Modena) See p.82.

Cheese

Grana This is the generic name for finely grained cheeses of which parmesan (more strictly *Parmigiano-Reggiano)* is the most famous. It is produced in the provinces of Parma, Reggio Emilia and Modena. The name *grana* appears quite often on menus as an eating (as distinct from a grating) cheese.

Grana padano *Grana* from the Po valley. It is made at Ferrara, Piacenza and Bologna. It is also made in Lombardy, further up the river.

Parmigiano See p.114.

Provolone del Pacentino *Provolone* (see p00) from the province of Piacenza.

Robiola all'olio Strictly speaking this is a Lombardy cheese, but the way we ate it near Parma – the soft creamy cheese made into a paste with olive oil – was absolutely delicious and so we regard it as a speciality of Emilia.

Wine

A rich, varied region that practically bisects Italy, stretching from the Adriatic coast almost as far as Genoa, Emilia-Romagna produces more wine than any other in Italy. In the west of the Region, Emilia, home of parmesan and Parma ham, *Lambusco* reigns supreme. In Romagna, between Bologna and Rimini, the fresh dry whites and the youthful, fruity reds are dominant, but throughout the region the wines are ideally matched with its rich and varied cuisine.

Albana di Romagna A white wine made from the Albana grape grown in the Eastern part of the region that can be either dry, sweet or sparkling. Rarely distinguished, it can rise above mediocrity when handled by producers such as *Fattoria Paradiso, Vallunga* or *Ferrucci.* The rich, nutty sweetness of the *amabile* version can be the ideal *digestif* to a Romagnan meal.

Cabernet Grown here for well over a century, the present vogue for this red grape is leading to an increase in its production. *Vallania, Vallunga* and the *Marchese Malaspina* are names to trust, especially in years such as '85, '83 and '82.

Colli-Bolognesi A DOC that encompasses the zone southwest of Bologna, where the name of the grape variety must also be shown on the label. *Sauvignon* and *Riesling Italico* are the most notable whites while *Cabernet Sauvignon, Merlot* and *Barbera* are the best reds. Producers such as *Vallania* and *Conti* lead the way in this promising zone.

Colli Piacentini A large zone on the Emilia-Lombardy border, with the style or grape variety distinguishing the many facets of the appellation. *Barbera,* Italy's most widely planted grape variety, giving young, acidic reds, and *Bonarda,* sometimes slightly frothing and bursting with fruit, are the better reds. Blended, they make *Gutturnio,* generous and rich when drunk young from years such as '85 and '83. The whites, *Trebbiano, Sauvignon* and *Pinot Grigio,* are increasing in popularity. Names to trust include *Fugazza, Pusterla* and *Romagnoli.*

Lambrusco Traditionally, in either its *secco* (dry) or *amabile* (sweet) version, *Lambrusco* was the the perfect wine to quaff with the rich dishes of the region, but now this frothing red wine also sells in enormous quantities as an all-purpose, low alcohol drink. A slightly higher level of quality may be indicated by one of the four DOC's *(di Sorbara, Grasparossa di Castelvetro, Reggiano* or *Salamino di Santa Croce)* being appended to *Lambrusco.* The best way to drink *Lambrusco* is young and slightly chilled with a rich *pasta* dish. The *secco* style is especially recommended. Names to trust include *Cavicchioli, Riunite, Giacobazzi, Chianti, San Prospero* and *Contessa Matilde.*

Lambrusco Bianco Increasingly popular as a sweet and fizzy white wine, this can, as a white wine from black grapes, made sparkling, be delicious, but most of the wine sold under this label hardly merits attention. Best drunk in the region from producers such as *Cavicchioli.*

Sangiovese di Romagna This widely planted red grape seldom produces wines of the same distinction as its Tuscan relation, *Fangioveto*, does in Chianti. From producers such as *Corovin* it is a light fresh wine best drunk young with a midday meal. From the top estates of the region *(Paradiso, Vallunga* or *Spalletti)* however, it reaches a level of quality that only the best *Chiantis* can match, and will improve with several years' ageing.

Trebbiano di Romagna This completes the trio of Romagnan DOC's, and is probably the least distinguished. *Trebbiano* is probably Italy's most widely planted white grape and, although it varies from region to region, usually produces high yields of neutral, dry white wine. Although the application of modern fermentation techniques have wrought a slight improvement in recent years, it is still a wine of little character, best drunk young. The sparkling and sweeter versions are seldom seen. Names to trust include *Paradiso, Vallunga* and *Corovin*.

RED

Lambrusco di Sorbara (the best)
Gutturnio dei Colli Piacentini
Colli Bolognesi
Barbarossa

WHITE

Colli Bolognesi
Albana (dry, sweet and sparkling)
Pagadebit (sweet)

FRIULI – VENEZIA GIULIA

Towns: Gorizia, Udine, Trieste

Regional Specialities

Boreto alla gradese Strongly spiced fish chowder from the island of Grado.

Cialsons *Ravioli* in Udine province.

Cotoletta alla viennese A *Wiener Schnitzel* no less – but remember that most of this region was Austrian until 1918 . . .

Golas/Gulyas/Goullash . . . and that it was part of an Austro-Hungarian Empire, where they ate *goulash.*

Iota triestina A soup of beans, potatoes, pickled cabbage boiled with pigs' trotters and ribs of smoked pork.

Luganega/Luganica   Pork sausage eaten cooked, or dried and eaten raw.

Pesse in saor   Fried fish marinated in wine, oil, herbs, garlic – in other words, *in carpione.*

Prosciutto di San Daniele   See p.31.

Cheese

Formagella pecorina   Ewe's milk cheese.
Montasio   Udine.

Wine

Tucked into the north-eastern corner of Italy, bordering Austria and Yugoslavia, this tiny region was once part of the Venetian Empire. Just as its gastronomic heritage is derived from a variety of sources (*goulash* from Hungary, *sauerkraut* from Bavaria, *San Daniele Prosciutto* from 'Italy'), so its vinous character is a similar hodge-podge, indelibly stamped with a regional character.

The wines from Friuli are clearly and simply labelled with the name of the grape variety and the district in which it is grown. The region has been carved up geographically into seven DOC zones, each of which has a different number of sub-denominations based (with one exception) on the grape variety. The seven DOC's are:

1. *Aquilea* – on the Adriatic coast
2. *Carso* – recently approved DOC, on a small strip of land on the Yugoslav border.
3. *Colli Orientali del Friuli* – runs from the Yugoslav border, north of Collio.
4. *Collio Goriziano* – in the easternmost part of the region, on the border, with Yugoslavia.
5. *Grave del Friuli* – by far the largest DOC, spreading from Udine in the east to the Veneto border.
6. *Isonzo* – nestled in the southeast corner.
7. *Latisana* – a small zone bordering the Veneto on the west and the Adriatic in the south,

Grape Varietico, White.   There is a great diversity of styles amongst the white wines of Friuli, simply because the grape varieties are mostly of French or German origin, with several striking indigenous exceptions. *Pinot Bianco* and *Pinot Grigio* are both widely planted, with the latter producing wines of the highest quality. *Chardonnay* is increasingly popular, giving light dry wines, while *Sauvignon* is making rapid improvements in quality. The great *Riesling* grape (*Riesling Renaro*, as distinct from wines that are labelled *Riesling Italico*, a much inferior grape of dubious provenance) produces dry aromatic wines of great distinction, similar to those of Alsace, while the *Traminer*, a relation to the *Gewürztraminer*, is producing wines with a soft spicey richness in the hands of some producers.

Of the native grape varieties, *Malvasia* has been approved for some DOC's, and is dry and characterful.

The small amount of *Verduzzo* produced can be either dry or sweet, but the latter is by far the finest. Another sweet wine of distinction is *Picolit*, stunningly individual (and expensive) and produced in miniscule amounts.

The best native grape is *Tocai*, unrelated to either the Hungarian or the Alsatian version, which produces dry, rich and distinctive wines throughout the north-east.

Red The Gallic brigade is led, of course, by *Cabernet*, mostly the *Franc* version, which gives fragrant, grassy wines, similar in style to those of the Loire. The *Merlot*, its Bordelais cousin, produces herbaceous, plummy wines of some distinction, while the *Pinot Noir* (*Nero* here) performs as well in Friuli as anywhere outside Burgundy, giving fragrant wines with a primary varietal style.

Of the native varieties, *Refosco*, soft and grapey, seldom disappoints, while *Schioppettino*, wild and fragrant, can be outstanding.

Names to trust: A multitude, but *Ca' Bolani, Dri, Jermann, Plozner, Prinai, Ronco Blanchis* and *Schiopetto* are amongst the best.

RED	WHITE
Grave del Friuli – Merlot	*Collio Goriziano – Tocai*
Colli Orientali – Refosco	*Colli Orientali*
	– Pinot Grigio
	– Picolit

LAZIO (Latium)

Towns: Rome, Latina, Frosinone, Rieti, Velletri, Viterbo

Regional Specialities

Abbacchio   Milk fed lamb (see Agnello, p.78).

Brodettato   A lamb stew.

Carciofi alla guida   Fried small artichokes, see p.24.

Carciofi alla romana   Artichokes stewed in oil. See p.25.

Coda di bue alla vaccinara   Oxtail, see p.70.

Coratella   See p.79.

Fagioli con le cotiche   White beans. See p.102.

Fave al guanciale   Broad beans with bacon and onion.

Fettucine   *Pasta*, see p.39.

Filletti di baccalá   Fillets of dried cod, coated with batter, and fried in oil.

Gnocchi alla romana   See p.39.

Maccheroni alla ciociara   See p.49.

Mazzancolle   Very large prawns. See p.28.

Pollo alla diavola   Grilled chicken. See p.87.

Saltimbocca   Veal, see p.75.

Spaghetti alla carbonara   See p.48.

Spaghetti alla carrettiera   See p.48.

Spaghetti alla matriciana   See all'amatriciana p.50.

Stracciatella   A broth. See p.37.

Suppli al telefono   Rice croquettes. See p.46.

Testarelle di abbacchio   Lamb's head. See p.78.

Trippa alla romana   Tripe (see p.77).

Cheese

Mozzarella   (see p.114)
Pecorino romano   Ewe's milk
Provatura   (see p.115)
Ricotta   Cottage cheese, ewe's milk
Scamorza   Cow

Wine

The Castelli Romani, the hills south of Rome, are home to the mostly neutral white wines (*Frascati, Est!Est!!Est!!!*) that predominate in this region. These ubiquitous whites would be enough to convince most people that the region had little else to offer, but the adventurous few would be amply rewarded if they persevered, for the reds of Latium, available in small amounts, can be very fine.

Castelli Romani   A name for table wines from the hills south of Rome which can, in the white version, be a suitable (and cheaper) alternative to *Frascati*.

Cesanese   A red grape variety that forms the basis for three DOC's, all similar in character, that are deep and warm and best drunk in the region.

Colli Albani A white DOC from the *Castelli Romani*, similar in style to an inferior *Frascati*. Best with seafood, or better still with mineral water.

Est!Est!!Est!!! di Montefiascone An easily forgotten wine with an unforgettable name, this dry white wine from the southern part of Latium is lighter and crisper than those from the *Castelli Romani*. It has benefited recently from the use of modern winemaking techniques, but seldom rises above the ordinary.

Frascati Any visitor to Rome will be hard-pressed to find anything other than *Frascati* in their local *trattoria*. They could do worse than this soft, faintly fruity dry white wine which slips down a treat under the hot Roman sun. The best version is the *secco*, although historically it was often slightly sweet *(cannellino)*. Names to trust: *Colli di Catone, Fontana Candida, Sotto d'Oro*.

Marino Similar to but slightly stronger and more flavoured than the wines from neighbouring *Frascati*. Best drunk young. The *Cantini Sociale (Co-operativi)* here is one of the best in the country.

Torre Ercolana A near legendary red, hailed by some authorities as one of Italy's greatest wines. Made from the local *Cesanese,* with equal parts of *Cabernet* and *Merlot*, it is rich and austere when young but unfolds gracefully into a wine of sublime character. '82, '79 and '78 are good recent vintages.

Velletri Another white from the *Castelli Romani*, but this can often be more flavoursome and better value than its more famous relations. The red, light and full of fruit, can be delicious when drunk young and slightly chilled.

RED	*WHITE*
Fiorano Rossa	*Fiorano Bianco*
	Firoano Semillon (sweet)

Very little is produced of these wines, but they are the best of the region. If you are lucky enough to spot one on a menu, treat yourself.

Cesanese di Affile	*Frascati*
Cesanese del Piglio	*Est!Est!!Est!!!*
(Both the above also	*Marino*
come in sweet versions.	*Colli Albani*
Check that you are	
getting the *secco*).	

LIGURIA

Towns: Genoa, Imperia, San Remo, Savona, La Spezia

Regional Specialities

Bagioi   Snails in a sauce of tomato flavoured with mint.

Buddego   Fish stew.

Burrida   See p.67.

Cappon magro   See p.83.

Cima alla genovese   See p.83.

Ciupin   Fish stew.

Condiglione   Mixed salad.

Cundium   Mixed green salad with tunny.

Fricassea di pollo   Chicken fricassée. See p.87.

Fritto alla stecco   *Fritto misto* – a mixed fry of veal, brains, sweetbreads, mushrooms, all dipped in egg and breadcrumbs and fried on a skewer.

Lumache alla genovese   Snails with basil, anchovy, garlic, oil, dry white wine.

Macchettaia   A kind of *pizza*.

Mitili   Mussels, eaten raw the lemon, like oysters.

Pesto   See p.51 – Likely to be served with all *minestre, paste asciutte* and other farinaceous dishes. One of the great sauces of the world.

Rascasse   Fish soup.

Riso arrosto alla genovese   Rice *timbale* with sausages, artichokes, peas, mushrooms and cheese.

Sardenaira   A kind of *pizza*, very typical of the Riviera, cooked with anchovies, tomatoes, black olives, onion, marjoram and flavoured with garlic.

Torta pasqualina   A pie of artichoke, onion, hard-boiled egg, *ricotta* cheese, and herbs; eaten on feast days.

Trenette   *Pasta* speciality of Genoa.

Triglie all'imperatrice   Red mullet cooked in tomato sauce with white wine, cognac, cream, onions and capers.

Zimino   A stew of fish with oil, parsley, fennel, celery, onion and tomatoes.

Zuppa di datteri   Shellfish soup (see *datteri*, p.26).

Cheese

In Liguria nearly all cheese is imported from other regions, but there is a *ricotta* (cottage cheese) made in Savona. Otherwise, the most popular cheese in Genoa and the neighbourhood is *Sardo* – the ewe's milk cheese from Sardinia, which is used for cooking and eating.

Wine

This tiny strip of land that curls around the coast from the French border to Tuscany is home to Genoa, some spectacular coastal scenery, some of Italy's best seafood and, of course, the wondrous *pesto genovese*. The little wine produced is more famous for the beauty of its names and its ability to enhance a magical meal on a terrace overlooking the sea than for its intrinsic quality.

Cinqueterre   A light, fresh, dry white, one of only two DOC's in the region, it is best on the spot, when the senses are transfixed by the scenery and the cuisine and are less concerned with what is being quaffed.

Pigato   A white grape that produces aromatic wines full of flavour, and high in alcohol. Often a better bet than *Cinqueterre*.

Rossese di Dolceacqua   The region's only red DOC can be surprisingly good. Depending on the style of vinification, it can be soft and fruity and best while young, or warm and well-structured, suitable for several years ageing and superb with rabbit. *Rossese di Albenga*, similar in style, can also be quite good.

Vermentino   This reliable white grape variety is none other than our old friend *Malvasia*, masquerading under another name. It is light, fresh and crisp, and probably produces the best white wines of the region.

RED	WHITE
Rossese di Dolceacqua	Pigato
Linero	Vermentino
Dolcetto	Cinqueterre
	Sciacchetra (sweet)

LOMBARDY (LOMBARDIA)

Towns: Milan, Bergamo, Brescia, Como, Cremona, Mantua, Pavia, Sondrio, Varese

Regional Specialities

Agnoli alla mantovana (Mantua) *Ravioli* filled with bacon, beef sauce, salamelle (small *salami*), chickens' livers, cheese, egg yolk, and cooked in broth.

Agoni al burro c salvia Small freshwater shad (*Alosa lacustris*) cooked in butter, flavoured with sage.

Busecca Tripe stewed with vegetables, herbs and spices; served with grated cheese.

Cassoeula/Cazzoeula Stew of pork, vegetables, sausage and cabbage.

Ceci con la tempia di maiale See p.80.

Costaletta alla milanese Veal cutlet, see p.72.

Lenticchie e cotechino Lentils and a sausage which is a poor relation of the *zampone* (see p.82).

Minestrone alla milanese A vegetable soup. See p.36.

Osso buco See p.74.

Panettone A sweet, light bread, made with butter, egg, candied peel and sultanas.

Polenta e osei (uccelli) Little roast birds served on slices of *polenta* (see p.41).

Polenta pasticciata See p.40.

Riso in cagnon Without the typical Milanese flavouring of saffron, but with more butter and cheese.

Risotto alla milanese A saffron-flavoured *risotto*. See p.45.

Risotto alla pilota (Manuta) A *risotto* with onion and butter.

Risotto con salamelle (Mantua) With small fresh *salami*.

Stufato Beef and vegetable stew.

Tinca carpionata Fried tench marinated in wine, vinegar, herbs and garlic.

Tortelli/tortellini di zucca alla mantovana *Ravioli* stuffed with pumpkin, cheese, nutmeg and egg yolk.

Zuppa pavese Broth with an egg. See p.37.

Cheese

Bel paese Needs no introduction.

Bitto A country cheese, mixture of cow and goat milk.
Branzi *Bergamo* – soft cheese like *taleggio,* qv below.
Crescenza Cow.
Gorgonzola
Grana padana Same type as parmesan.
Groviera Gruyère.
Mascarpone Very creamy soft cheese.
Robiola Very soft.
Stracchino Soft creamy.
Taleggio Soft.

Wine

Lombardy, Italy's wealthiest region, with Milan as its capital, spreads from the Alps on the Swiss border to Piemonte in the east and Veneto in the east, with Emilia and the rest of Italy at its feet. From the Alpine valleys to the shores of Lake Garda and the hills of the Po Valley, Lombardy produces a brilliant and bewildering array of wines that, like its cuisine, is highly individual and varied.

Franciacorta The star of this DOC, north of Brescia, is in the ascendant. The still white is dry and slightly biscuity, while the *spumante* can be a very decent glass of fizz or a rival to many Champagnes. *Ca' del Bosco* produces the best *spumante,* but at prices that would embarrass many a Champenois.

The *rosso* is a bizarre mixture of four grape varieties (*Cabernet Franc, Barbera, Nebbiolo* and *Merlot*) producing a classy wine with a fresh, herbaceous character. '85, '83 and '82 were all superb years.

Names to trust: *Ca' del Bosco, Berlucchi, Contessa Maggi, Longhi- De Carli.*

Lugana Grown around Lake Garda, this distinctive dry white is often better than its relative from the Veneto, *Soave.* It is more aromatic and has a greater depth of flavour than many Italian whites. Names to trust include *Dal Cero, Zenato, Lamberti, Co' de Fer.*

Oltrepo Pavese A huge zone in south-west Lombardy that borders Piemonte, this DOC produces a prodigious amount of wine under ten sub-denominations. Some of the best and most widely spread are:

Barbera Probably the best version outside Piemonte which, though lighter, is still full of character.

Bonarda Inky purple with soft grapey fruit and a slight *frizzante* character from some producers, this is an artisanal wine of good quality and supreme character.

Buttafuoco Great name, good rich red wine.

Moscato Sweet and usually sparkling this is the

type of peachy and hedonistic wine at which the Italians excel.

Pinot Both *Nero*, which can produce the smokey, decadent character that is the hallmark of great Burgundy, but is also vinified white and made sparkling as a *blanc de noir*, and *Grigio*, which is quite rich yet with a pleasant crispness, and is sometimes blended and used as a base for sparkling wine.

Rosso A variety of styles with a surprisingly high standard. Can be trusted.

Names to trust: *G. Agnes, Castello di Luzzano, Martini, Alberici.*

Ronco di Monpiano A rich, robust red from the province of Buscia, made with one-third *Merlot* and two-thirds *Marzemino*. One of the region's finest wines, especially from years like '85, '83 and '82. Don Giovanni, incidentally, sings lovingly of the wines of the *Marzemino* grape.

Valcalepio A fresh if rather neutral white and a rich, plummy red make this DOC of some interest.

Valtellina Superiore A DOC on steep slopes near the Swiss border, this is one of the few areas outside Piemonte where the noble *Nebbiolo* grape thrives. The four sub-denominations are *Grumello, Inferno, Fassella* and *Valgella*.

These wines, at their best, are lighter than *Barolo* but have rich tarry character with a tightly knit, tannic fruit on the palate, and are capable of ageing from 7-10 years, or even longer.

Sforzato, a variation on the theme that involves the addition of semi-dried grapes, is fuller and stronger, superb with strong cheeses or as a digestif.

RED	WHITE
Valtellina Superiore	*Oltrepo Pavese*
– *Grumello*	– *Pinot*
– *Inferno*	– *Riesling*
– *Sassella*	*Lugana*
– *Valgella*	*Pinot di Franciacorta*
Oltrepo Pavese	*(methode champenoise)*
– *Buttafuoco*	
– *Barbera*	
Botticino	

Frecciarossa (Red Arrow) is a good producer's name to look out for in this area.

PIEDMONT (PIEMONTE) – VALLE D'AOSTA

Towns: Turin, Aosta, Asti, Alessandria, Cuneo, Novara, Vercelli

Regional Specialities

Agnolotti   See p.38.

Bagna caoda   A hot sauce, see p.23.

Bagnet verd   See under *salsa verde* (p.108).

Bollito   Boiled meats with vegetables.

Bue al barolo   See p.70.

Camoscio in salmí   See p.94.

Camoscio stufato   A stew of *chamoix*, well flavoured with herbs, vegetables and wine.

Castellana gratinata   Poultry or veal *alla castellana* (see p.72)

Faseui   Dialect for white beans (*fagioli*)

Finanziera di pollo   See p.85.

Fondua   Fonduta – see p.27.

Gnocchi alla fontina   Semolina dumplings cooked in milk, to which *fontina* cheese and spices have been added, then rolled in egg and breadcrumbs and fried.

Gnocchi di patate alla bava   Dumplings made of potato, egg, flour and nutmeg, served in a 'cream' of melted *fontina* cheese.

Grissini   (Turin) The famous breadsticks found on Italian restaurant tables all over the world.

Insalata con tartufi   A salad of endive, celery hearts and finely sliced white truffles, dressed with oil, and vinegar.

Mocetta/Moretta di camoscio   *Chamoix*, salted and preserved (Valle d'Aosta).

Polenta alla valdostana   See p.41.

Pollanca ripiena alla piemontese   Young turkey hen (or pullet) stuffed with veal, liver, grated parmesan, truffles, flavoured with nutmeg and Marsala and cooked in the oven.

Pollo alla baby   See p.86.

Rane dorate   Fried frogs' legs.

Riso e ceci   Rice and chick-peas cooked with tomato and flavoured with spices.

Risotto campagnolo   A *risotto* with asparagus tips, fresh peas, red peppers and mushrooms.

Risotto alla valdostana See p.46.

Tortino di tartufi alla piemontese Alternate layers of truffles and game on toast, with a wine and game sauce poured over it.

Trota alla baby Trout split open and sautéed in oil, flavoured with bayleaf and onion.

Trota alla piemontese Trout poached with herbs, together with grated lemon and sultanas, and served with a sauce made from the liquid it was poached in.

Cheese

Fontina Full cow's milk, from one milking.
Paglierina Cow – matured on straw.
Toma and tomini Cow – first cousin of the Tomme of Savoy.

Piedmont is famous for what it calls *elaborati di formaggi*. There is no foreign equivalent; the nearest we get to it is mixing chives with cream cheese for spreading on crackers at cocktail parties. The Piedmontese, on the other hand, make a whole dish out of their elaborations, of which the following three are perhaps the best known:

Fracet Curdled milk and parmesan with *grappa* (the fierce 84 proof spirit distilled from the pressed husks of grapes), a little salt and a lot of pepper.

Sernium Gorgonzola and parmesan grated and mixed with oil, vinegar and salt.

Tomini elettrici *Tomini* cheese (cow's milk) steeped 'for at least ten days' in oil, vinegar, sliced garlic and ground hot red peppers.

Wine

Piedmont stands alone as the region containing Italy's finest red wines; with its *Barolo* and *Barbaresco* producing wines that are rivalled only the great growths of Bordeaux and the small domaines of the Cote d'Or. But if *Nebbiolo*, the grape used to make *Barolo*, reigns supreme in Piedmont, the region also has several other grape varieties that are capable of producing wines of stellar quality.

As a region, Piedmont has well over thirty DOC's, by far the most of any in Italy. As almost all are from single grape varieties, it seems easier to use these names as signposts in order to navigate our way through the region.

White Grapes

Arneis A small amount of wine is made from this indigenous vine around Alba. The best has a rich, nutty creaminess and stunning complexity. Worth a detour, especially from a producer like *Castello di Neive*.

Chardonnay As with the rest of the world, the Piemontese have become fascinated by this great grape, so it will be of growing importance in the near future.

Cortese This indigenous grape forms the base for two DOC's, the best known and most fashionable of which is *Gavi*, a dry citrussy wine that can be good, but seldom merits the exhorbitant prices charged for it. Names to trust include *La Chiara*, *La Scolca*, *Villa Banfi*, *Pio Cesare*.

Erbaluce A DOC from Caluso, this grape makes a dry white which usually surpasses *Gavi* and a sweet *(Passito)* version that is highly distinctive.

Malvasia Forms the base for a couple of uninspired DOC's that seldom travel beyond the confines of the region.

Moscato The Moscato grape *(Muscat)* is one of the oldest known and most distinctive wine grapes. It excels in Piemonte, especially around Asti, lending to wines a sweet, zingy peachiness that is irresistible. Some is sparkling *(Asti Spumante)* and some still *(Moscato d'Asti naturale)*, but all of it is fresh, low in alcohol and, when made properly, delicious.

Names to trust include *Ascheri*, *Contratto*, *Fontanafredda* and *Vietti*.

South of Asti, near Acqui, the *Moscato* grown around Strevi has achieved fame. The wines of Ivaldi are especially notable.

Red Grapes

Barbera By far Piedmont's most widely planted grape variety, *Barbera* is often despised but can produce wines of great style and longevity. It has a distinctive 'farmyard' character and marked sharpness (acidity in winespeak), and reaches its apogee around Alba. *Barbera d'Asti* can also be superb, while that from *Monferrato* is usually lighter. Those from *Giacosa*, *G. Mascarello*, *G. Bologna*, *Gaja* and *Ronco* are especially good.

Brachetto An unusual but intriguing light red, at its best around Acqui, that is usually sparkling and slightly sweet, and is ideal with *Panettone* at Christmas.

Cabernet Sauvignon As with *Chardonnay*, fashion dictates that this noble grape should be planted, but *Gaja*, amongst others, has proved that it can flourish.

Dolcetto An inky purple colour, rich damsony fruit

and a low acidity give this wine a delicious character unrivalled elsewhere, and makes it an ideal partner to every course of the meal. It is grown throughout the southern part of the region, but is at its best around Alba (*Ascheri, Brovia, G. Conterno, Gaja*) and Ovada (*Poggio*).

Freisa Several producers have dragged this light red grape back from the brink of extinction and are now making dry wines, some sparkling, of character. *Pio Cesare,* the *Conterno* brothers and *G. Bologna* are amongst the best producers.

Grignolino Another of Piemonte's highly individual red grape varieties, although this is more of a *rosé* than anything else. It is grown around Asti and Monferrato, and makes an ideal and unusual aperitif.

Nebbiolo It is only in Piemonte that this fickle grape variety performs at its best, but at its best it ranks with the great wines of the world. *Barolo* and *Barbaresco,* hard and austere when young mature into rich, complex wines that have an intriguing aroma of white truffles, tar and violets. Great years include '85, '82, '78, '74 and '71, while '83, '80, '79 and '70 are all good.

As in Burgundy, the style and quality of the wine depends more upon the person who makes it than anything else, so producers should be chosen with care. *Cavallotto, the Conterno Brothers, Cordero, Marcarini, Oddero, Prunotto, Pio Cesare, Ratti* and *Vietti* are all names to trust in Barolo, while *Fontanafredda, Gaja, Giacosa, di Gresy* and the *Produttori* lead the way in Barbaresco.

While *Nebbiolo* is epitomised around Alba, it flourishes throughout the region. The rare but subtle *Carema* is superb from Ferrando, while *Gattinara* can surpass many a *Barolo. Ghemme,* neighbour to *Gattinara,* is lighter but more elegant, while *Lessona* and *Sizzano* can both be fine.

Around Alba, the humble sounding *Nebbiolo d'Alba* can produce superb results, while further north the local name for the grape, *Spanna,* is used for a number of wines, some no better than plonk, others as good as many a *Barbaresco.* Everywhere, through, from the humblest *Spanna* to the most exalted *Barolo,* the *Nebbiolo* gives its distinctive character to the wine: garnet colour, violets, tar, beef extract and truffles on the nose and on the palate, a kernel of rich fruit encased in a layer of hard tannin that is eroded with age as the wine develops a velvety, savoury character.

The beginner would be well-advised to start with the lighter, more accessible versions of *Nebbiolo (Lessona, Nebbiolo d'Alba)* before progressing to the great *Barolos,* as their overwhelming character can be off-putting at first. But whatever you do, don't let that initial obstacle defeat you, for once over it, there is the fascinating world of a great grape variety to be discovered.

RED

Barolo
Barbaresco
Nebbiolo d'Alba
Barnera
Gattinara
Dolcetto
Grignolino

WHITE

Gavi (Cortese di)
Erbaluce di Caluso
Asti Spumante
   (sparkling sweet)
Moscato d'Asti
   (sparkling sweet)
(Dryer *methode champenoise* versions of these last are now being made and are worth looking out for)

PUGLIA (APULIA)

Towns: Bari, Brindisi, Foggia, Lecce, Taranto

Regional Specialities

Agnello al forno con patate e pomodori Chopped-up pieces of lamb cooked in the oven with white wine, onions, rosemary, tomato and – most important – very small new potatoes.

Alici crude alla brindisina Tiny anchovies soaked in oil, pepper and lemon juice and eaten raw.

Biancomangiare Literally 'blancmange'; but culinarily it is rice cooked in almond water (Lecce).

Calzone ripieno Pie filled with such things as onion, olives, anchovies, *pecorino* cheese, boiled dried cod and tomatoes.

Capitone A large eel, either roast or done in *carpione* – that is, fried then marinated in wine, oil, vinegar, herbs, etc.

Capretto ripieno Kid stuffed with herbs and spices and roasted.

Capriata Pungent vegetable stew.

Cavatelli/Cavatieddi Home-rolled traditional *pasta* served with *ricotta, pecorino* and rue.

Cozze alla marinara Mussel stew flavoured with pepper or ginger.

Cozze gratinate Mussels with oil, parsley, garlic and breadcrumbs, baked in the oven.

Gnummarieddi   Offals and lights of kid cooked on a skewer with sage leaves.

Marro   A piece of meat (usually leg of veal) pierced and stuffed with ham, salami, garlic and anchovies mixed with cheese.

Minuicchi/Minuit   *Gnocchi.*

Orecchiette e cima di rape   *Pasta* shaped like 'little ears', with turnip tops, anchovies, oil, garlic.

Ostriche alla tarantina   Raw oysters on the half shell with mussels and slices of smoked salmon.

Pasta con cavolfiore   Layers of *pasta* with *ricotta* cheese and fried flowers of cauliflower.

Richitelle   Dialect word for *orecchiette* (see above).

Risotto alla marinara   With prawns, mussels, tomato, oil, garlic, parsley, wild marjoram and white wine. .

Scazzecappetit   Dialect word for *stuzzica appetito* – something to provoke or stir up the appetite. In other words, *antipasti.*

Spiedini di capretto   Pieces of kid cooked on skewers in the oven.

Stacchiodde   Dialect word for *orecchiette* (see above).

Torcinelli/Turncinielli   See *gnummarieddi* above.

Tortiera pugliese, la   Rice, potato, courgette and pimento casserole.

Cheese

Burrata   With a butter filling.
Cacirotta   Whey cheese from Brindisi.
Menteca   Cow, very fatty.
Mozzarella   See p.114.
Provola   Cow, mild, sometimes smoked.
Provolina   Name used in Bari for *mozzarella*.
Ricotta   Ewe's milk
Ricotella   Ewe.
Scamorzella   Cow.

Wine

Puglia, the heel of Italy, has traditionally produced vast amounts of wine, most of it indifferent in quality and destined to add to the European wine lake. But this image is changing as a few intrepid producers have set out to sculpt a distinct Puglian identity from the grape varieties that once produced wines that were only suitable for blending with those of the north. If not gentrified yet, Puglia is certainly on the up and up.

Aleatico di Puglia A limited amount of this sweet fortified wine is made, but the quality is usually high. Worth a try.

Alezio A new DOC for a full red and a fine *rosato*, which will now include *Rosa del Golfo*, one of Italy's most distinguished rosés.

Castel del Monte This DOC consists of a firm red, capable of ageing, yet another excellent *rosato* (Puglia is the region for rosé lovers) and a rather uninteresting white. Under this denomination, *Il Falcone*, the *reserva* of Rivera, is particularly outstanding.

Copertino A deep-coloured, full-flavoured red wine with a warm velvety richness is the hallmark of this DOC, while the pink is fragrant and flavoursome but less impressive.

Favonio Not a wine but the name of the estate run by winemaker A. Simonini, whose wines defy classification. Easily mistaken as *Friulian* by their style, their elegance is all the more surprising given the hot sun under which they are grown. His *Chardonnay* and *Pinot Bianco* are quite interesting, his *Cabernet Franc* is usually distinguished and his *Pinot Nero*, surprisingly, can be the best of the lot. Certainly worth a detour.

Five Rosés A rosé from Salento, famous for the rich penetrating character that it derives from several years' ageing in cask.

Locorotondo Perhaps the best of Puglia's growing band of white wines, it has a clear, fresh, crisp style that belies its southern origins. The *Cantina Sociale* produces a good version.

Moscato di Trani The versatility of this grape is displayed by this rich, deep coloured sweet wine that is sometimes fortified. Delicious with dessert.

Primitivo di Manduria *Primitivo* is a native Puglian variety (thought to be the antecedent of the Californian *Zinfandel*) that could produce wines of good quality. In this DOC it does, giving either dry and sweet but always robust, strapping wines that are well-matched to highly flavoured meat dishes.

Rosso Barletta One of three northern Puglian DOC's based on the *Uva di Troia* grape, which are distinctive if unremarkable. Of the other two, *Rosso Canosa* and *di Cerignola*, the latter is probably the finest.

Salice Salentino One of the region's better DOC's with a fine rich red and a distinctive *rosato* along the lines of *Five Rosés*. *De Castris* is one of the best producers.

San Severo A DOC for whites and reds, usually producing vast amounts of plonk on the plains. Can, however, be of surprisingly high quality and exceptionally good value, especially from a producer like *D'Alfonso del Sordo*.

Squinzano Another good Salento wine, again based on the *Negroamaro* grape. The DOC is for red and *rosato*, the best producer probably being *Strippoli*.

Torre Quarto A fine, rich, slightly bitter red of distinctive character that is one of southern Italy's finest reds. Ages for up to a decade, the '83 and '81 being particularly good.

RED	WHITE
Rosso di Cerignola	*Locorotondo*
Torre Quarto	*Castel del Monte Bianco*
Salice Salentino	*Moscato di Trani* (sweet)
Castel del Monte (Rivera) *rosé*	

SARDINIA (SARDEGNA)

Towns: Cagliari, Nuoro, Sassari

Regional Specialities

Bottarga/Botterigo/Buttariga Smoked tunny fish or mullet roe, eaten with lemon.

Burrida Roughly the same as in Genoa (see p.67) but serve cold.

Carne a carrargiu/carraxiu This typical Sardinian way of cooking meat, and particularly suckling pig, is best described in one of the island's tourist pamphlets: 'The sucking pig is placed inside a sheep's stomach and the whole wrapped in herbs and aromatic shoots and roasted in a hole in the ground containing glowing embers and covered over, with a fire lit on top'.

Carta da musica 'Music paper' – a name given to mean the thin circular sheets of unleavened bread, about 18 inches in diameter. Rather like very large *motsas*.

Cassola Fish stew.

Cauddada Dialect for *cavolata*, a cabbage soup.

Chibarzu/Chivarzu See *pane di sanluri* below.

Coccoidu appienu Large snails with tomato sauce.

Cordulas alla sarda Tripe, or sheep's liver, and kidneys cooked on a skewer.

Culinzones/Curligiones/Culurroues *Ravioli,* filled

with meat, cheese and beet, served with sausage and tomato sauce.

Favata *Minestrone* of broad beans and pork.

Filotrottas Eel folded into an S and cooked on a skewer with bay leaves over charcoal.

Fegula Small balls of *pasta*, coloured with saffron.

Fricassadu Fricassée of offal.

Grive Thrushes and blackbirds. Eaten when they have been boiled, salted and preserved with myrtle, and served cold with salt olives as an *antipasto*.

Lumaconi ripieni Large stuffed snails.

Malloreddus Very small dumplings flavoured with saffron, served with tomato or game sauce.

Monzettas/Monzette/Munzettas alla sassarese Snail dishes.

Pane carasau See *carta da musica* above.

Pane di sanluri A large wholemeal loaf.

Porceddu/Porchetta Sucking pig.

Porcheddu is'ispidu Sucking pig on the spit.

Presuttu di sirbone Wild-boar ham.

Puddinghinos a pienu See p.90.

Succu See *fregula* above.

Tacculas Small birds roasted, flavoured with myrtle.

Ziminu Fish stew similar to *zimino* (see p.142). An officially published tourist guide states, however, that in Sassari *ziminu* is a dish of offal cooked with spices. As we have never eaten a Sassari *ziminu* we cannot confirm this, but it sounds to us a little like an example of the characteristic confusion into which the nomenclature of Italian gastronomy can throw even the Italians.

Cheese

Caciotta fiore Soft ewe's milk cheese.
Casu novu 'New cheese' – fresh ewe's milk cheese.
Fiore sardo Fresh cheese.
Fresa
Mozzarella (see p.114)
Pardulas Small mild cheeses.
Pecorino Ewe.
Ricotta Ewe.

Wine

Island cultures, as we know, tend to develop differently than those less isolated, and this fact is very much in evidence in the idiosyncratic nature of Sardinia's vinous culture. Although similar to, it is quite different from 'Italy's', but thanks to the foresight of several individuals it has become modern and commercially viable while retaining and improving its great traditional wines.

Here, as in Piemonte, a knowledge of the grape varieties grown is the key to understanding the island's wines.

White

Malvasia Very good examples of this grape are produced in two DOC zones, *Bosa* and *Cagliari*. They can be either dry or sweet, fortified or unfortified, so can be drunk throughout the meal.

Moscato Although a relatively new DOC exists for an *Asti Spumante* taste-alike called *Moscato di Sardegna,* the grape has traditionally made sweet dessert wines around Cagliari and Sorso and Sennori.

Nasco A distinctive DOC, *Nasco di Cagliari,* covers high strength whites that may be dry, which is nutty and full of character.

Nuragus Although probably the island's most widely planted grape variety, the wine produced is amongst the least distinctive, although the *Cantina Sociale* at Dolianova produce a passable version.

Torbato A localised clone of the *Malvasio,* the *Torbato* made by Sella e Mosca is a decent dry white, while that from their single vineyard, *Terre Bianche,* is the island's best modern white wine. It is dry with a good depth of biscuity fruit, with good balance and a long finish. Worth searching for.

Vermentino Another variation of *Malvasia,* producing wines which are crisp, clean and slightly nutty, ideal with seafood.

Vernaccia di Oristano One of the island's great wines, rich, nutty and dry, similar to a *fino* sherry. Worth a detour.

Red

Cannonau Produced in a bewildering array of styles, from the dry red, rich and peppery, to a sweet and fortified, port-like wine. *Sella e Mosca* make a good version of the former while their latter, called *Angelu Ruju* is strong, sweet and spicey.

Carignano While the *Cannonau* is thought to be the *Grenache* of southern France, this grape came to Sardinia from Spain, via the Carignan of France, and produces a fairly robust, peppery wine which can be very good. Also made as a rosé.

Monica When made around Cagliari it is usually sweet, but the DOC for *Monica di Sardegna* is always dry. The *Cantina Sociale di Dolianova* make a soft, forward and quite good version.

RED	WHITE
Cannonau	*Naragus di Cagliari*
Carignano del Sulcis	*Torbato di Alghero*
(also *rosé*)	*Malvasia di Bosa*
	(sweet)
	Vernaccia di Oristano
	– in effect, sherry

SICILY (SICILIA)

Towns: Palermo, Agrigento, Catania, Caltanissetta, Enna, Messina, Siracusa (Syracuse), Trapani

Regional Specialities

Anelletti gratinati Rings of cuttlefish dipped in breadcrumbs and cooked in the oven with oil, garlic and parsley.

Anghellini Small *ravioli*.

Arancini See p.38.

Bottarga Tunny-fish roe, boiled and served with oil and lemon or grilled.

Cannoli Cases of pastry filled with cheese, candied fruit or chocolate.

Caponata/Caponatina See *alla siciliana, alla siracusana* under *Melanzane*, p.29.

Cassata (dolce) See p.109.

Cassata (gelato) See p.109.

Crispeddi Meat fritters.

Cuscusu Fish soup with semolina.

Farsumagru See p.70.

Friteddi Meat fritters.

Frittura di sciabacheddu Fry of tiny fish (very small fry)

Maccheroni con gamberi With fresh prawns in a tomato sauce.

Maccheroni con le sarde See p.52.

Maccu Soup of dried beans.

Micuzzi Aubergines fried in oil.

Pasta con le sarde *Pasta* with sardines.

Pesce spada Swordfish.

Pizza alla siciliana *Pizza* stuffed with anchovies or *ricotta* cheese.

Pumaruoro e gratte Tomatoes stuffed into capers, anchovies and *salame,* and topped with breadcrumbs.

Scursumera Jasmine-flavoured ice-water.

Spaghetti alla Norma (Catania) With tomato sauce, slices of aubergine, local *ricotta* cheese. Norma was written by Bellini, who was born in Catania.

Stocco palermitana Dried cod, sautéed in a sauce of tomatoes, potatoes, celery, onion, olives and capers, olive oil.

Zuso Brawn served with lemon juice.

Cheese

Caciocavallo See p.113.
Canestrato Ewe's milk.
Provola See p.115.

Wine

Unlike those of Sardinia, the wines of Sicily, the largest Mediterranean island, are made by mixing several different grape varieties. But like Sardinia's, Sicily's wines have also undergone a technological revolution that has wrought a great improvement in quality – while also bringing many of the attendant problems of modernisation. Over-production is one, so much so that Sicily is now the largest contributor to Europe's wine surplus. It is to be hoped, therefore, that the continuing emphasis on quality will alleviate this problem and add new stars to a Sicilian firmament that already glitters brightly.

Alcamo   A usually rather neutral, dry white wine, that can be quite flavoursome and nutty from some producers. *Rapitala* is similar in style but better than most of the DOC wines. Names to trust include *Gatinais* and *Rincione*.

Carasuolo di Vittoria   A DOC from the south-eastern part of the island, this is a red wine light in colour but fairly full in body that can be very good. From Coria, it is both good and expensive, as is his highly individual *Stravecchio Siciliano*, a dry aperitif wine.

Corvo   The name used for the consistently reliable wines from the estate of the Duca di Salaparuta. The white is light, dry and fresh, while the red is soft, warm and generously flavoured. There is also a good *spumante* and a remarkable *Stravicchio di Sicilia*. When in doubt as to which Italian wine to choose, *Corvo*, because of its remarkable consistency, seems an obvious choice.

Etna   A DOC for red, white and rosé wines grown on the slopes of Mount Etna. Fortunately the red, which is the best of the three, is also the largest component of the DOC.

Malvasia delle Lipari   Another of southern Italy's exquisite dessert wines, this is made on Lipari, one of the small islands off the north-east coast of Sicily. It has a deep colour, a rich, luscious flavour, and is great with dessert or on its own at the end of a meal. Hauner is the best producer.

Marsala   *Marsala*, Sicily's most fabled wine, seems on the verge of a comeback after years of neglect and use solely as a cooking wine. While the *Fine* and *Specials* versions are best used for cooking, the *Superiors*, either dry or sweet, is superb, while the *Vergine* dry, nutty and complex is one of the world's great fortified wines. The best versions are from Lombardo, Pelegrino and Rallo, and recently de Bartoli.

De Bartoli is also responsible for the exquisite *Vecchio Samperi*, unfortified and produced in minute quantities, which he claims is the true *Marsala*. Whatever it is it's certainly worth paying the high price.

Moscato di Pantelleria   Closer to Africa than Italy, this is a sweet, fine Moscato that can be fortified or made sparkling. Very little is made except by the co-op, which calls it *Tanit*.

Regaleali   Like *Corvo*, the name for wines made on the estate of the Conte Tasca d'Almerta. An excellent white, nutty and baked yet fresh and singy, a fairly full, gutsy red and the *Rosso del Conte*, a red of great depth and finesse that is probably Sicily's finest, is the extent of their considerable achievement.

RED	WHITE
Corvo di Salapuruta rosso	*Corvo di Salapuruta bianco*
Etna rosso (also rosé)	*Regaleali*
Marsala	*Etna bianco*
	Moscato di Noto (sweet)

TRENTINO – ALTO ADIGE

Towns. Bolzano, Trento

Regional Specialities

Canederli   A corruption of the Austrian Knoderln – *gnocchi* made with breadcrumbs.

Crauti con carne di maiale e luganeghe   Loin of pork, with sausage and sauerkraut.

Fritelle di segala   Rye-flour rolls spiced and fried in oil.

Gnocchi   See p.39.

Gulasch di selvaggina   A goulash of game.

Lepre alla trentina   Jugged hare.

Omelette di patate e maiale   Potato and pork omelette.

Pane tirolese   A sweet, light bread, with almonds, cinnamon and lemon peel in it.

Ravioli alla trentina   *Ravioli* filled with meat or vegetables and curds.

Speck   Cured ham – subtly different from any other kind of *prosciutto*.

Strudel   *Apfelstrudel* – Austrian apple flan.

Würstel con crauti   German sausage and sauerkraut.

Zuppa acida   Soup of pickled tripe.

Zuppa di farina abbrustolita   Soup with toasted grain in it.

Cheese

Ricotta   ewe's milk.

Wine

Stretching from the Swiss and Austrian border to the northern tip of Lake Garda, this is in fact two distinctly different regions. In the northern Alto Adige we have the South Tyrol, which is Germanic in character, approach and language. Moving south, the approach becomes more Italian as the Dolomiti give way to a more gently undulating countryside.

The thread that connects the two is wine. In most cases, the wines are made from single grape varieties in the region's twelve DOC zones. The Teutonic predilection for order is evidenced by the fact that this zone has one of the most comprehensive and understandable set of laws – if, that is, you can separate the German from the Italian names!

White Grapes

Chardonnay Recently promoted to DOC, this region should be producing Italy's best *Chardonnays* before long. The style is light and crisp and green, but a few producers are experimenting with small oak barrels *(barriques)* in an attempt to give the wine a smokey richness. The former is the style best suited to food, and like the *Chablis'* that they resemble they are ideal with seafood.

Moscato A dry white DOC exists for this wine in Trentino, where *Conte Martini* excel, but the dry *Goldmuskateller* made in the South Tyrol by *Tiefenbrunner* is an aromatic, nettley delight. The sweet *Goldmuskateller*, DOC in the South Tyrol, is a good dessert wine.

Muller Thurgau Some very good dry versions of this run-of-the-mill German variety are made by *Tiefenbrunner* and *Pojere e Sandri*.

Pinot Both *Bianco* and *Grigio* excel here, and are produced under the *Trentino, Terlano* and *Alto Adige* DOC's. The *Pinot Bianco* is often better than most *Chardonnays*, with which many growers have got it confused.

Rhineriesling Italy's finest examples of this noble grape variety are produced in the South Tyrol. Fragrant, mountain fresh, they are superb as *aperitifs* or with delicate fish dishes, especially salmon.

Sauvignon Although included in two South Tyrolean DOC's they have yet to succeed in making a *Sauvignon* that can match a *Sancerre*. Some producers have vowed to succeed.

Traminer Thought to have originated in the local village of Tramin and to have travelled north to become the great Alsatian *Gewurz* (spicy) *traminer*. The local version is only lightly spicy, restrained and elegant rather than rich and opulent.

Red Grapes

Cabernet Both *Franc* and *Sauvignon* are grown and are DOC in Trentino and South Tyrol, where they are light and grassy, and will mature for several years. Several producers have used it to produce Bordeaux blends, notably *Maso Lodron* and *Castel San Michele*.

Lagrein An oddball of a native grape variety which can be either *Dunkel* (dark) or *Kretzer* (rosé). The former is deep coloured with a supple, wild raspberry fruit and a delicious richness, while the latter has a robust, penetrating fruit that makes it a fine rosé. *Conte Martini* make the best version in Trentino.

Rosenmuskateller Occasionally dry but usally sweet, this wine lives up to its name and has a splendid perfume of roses. The sweet wine from *Graf Kuenburg*, a concentrated nectar, is one of the world's greatest sweet wines.

Pinot Nero Usually pedestrian, but when handled by *Hofstatter* in the South Tyrol it surpasses many a Burgundy.

Schiava Called *Vernatsch* by the Germans, this is the region's most widely planted vine. It generally produces light, rather anonymous wines, and is the base for *Lago di Caldaro (Kalterersee)* and *St Magdalener*. It is probably at its best in the latter, especially with a judicious addition of *Lagrein* to give it backbone. Serve lightly chilled to show at its best.

Teroldego Grown only in a small part of Trentino, *Teroldego Rotaliano* is a deep coloured, rich gripping wine of some distinction. From a good vintage ('85 or ('83) and a top producer *(Conti Martini, Zeni, de Cles)* it is very fine indeed. Worth a detour.

RED	WHITE
Lagrein Dunkel	Alto Adige/Sudtiroler
Lagrein kretzer (rosé)	Gewurztraminer
Teroldego	(also *Sylvaner*, *Pinot*
Santa Maddalena	etc:
	Austrian taste-alikes)
	Goldmuskateller
	Ferrari Gran Spumante
	(Champagne – nearly)

TUSCANY (TOSCANA)

Towns: Florence, Arezzo, Grosseto, Livorno (Leghorn), Lucca, Pisa, Pistoia

Regional Specialities

Acquacotta (Grosseto) 'Cooked water' – a thick vegetable broth poured over large pieces of bread soaked in beaten egg.

Arista all'aretina Loin of pork, with garlic and rosemary, cooked on a spit.

Arista alla fiorentina   Loin of pork, see p.79.

Baccalá alla livornese   Dried cod cooked with tomato and potatoes.

Bistecca alla fiorentina   A rib steak, see p.69.

Cacciucco   See p.67.

Cee/Ceche alla pisana (Pisa)   Eel-fry cooked with sage, lemon, garlic, pimento and *parmesan*.

Fagioli all'aretina   White beans flavoured with sage, rosemary, garlic, bayleaf and oil; baked in the oven with juniper faggots.

Fagioli al fiasco   See p.102.

Fagioli alla fiorentina   See p.102.

Fagioli alla toscana   See p.102.

Fegatelli di maiale all'uccelletto   Pieces of pig's liver between pieces of bread and bayleaf, cooked on a skewer over charcoal.

Fegatini di maiale   The same as *fegatelli di maiale* above.

Finocchiona   A *salame* flavoured with fennel, delicious.

Fricassea   A veal stew, see p.73.

Fritto misto alla fiorentina   See p.82.

Pappa con pomidoro freschi   A thick mush of bread with oil and fresh tomatoes. Found in Florence under the *minestre*.

Pollo alla diavola   See p.87.

Prosciutto del senese   Ham from the province of Siena.

Salsiccia di cinghiale di Maremma   Wild boar sausage.

Spaghettini con le telline (Viareggio)   Thin spaghetti with clams, garlic, tomato, parsley, oil, pepper and small hot peppers.

Stracotto alla fiorentina   Veal stew.

Tagliatelle al ragu   *Pasta*, see p.51.

Topini di patate all'aretina   Small dumplings of potato, served with meat and a tomato sauce.

Tortino di carciofi   In effect an artichoke omelette, but baked in the oven.

Triglie alla livornese   Red mullet cooked in a tomato sauce and flavoured with garlic and ginger.

Trippa alla fiorentina   See p.77.

Trippa alla senese See p.77, but it can also be rather like trippa alla fiorentina, served with a meat sauce, sometimes with and sometimes 'without *parmesan*.

Uccelletti Little birds (usually larks) on skewers, with bread and a bayleaf between each pair of birds.

Ventresca di tonno con fagioli The stomach of tunny (the best part of the fish) with white beans.

Zuppa di datteri alla viareggina Soup of *datteri di mare* (see p.27) with tomatoes and garlic.

Cheese

In spite of all the veal that's eaten, cow's milk is rare in Tuscany and is not used for cheese – at least, only in small quantities, when it is nearly always mixed with ewe's milk. The cheeses listed below are virtually all pure ewe's milk products.

Caciofiore di Maremma
Cacio toscano
Caciotto di pecorino del Chianti
Giuncata
Pecorino di Asciano fresco
Pecorino dolce di Siena
Pecorino pizzicante Maremmano   (piquant)
Raviggiolo
Ricottine del Casentino   (small form of *ricotta*)

Wine

Tuscany has a long and noble history. Dante was the first modern European poet to write in the vernacular, and is probably still the greatest, while the court that followed Catherine de Medici to France laid the foundation for the great cuisine that the French enjoy today. In wine, the region of Chianti and Brunello di Montalcino was the first to introduce controls on origin when Carmignano was delimited by Cosimo de Medici III in 1716.

Today, Tuscany is the most dynamic of any of Italy's regions in the field of wine. The character and style of the wines, especially in Chianti, is constantly changing and being re-defined while, thankfully, retaining a clearly identifiable Tuscan style. The 'Super-Tuscans', the flagship red of many Chianti estates is seen by some as the way forward, while the whites, dull and directionless until a few years ago, are now beginning to generate some interest.

White

Bianco Simply meaning white, this is used as a prefix for the great number of white wines marketed either by individual estates (*Bianco di Volpaia*) or under a DOC *(Bianco Vergine della Valdichiana)*. As more producers use less of the white grapes in their *Chianti*, the surplus increases and the search for an acceptable style of white wine continues. The best are fresh and pleasant if rather neutral although the *Bianco Vergine* of Avignonesi is an exception.

Chardonnay Seen by some as the way forward for Tuscan whites, *Chardonnay* has had some success already in *Pomino 'Benefizio'* from Frescobaldi, rich and smokey, and the *Fontanelle* from Villa Banfi, smokey and international in style.

Galestro A dry white of imperceptible character pioneered by several large producers *(Antinori, Ricasoli, Frescobaldi)* as a means of disposing of their surplus of white grapes.

Montecarlo The most interesting of the Tuscan whites, simply because the Trebbiano grape is supplemented by several more characterful varieties to give a flavoursome, dry and sometimes flowery wine.

Moscadello di Montalcino A denomination that had lapsed until recently revived by Villa Banfi, this sweet, peachy, frothy white is delicious. Ideal as a refresher before or after the meal.

Pomino A DOC for red as well as white wines, of which *Frescobaldi* are the best (and only) producer. The white, made with a bit of *Trebbiano* suitably bolstered by *Pinot Bianco* and *Chardonnay*, improves yearly (the '85 was good), and their premium *Pomino 'Il Benefizio'* is a superb, rich, honeyed white that is aged in new oak.

Vernaccia di San Gimignano The best of the traditional Tuscan whites, made from the Vernaccia grape (different from the Sardinian one, as the name derives from the same root as the vernacular) grown around the beautiful hill-top town. Although the modernists are trying to make it light and clean, the best versions are those that have a deep colour, allied with a rich, nutty character. *Teruzzi e Puthod* and *Pietrafitta* are the best producers of this style.

Vin Santo A Tuscan masterpiece, this amber wine of great sweetness is made from dried grapes that are pressed, added to some older wine and then sealed in a vessel for several years. The result is one of Italy's great dessert wines. From a producer such as *Avignonese*, it is incomparable.

Red

Brunello di Montalcino This fabled wine, now a DOC, is made from a local strain of *Sangioveto* and is renowned for its hard tannic character and muscular structure when that unfolds gradually into a fine, rich and distinguished wine with age. From a producer like *Biondi-Santi*, in a great vintage like 1964, the wine seems capable of lasting for at least a century. Many newer producers are now aiming to make a wine that is more approachable in youth, and *Altesino* and *Caparzo* have succeeded admirably. Good recent vintages include '85, '83 '82, '80, '79, '78 and '77. Other names to trust include *Castelgiocondo, Villa Banfi* and *Il Poggione*.

Cabernet Sauvignon This grape variety has received honorary Tuscan status in the last decade, and is now probably the second most widely planted vine in the region, after Sangiovese. It is used either on its own in wines like *Sassicaia, Tavernelle (Villa Banfi)* or *Sammarco (Rampolla)*, or with *Cabernet Franc* or *Merlot*, as in *Solaia* or *Ghaia della Furba (Capezzana)*. These wines, aged in small new oak barrels, are usually rich and smokey, with a flavour of mint and blackcurrants, and are usually more in the style of Californian or Australian *Cabernet* than of Bordeaux. It seems to be more effective when used in conjunction with the local *Sangioveto*, as even a little *Cabernet* goes a long way towards softening the rough edges of the native grape. *Tignanello* was the first wine of this style, and others to succeed include *Grifi (Avignonesi)* and a host of *Chianti* estates taking advantage of the DOC G loophole for 10% of other grape varieties (see *Chianti*).

Carmignano Probably the world's oldest delimited wine region, this tiny enclave uses *Cabernet Sauvignon* (up to 10%) to temper the youthful austerity of *Sangioveto*, with the result being a wine of real breeding and finesse. It is best about 5-8 years after the vintage, and is an ideal partner to game. *Villa di Capezzana* is the best known producer, while *Artimino* and *Villa di Trefiano* are both excellent.

Chianti This wine can, from certain estates, be one of the world's great wines, rich, classy and long-lived, while from other producers it is often barely drinkable. This paradox makes *Chianti* endlessly fascinating and often infuriating, and a knowledge of what estates are producing the best wine (as in Bordeaux) is the only true guide.

DOC G was brought in with the abysmal 1984 vintage, and reduced the proportion of white grapes necessary in the blend leaving the door open for up to 10% of 'other grapes' (*Cabernet Sauvignon*) to be used to complement the *Sangioveto*, which is the major component. Each estate usually produces a *Riserva* (their best wines that undergo a longer period of ageing) and a *non-Riserva*, a wine meant for younger drinking. The former, given a bit of bottle-age, is usually the better wine.

Although *Chianti Classico*, in the heart of the region, is the best known, producing ideally wines of class that age well, other zones, especially *Rufina*, which produces a more robust style, can match it for quality. Other zones are *Colli Aretini*, *Colli Fiorentini*, *Colli Senesi*, *Colline Pisane* and *Montalbano*. Wines from the *Classico* region can (if the estate belongs to the consortium) be identified by the black cockerel on the neck label, while those from the other zones are grouped under *Chianti Putto*, symbolised by a cherub.

A comprehensive list of names to trust is impossible, but would include *Badia a Coltibuono, Brolio, Castellare, Isole e Olena, Castello in Villa, Rampolla, Volpaia, Vicchiomaggio, Monte Vertine, Rocca della Macie, Riecine, Pagliarese* and *Villa Antinori*.

In *Putto, Artimino, Capezzana, Vetrici* and *Frescobaldi (Remole, Montesodi* and *Nipozzano)* are all good bets.

Morellino di Scansano Solely *Sangiovese* from southern Tuscany, this DOC gives full, elegant but robust wines, and deserves a wider audience. The *Cantina Sociale* and *Le Pupille* are amongst the names to trust.

Predicato A new denomination set up by a group of large producers, led by *Antinori, Frescobaldi* and *Ruffino*, who have decided to opt out of the recently introduced DOC G. The whites, based on *Pinot Grigio* and *Chardonnay* seem destined to be less successful than the reds, made with *Sangiovese* and *Cabernet*. It is still too early to predict how it will turn out but the names that have backed it auger well for the success of the venture.

Rosso di Montalcino From the same region as *Brunello* but made from younger vines and wines not aged long enough to qualify for the higher appelation. Elevated to DOC in 1983, the wines are robust and youthful, retaining the fruit that many *Brunello* lose through protracted cask ageing. Can give very good value from producers like *Altesino, Villa Banfi, Argiano, Caparzo, Cal d'Orcia*.

Super Tuscans A term applied to some of the best and most expensive wines of the *Chianti* region, almost all of which are labelled as *Vino da Tavola* because they don't conform with the DOC G regulations. They are of three types: 100% *Sangiovese; Sangiovese* mixed with another grape, usually *Cabernet;* or *Cabernet* based wines. The trend started with *Tignanello* and *Sassicaia* (the second and third categories respectively) in the '70's, and has blossomed into a fantastic range of wines. In the first category, the best are *Flaccianello (Fontodi), Il Soldaccio (Monte Vertini),*

Vinatierri Rosso, Palazzo Altesi, Sangiovieto di Coltibuono and *Cepparello;* in the second, *Ca' del Pazzo, Gifi (Avignonesi), I Sodi di San Niccolo (Castellare, Sangioveto* and *Malvasia Nera);* while in the third, *Sammarco, Solaia* and *Tavernelle* have followed the example set by *Sassicaia.* Certainly these are exciting wines, but the dynamism of the region makes it difficult to remain abreast of new developments.

Vino Nobile di Montepulciano The noble wine of Montepulciano, a village in south-eastern Tuscany, is a DOC G that bears no relation to the grape of the same name that is grown in the *Abruzzi. Sangiovese* predominates in the blend, and the wines are more austere than those of those of *Chianti* but more approachable than *Brunello.* Quality is variable, but dependable, names include *Avignonese, Podei Boscarelli* and *Poliziano.*

Tuscan vintages:
White   usually the youngest available.
Red   '86, '85, '83, '82, '78 and '77 are all excellent, while '81, '80 and '79 are good. '75, '70 and '64 are the best of older vintages in *Brunello.*

RED	WHITE
Chianti Classico	*Vernaccia di San Gimignano*
Chianti Putto	
Brunello di Montalcino	*Montecarlo*
Carmignano	*Galestro*
Tignanello	*Bianco della Laga*
Sassicaia	*Bianco di Pitigliano*
Vino Nobile di Montepulciano	

UMBRIA – LE MARCHE (THE MARCHES)

Towns in Umbria: Perugia, Assisi, Orvieto.
Towns in The Marches: Ancona, Ascoli Piceno, Macerata, Pesaro, Urbino

Regional Specialities

Brodetto   Fish stew (see p.66)

Brodetto all'anconetana   Fish stew, speciality of Ancona.

Calcioni   Regional name for *ravioli.*

Cardi alla perugina   Chards that have been dipped in batter and fried, cooked in the oven with a meat-and-tomato sauce.

Ciriole   *Pasta* served with oil and garlic.

Colombi Wild pigeons.

Coneglio in potacchietto A casserole of rabbit cooked with wine and garlic, flavoured with rosemary.

Fave alla campagnola Broad beans cooked slowly so that they absorb the water they're cooked in; served with a lot of olive oil poured over them and a *purée* of onion.

Mazzafegati Pig's liver sausage flavoured with garlic and coriander; eaten fried.

Medaglione alla Rossini Fillet of beef cooked in butter with a *Marsala* sauce, with slices of ham and cheese on top.

Olive al forno Green olives wrapped in bacon and cooked in the oven.

Olive alla marchigiana/Olive ripiene fritte Speciality of Ascoli Piceno. Large green olives stuffed with a forcemeat, dipped in egg and breadcrumbs and fried.

Olivette di vitello Little rolls of thinly sliced veal stuffed with anchovy and capers, dipped in batter and fried in butter.

Omelette con tartufi Omelette with black Umbrian truffles which do not grow anywhere else in Italy.

Palombacce Large hen-pigeons as big as wood-pigeons.

Palombacce all' uso di Foligno Pigeon cooked whole (with intestines) in a casserole with spices, herbs, vegetables, ham, black olives, pickles, red wine and vinegar.

Piconi *Ravioli* in Umbria.

Pizza rustica See p.30

Porchetta Sucking pig stuffed with fennel, garlic, rosemary and nutmeg, and roasted whole over an open fire or in the oven.

Poveracci Regional slang for clams.

Ravioli verdi ripieni di cervella *Ravioli* stuffed with brains, smoked ham and fresh peas; eaten with cream and grated parmesan.

Regina in porchetta A giant carp, weighing between 20 and 30 lbs and found in Lake Trasimeno, cooked on a spit over a wood fire with ham fat, wild fennel, rosemary, garlic and lemon.

Risotto alla Rossino (Pesaro) A mushroom-and-egg *risotto* from Rossini's native city.

Salume di Norcia Norcia is famous for its pork butchery.

Sedani di Trevi Speciality of Trevi – celery stewed in tomato sauce.

Sogliola alla Rossini Fillet of sole with white-wine sauce and *foie gras*.

Spaghetti aromatici With a sauce of garlic, oil, anchovy, mint, black olives, capers and parsley.

Spaghetti alle noci With walnuts, pine-nuts and garlic.

Spaghetti ai tartufi neri With the famous Umbrian black truffles.

Spiedi misti spoletini A 'mixed spit' of sausage, lamb, baby chicken, pig's liver, bacon, sage and rosemary cooked on a spit.

Stoccafisso all'anconetana Dried cod cooked with onions, tomatoes, garlic, oil and pounded anchovies.

Strangozzi di Spoleto Home-made flat *pasta* served with oil, garlic, basil and tomato.

Triglie all'anconetana Red mullet marinated in oil, lemon juice and herbs, wrapped in a slice of raw ham and baked.

Trippa alla marchigiana See p.77.

Uccelletti di mare allo spiedo (Adriatic) Not veal, certainly not birds; but small fish on a skewer.

Vincisgrassi See p.47.

Zuppa di arselle Clam or mussel soup. See *arselle* (p.60).

Cheese

Caciotto Cow.
Pecorino Ewe.
Salto A hard *pecorino* that looks like parmesan and is imported from Sardinia.

Wine

Umbria

Umbria, the only land-locked region south of the Po, is often seen enviously as little more than an extension of Tuscany. This is unfair for, although it may be overshadowed by its northern neighbour, Umbria has a distinct character of its own, and boasts a couple of Italy's finest wines in *Torgiano* and, surprisingly, *Orvieto*.

Despite the attractions of Perugia and Assisi and the strikingly green hills, Umbria remains rather unspoiled and isolated. Despite this, *Chardonnay* and

Cabernet Sauvignon have crept in here and are of increasing importance, but the local varieties, the red *Sagrantino* and the white *Grechetto*, continue to flourish alongside the ubiquitous *Sangiovese*. Hopefully these wines will one day recieve the same acclaim as is presently reserved for the splendid olive oil of the region, arguably Italy's finest.

Colli Altotiberini   A recently approved DOC for a red, white and *rosato* wine produced in northern Umbria. It is seldom seen outside the region as yet, although the red, based on *Merlot* and *Sangiovese* (with a bit of *Barbera* and *Gamay* (!), the *Beaujolais* grape, used by some producers), can be good. *Colle del Sole* make a very good red, an interesting white (with *Chardonnay* supplementing the *Trebbaiano*) and a decent *rosato*. The red should last for several years, but the white and rosato should be drunk while young.

Colli del Trasimeno   Touted as a zone to watch, punters would be well-advised to note that the form is still too patchy to consider this recent DOC a safe bet. The white can be good, depending on the proportion of *Grechetto* used in the blend, while the red, from *Sangiovese* and *Gamay*, has a medium richness of fruit at its best.

Grechetto   The premier white grape of Umbria, used in *Orvieto* and on its own. It produces rich, distinctively flavoured wines that have a good breadth and penetration of nutty flavour.

Good producers of *Grechetto* are *Benincasa, Caprai* and *Vagniluca*, who produce the best one that I've come across.

Montefalco A DOC for two characterful reds that are undiscovered, under-rated and under-priced. The *Rosso di Montefalco*, mainly *Sangiovese*, has a robust, peppery fruit with good penetration. The *Sagrantino di Montefalco* has a velvety, bitter-sweet fruit and distinctive breeding. The *passito* version, sweet and luscious, is superb. Names to trust include *Benincasa*, *Caprai* and *Fongoli*. Good recent vintages are '85, '83 and '82.

Orvieto Traditionally sweet, *Orvieto* has gained in popularity in recent years as a rather neutral but quaffable dry white. One of the most neutral until recently was *Bigi*, but they have, in the last couple of years, burst on the scene with a single vineyard *Orvieto* called *Vigneto Torricella* that stands as one of Italy's best, new-style white wines. They achieved this largely by increasing the proportion of *Grechetto* at the expense of the neutral *Trebbiano*. The *abboccato* has a light, fresh sweetness that is in no way cloying, as exemplified by Bigi's *Vigneto Orzalume* and *Decugnano dei Barbi*. Other good producers are *Antinori*, *Barbermani* and *Ortu*.

San Giorgio The Umbrian wizard, Giorgio Lungarotti, has produced this remarkable wine (*Torgiano* with a goodly dollop of *Cabernet*) that rivals the best of *Super Tuscans*.

Torgiano This DOC in central Umbria is the domain of Lungarotti. His white, *Torre di Giano*, continues to improve as he increases the amount of *Grechetto* in the blend, while the red, from *Sangiovese*, *Montepulciano* and *Canaiolo*, has more body and character than most *Chianti*, and ages well (the '78 was at its peak in 1986). It is the *Riserva*, however, that steals the show. Called *Rubesco*, from the Monticchio vineyard, it is aged in small oak barrels and develops a spicey warmth and a rich savoury fruit, nuanced and long on the finish. It needs 8-10 years from a good vintage to show its true breed, but it is well worth waiting for. The '83, '82, '80, '78, '77, '75 and '71 are all recommended.

Le Marche

With Umbria on one side and the Adriatic on the other, the Marches are a region of great national beauty. It is known largely for its white wine, especially *Verdicchio*, but produces a couple of reds that are of much greater intrinsic interest, as well as a sparkling red that rates highly in the 'weird and wonderful' category. When in the region though, especially on the beautiful Adriatic coast, it is more likely that white will suit the occasion and quench the thist.

Bianchello del Metauro A fresh, dry white, rather neutral but ideal with seafood, from the *Bianchello* grape.

Rosso Conero A red based on the *Montepulciano* grape that performs so well in the Abruzzi to the south. Although there is a provision in the DOC regulations for the addition of up to 15% *Sangiovese*, the best are made solely from *Montepulciano*. It is rich, robust and austere, and is well-matched with game. Names to trust include *Marchetti* and *Bianchi's Vigneto San Lorenzo*.

Rosso Piceno Made from 60% *Sangiovese* and 40% *Montepulciano*, this is lighter but more elegant than *Rosso Conero*. Vast quantities are produced in a DOC zone that covers a large expanse in the south-eastern Marche, but quality is usually high. Although some prefer it, it seems to lack the intrinsic quality of *Rosso Conero*, probably due to the lower proportion of *Montepulciano*. Names to trust include *Fazi-Battaglia* and *Umani Ronchi*.

Verdicchio The most widely planted white grape in the Marche is DOC in *Matelic* and in the famous *Castelli di Jesi*. Easily recognised in its amphora shaped bottle, the latter seems to be moving away from that image with the emergence of a small band of producers who contend that *Verdicchio* can produce wines of character, despite the neutral product in the Lollabrigida bottle. The leading wines of the emergent style are Monte Schiavo's *Il Pallio* and *Coste del Molino, Ca' Sal di Serra, Bucci* and *Brunori*. Garofoli produce a good version in the amphora as well as their cru *Macrina*.

In the Matelica zone, names to trust include *Villa Pigna* and *Fabrini*. For both wines, drink the most recent vintage, as a capacity for ageing is not one of the *Verdicchio's* few attributes.

Vernaccia di Serrapetrona A sparkling red wine from *Vernaccia di Serrapetrona* grapes that can be either dry or sweet, and has tremendous character in either version. Worth seeking out as an oddity. Fabrini produce a *Champagne* method wine that is the best. Very good as a dessert wine.

RED	*WHITE*
Montepulciano	*Orvieto (secco – dry*
Torgiano	*abboccato –* sweet)
Sangiovese dei Colli Pesaresi	*Grechetto*
	Verdicchio dei Castelli
	di Jesi

VENETO (VENETIA)

Towns: Venice, Padua, Treviso, Verona, Vicenza

Regional Specialities

Baccalá mantecato   A purée of salt cod.

Baccalá alla vicentina   Salt cod cooked with onions, spices and herbs.

Bigoli   *Spaghetti.*

Bigoli in salsa   Wholemeal *spaghetti* with an onion and anchovy sauce.

Bisato   Eel, boiled, fried or grilled, over a wood fire.

Bottargo   Hard roe of tuna-fish eaten with oil and lemon, or baked.

Bovoloni   Snails.

Canderli   *Gnocchi* made of bread, egg, cheese and *salami* or bacon, served in broth or with a sauce. See p.159.

Capon alla canevera   Roast capon in a pig's bladder.

Fegato alla veneziana   See p.73.

Granceole/Grancevole   Large Adriatic crabs.

Marsoni   Small fish from the River Astico (Vicentino).

Masantete   Female crabs.

Moleche   Shell-less crabs, fried.

Osei scampai   Slices of veal on a skewer. See *Uccelli scappati* (p.77).

Paetarosta col magaragno   (Vicenza) Turkey roast on a spit and flavoured with pomegranate juice.

Pasta e fasoi (fagioli)   See p.37. Often eaten *semifreddo* – half-cold (or half-warm).

Polenta e osei   See p.41.

Pollo alla padovana   See p.88.

Radicchio rosso   A red chicory which makes excellent winter salads.

Rafoi   Dialect for *ravioli*. See p.41.

Risi con la luganega   Rice with a local highly spiced sausage from Treviso.

Risi e bisi   See p.37.

Riso e zucca   (Padua)   Rice and pumpkin.

Salsa peverada   Sausage and herb sauce.

Soppressa   Salted meat.

Tacchino con la melagrana See *paetarosta col malgaragno* above.

Torresani allo spiedo Pigeons roast on a spit.

Cheese

Asiago Cow.
Ricotta Ewe.
Vezzena stravecchio

Wine

This is a region that can easily detain the tourist, with the beauty of Venice, the splendour of Palladian architecture and the richness and diversity of the cuisine. Wine seems almost incidental in this context, yet the region produces some the the great wines of Italy – as well as the worst. It ranks among the top three regions in terms of quantity, as well as rivalling Tuscany as the leading producer of DOC wines. While the whites, led by *Soave*, have achieved a good measure of commercial success, it is the reds, led by the revitalized *Valpolicella*, that have brought the region from its post-war status as a source of industrial plonk in double litre, screw cap bottles, to its present position in the vanguard of Italian viniculture.

Bardolino A DOC from the same grapes and in the same style (if lighter) as *Valpolicella*. The wine has an aroma of bitter cherries, a light easy fruit and bitter twist on the finish. The *chiaretto (rosé)* can be delicious. Both should be drunk young and slightly chilled. Names to trust include *Anselmi, Bertani, Boscani, Guerrieri-Rizardi, Santa Sofia, Tedeschi* and *Portalupi*. This wine should be chosen with care, preferably from a producer you know, as a great deal of it is still the rather anaemic and neutral industrial product that held sway a quarter of a century ago.

Bianco di Custoza A dry white that often bears a familial resemblance to Soave, but, because of the addition of *Tocai*, has extra flavour and an added dimension that its neighbour seldom does. *Arvedi d'Emelia* and *Tedeschi* both produce excellent version – worth a detour.

Breganze A DOC covering seven styles, produced in a zone in the north eastern part of the region. The varietals are *Pinot Grigio, Pinot Bianco* and *Vespaiolo*, with *Pinot Nero*. The *Bianco* is made with *Tocai*, and Maculan's *Breganze di Breganze* is improving yearly, while the red, a chunky *Merlot*-based wine, dominates production. *Maculan* is the best producer.

Colli-Berici This DOC zone in the Berici hills produces seven varietals, with *Cabernet, Pinot Bianco* and an intriguing *Tocai Rosso* being the most interesting.

Colli Euganei   Seven is obviously a number of mystical significance in the Veneto, as this DOC also covers seven styles including a *Moscato* and a good *Pinot Bianco*.

Gambellara   Like its neighbouring *Soave*, *Gambellara* is made principally with the *Garganega* grape, and produces a dry, rather neutral white, a *Recioto* (a sweet dessert wine) and an unusual *Vin Santo*. The *Cantina Sociale* is highly regarded.

Piave   The wines of Piave are responsible, with the Adriatic, of course, for keeping Venice afloat. Large quantities of the eight different varietals are produced on this plain, often with a surprisingly high level of quality. The *Pinot Bianco* and *Tocai* lead the whites, while *Raboso*, an obscure indigenous red, produces full, well-structured wines of character. *Maccari* and *Cescon* are names to note.

Pramaggiore   A DOC on the Friuli border that produces some of the best *Cabernet* and *Merlot* in the north east. *La Fattoria* is outstanding.

Prosecco   This white grape gives light, dry wines that seem to be ideally suited a a base for sparkling wine. The DOC zone is based around Conegliano, with a superior zone delimited as *Valdobbiadene Superiore di Cartizze*. If after try to pronounce that mouthful you need a drink, it is a good sparkler to drink while in Venice.

Soave   Most of the enormous production of this dry white is undistinguished, but it is one of Italy's best known wines. Although much of the production was dominated by the large firms in the post-war period, several smaller producers have recently come to the fore with wines of distinct character that are often said to be 'too good for *Soave*'! Pieropan, Masi's *Col Baraca* and Anselini's *Capitel Foserino* are exceptional wines. Other names to trust include *Campagnola*, *Santa Sofia*, *Zenato*, *Boscaini* and *Tedeschi*.

Tocai di Lison   Overlapping with *pramaggiori*, the *Tocai* here rises to great heights, with the one from *La Fattoria* being rich, spicy and deeply flavoured.

Torcolato   A sweet wine made in Breganze from semi-dried grapes. Has a good capacity for ageing, and is often rated highly by the experts. *Maculan* is the producer.

Valpolicella   This cherry-coloured, cherry-scented wine with a light, fragrant fruit cut by a twist of bitterness is the last of the trio of popular Veronese wines, and is made in four styles. The first is the basic

DOC, a light quaffing wine similar to but with more depth than *Bardolino*.

When the ripest *Corvina*, *Rondinella* and *Molinara* grapes are taken and dried for several months before pressing, the result is either the sweet *Recioto della Valpolicella*, a rich concentrated wine with an intense flavour and an appealing bitter sweetness, or the *Recioto della Valpolicella Amarone*, a strong (16%) dry wine of great power allied with a lingering flavour of great delicacy. The former is an ideal replacement for port (and it won't produce the killer hangover that port does) while the latter, known locally as a *Vino da Meditazione* (Meditation wine) is best savoured with a strong cheese, or simply on its own, sipped and marvelled at. With *Barolo*, the *Amarone* is the greatest and most individual of Italian wines. Masters of the art of making *Recioto* and *Amarone* include *Masi*, *Tedeschi* (best with *Recioto*) and *Quintarelli*.

The fourth version, unrecognized by law yet tradional to the region is called *Ripasso*. It involves fermenting the wine on the lees of the *Recioto*, thus giving a fuller flavoured wine that has some of the complexity and depth of *Amarone* without the raw power. Masi's *Campo Fiorin*, Boscanini's *Le Cane*, Serego Alighieri Valpolicella* and Quintarelli's *'normale'* are all fine examples of *Ripasso* wines.

Names to trust generally include *Allegrini* (their *Fieramonte Amarone* is superb) *Bertani*, *Bolla*, *Campagnola*, *Masi*, *Santa Sofia*, *Tedeschi* and *Zenato*.

While most *Valpolicella* should be drunk young ('85 was a good year), the *Amarone* can age superbly, with '82, '79, '78, '77 and '74 all being good vintages.

Venegazzu   A model estate in the Veneto, producing some decent whites, a good sparkler and a deservedly acclaimed red, *della Casa*, made with the Bordeaux mixture of grapes. Their *Etichetta Nera*, a more intense version of the *della Casa*, is superb, but carries a price tag to match. '85, '83, '82, '80 and '79 have all been good vintages.

RED	WHITE
Bardolino	Soave
Gambellara	Tocai di Lison
Venegazzu	Prosecco di Conegliano
Cabernet/Merlot	(sparkling)
di Pramaggiore	Cartizze (superior version
Valpolicella	of above)
Clinton	

SECTION THREE

Shopping Guide

Shopping Guide

To foreign eyes food shops in Italy may seem to be open day and night, six days a week, except in the early afternoon when they all close for two or three hours from one o'clock. However, butchers – like butchers all over the world – have to be watched carefully, for they observe religious or vocational festivals all their own, shutting down without any warning on days never mentioned in any Calendar of the Saints. *Festas* have to be watched out for at all times, of course, but they do not as a rule affect food sellers before midday. In the height of the summer, butchers and *pollerie* may not open at all in the afternoons.

Baker's   *La panetteria*

Butcher's   *La macellaria*

Cakes and Pastries   *La pasticceria*

Cooked meats   *La salumeria/la rosticceria*

Dairy   *La latteria*

Fishmonger's   *La pescheria*

Fruit and Vegetables   *Frutta e verdura*

General groceries   *Generi alimentari/Generi coloniali/la drogheria*

Poultry and game   *La polleria*

Vegetables and herbs   *Verdue, erbe* (These are always best bought in the market – *il mercato* – especially if you happen to be near the great covered food market of Florence; otherwise fruit-and-veg shops are ubiquitous).

WEIGHTS

The metric system of weights and measures is something that English and American visitors to Italy may feel uncomfortable with. Instead of endless mental calculation it is better, however, to try and *think* in metric quantities right from the start, and there is one weight in Italy that makes life much less difficult for the shopper: this is the *etto*, short for ettogrammo or hectogramme, and equivalent to 100 grammes. The *etto* (plural *etti*) is an extremely convenient weight, and its use saves one trying to remember too many Italian numbers. 'Un etto e mezzo' is much easier to say and calculate than 'cento-cinquanta grammi'. The *etto* can be used as a unit right up to 950 grammes if necessary ('nove etti e mezzo'), at which point the kilo takes over. This is spelt *chilo* in Italy but pronounced *keelō* as everywhere else in Europe.

Approximate weight conversions

1 ounce	– 30 *grammi*	30 *grammi*	– 1 oz
2 oz	– 60 *g*	100 g } un *etto* }	– 3½ oz
4 oz	– 120 *g*	un *quarto* (250 g)	– 9 oz
8 oz	– 240 *g*	un *mezzo chilo*	– 1 lb 2 oz
1 lb	– 480 *g*	un *chilo*	– 2 lb 4 oz

A slice *Una fetta*   **A dozen** *Una dozzina*
A packet *Un pacchetto*   **A tin (can)** *Una scatola*

Liquid measures are shown in the *Lista dei vini* **on page 119.**

BAKER — *Il pannetiere (la panetteria, il panificio)*

The baker in Italy bakes twice a day, six days a week. In some areas you may find a baker open on Sunday morning, although this is uncommon. But there seems to be none of that confusing business one encounters in France of a rota for bakers on Mondays. On the other hand, the Italian baker is not half the artist his French counterpart is; the Italians use remarkably little imagination in designing the shape of their loaves compared with the perennial preoccupation with the invention of new shapes and names for *pasta*.

Brown read *Pane integrale*   **Rolls** *Panini*
Milk bread *Pane al latte*   **Rye bread** *Pane di segale*
Oil bread *Pane al olio*   **Wholemeal bread** *Pane*
(crustier and crisper than milk   *integrale*
bread but made only as rolls)

The quality of the bread in Italy varies greatly from district to district: Venetian bread is like cotton-wool. When it is good, however, it can be most appetizing. In the last few years an enterprising chain called 'Il Forno' has contracted with bakers all over Italy (and beyond – there is one in London's Fulham Road!) to supply modern pine fittings and their own flour varieties on condition that a wide range of bread types is produced, to their specifications. Where the local bread has not been good, these easy-to-recognize stores have been a godsend.

BUTCHER – *Il macellaio (la macellaria, la beccheria)*

Italian butchers, like Italian bakers, cannot compare with the French in the matter of presenting their wares in an artistic manner. In a way this makes things a little easier for the shopper, who is not faced with puzzles like *Épaule d'agneau en musette*, which is tied up with string to look like an aerial balloon.

Beef – *bue, manzo*

As far as beef is concerned, *bue* describes the animal and *manzo* the flesh, so that as we would say oxtail and not beeftail the Italians say *coda di bue*, and not *coda di manzo*.

Offal *Interiora*
Heart *Cuore di bue*
Kidney *Rognone di bue* (pl. *rognoni*)
Liver *Fegato di bue*

Oxtail *Coda di bue*
Tongue *Linguia di bue*
Tripe *Trippa di bue*
Tripe, honeycomb *Centopelle*

CUTS

Braising beef *Manzo da brasare*
Brisket *Il petto di bue*
Chateubriand (steak from top of sirloin) *Chateaubriand*
Fillet *Il filetto*

Rib steak *Costata di manzo/bue*
Rump steak *La culatta*
Sirloin *La lombata di bue*
Skirt *La copertina*
Tournedos *Il turnedò/la coda del filetto*

Lamb – *Abbacchio* (milk-fed), *agnello*
Mutton – *Montone, castrato*

Offal *Interiora*
Brains *Cervella di abbacchio*
Sweetbreads *Animelle di abbacchio*

Trotters *Piedini di montone*

CUTS

Breast *Il petto*
Chop/cutlet *La costola nel filetto/una cotoletta*
Leg *La coscia/il cosciotto*
Loin *Il lombo*

Neck cutlet *La seconda costola*
Shoulder *La spalla*
Shoulder, boned *Spalla disossata*

Pork – *Maiale*

Offal *Interiora*
Brains *Cervella di maiale*

Kidney *Rognone di maiale* (pl. *rognoni*)
Liver *Fegato di maiale*

CUTS

Bath chap *Guancia di maiale*
Chine/loin/saddle *Àrista*
Cutlet *La Costeletta nella schiena*

Front loin *Carré di maiale*
Loin chop *La prima costoletta*
Trotters *Piedini di maiale*

Veal – *Vitella, vitello*

Vitella, though strictly speaking the Italian for a heifer, is the word used by the Tuscans to denote the best-quality veal – milk-fed and killed between two and four weeks old. *Vitello* they regard as anything older than that – an animal which, whether it lives two months or two years, lives a life of idleness, growing fat and tender from not working in the fields or pulling carts. Increasingly, however, the distinction between the two words is becoming blurred.

The famous *bistecca alla fiorentina* has no counterpart in non-Italian butchery. It is taken from the carcase of the *vitellone* or 'large veal' – that is, from an animal not more than three years old and which, like the *vitello*, has not been out to work. The cut itself is a large rib steak with the bone attached.

Anyone expecting a *bistecca* to resemble what an American would call a steak – red, juicy and inches thick – will be disappointed. It is, however, a piece of meat well worth eating – in its own right, as it were.

Offal *Interiora*	**Liver** *Fegato di vitello*
Brains *Cervella di vitello*	**Sweetbread** *Animelle di*
Feet *Piedini di vitello*	*vitello*
Head *Testina di vitello*	**Tongue** *La lingua di vitello*
Kidneys *Rognoncini di vitello*	

CUTS

Best end of neck See **Rib** below	**Escalope** *Una scaloppina*
Breast *Il petto di vitello*	**Fillet** *Il filetto*
Chop/cutlet *Una costoletta/ cotoletta*	**Knuckle** *Il garretto*
	Loin *Il lombo*
Chump end of loin *Pezzo grosso del lombo*	**Rib** *Carré di vitello*
	Rib steak *Una bistecca*
	Saddle *La sella di vitello*
	Shoulder *La spalla*

Cakes, Pastries, Sweets and Candy – *La pasticceria*

All the naïve delight in tinsel and coloured ribbons that goes into the extravagantly sentimental decorations of small Italian churches is found in the cake- and sweet-shops of Italy. The presentation and packaging, the bright festoons and bows and cellophane wrappings are too gaudy for some people's taste, but to others they could not be more in keeping with what is, after all, an essentially saccharine trade. The quickest way to get what you want is to point at it.

The only important names to know are Campari, Cinzano, Punt e Mes and Martini, for these shops also sell *aperitives*, as well as all the most popular and sticky liqueurs that the Italians drink as a *digestivo* – and a *digestivo* is about all; the Italians have never yet produced an after-dinner liqueur that anybody would call a drink.

COOKED MEATS/PORK BUTCHER – *Il salumaio (la salumeria, la rosticceria*

Italian delicatessen shops, like those in Europe and America, stock virtually everything that you would eat as a cold *hors d'oeuvre* and a great deal else besides. To list the items you are likely to encounter in a *salumerie* in Italy is hardly a practical proposition; we suggest that the best thing to do is go into the shop, look around and then point at what you want – remembering that the easiest unit of weight is the *etto* (3½ ounces), and that a slice is *una fetta* (pl. *fette*),

DAIRY – *La latteria*

Butter *Il burro* (which will invariably be unsalted. If you want salted, ask for *burro salato*, though in smaller *latterie* they may not stock it).
Cream *La panna*

Cheese *Il formaggio*
Eggs *Uova* (sing. uovo; a dozen *una dozzina*)
Milk *Il latte* (1 litre: 1.7 pints). Milk is also sold at general grocery stores

FISHMONGER – *Il peschivendolo* (la pescheria)

Anchovies *Acciughe/alici*
Angler-fish *Boldrò/rana pescatrice/rospo*
Barbel *Barbio*
Bass *Branzino/spigola*
Bream *sea (Dentex) Dorata/orata/pagello/dentice*
Brill *Rombo liscio*
Carp *Carpa/carpione*
Chub *Cavadano*
Clams *Vongole/telline* in Tuscany/*poveracci* in The Marches
Cockles *Venere/tartufi*
Cod (Gadus morrhua) *Merzullo*
Cod, salt *Baccala*
Conger eel *Grongo*
Crab *Granchio/*in Venice *graneole* and *grancevole*
Crawfish (langouste) *Aragosto* (this is the real name for a *langouste*, but it is now used for lobster too)/*palinuro*
Crayfish *Gamberi di fiume*
Dogfish *Pescecane/palombo*
John Dory *Pesci di San Pietro/sampietro*
Dublin Bay prawns *Scampi*
Eels *Anguille/capitoni/ceche/ciechine*
Flounder *Passera* ('sparrow')
Frogs *Rane*
Garfish *Aguglia*
Grayling *Ombrina*
Gidgeon *Chiozzo*
Hake *(Merlucci nerluccius)* **Merluzzo/merlango/merlucci-**
Herring *Aringa*

Lamprey *Murena/morena/lampre*
Lobster *Aragosta*
Mackerel *Sgombro/maccarello*
Mullet, grey *Muggine/cefalo*
Mullet, red *Triglia*
Mussels *Muscoli/mitili/cozze*
Octopus *Polipo*
Oysters *Ostriche/*in Venice *ostriche*
Perch *Pesce persico, perca*
Pike *Luccio*
Plaice *Passerino*
Prawns *Gamberetti*
Roach *Lasca*
Salmon *Salmone*
Salmon trout *Trota salmonata*
Sardines *Sardine*
Scallop *Conchiglia*
Sea-urchins *Ricci di mare*
Shad *Alosa/cheppia*
Shad roe *Uova di alosa*
Shrimps *Gamerettini di mare*
Skate/ray *Razza*
Sole *Sogliola*
Sturgeon *Storione*
Swordfish *Pesce spada*
Tench *Tinca*
Trout *Trota*
Tuna/tunny *Tonno*
Turbot *Rombo maggiore*
Turtle *Tartaruga*
Whitebait No Italian equivalent, but a request for *pesciolini* could produce a small-fry substitute
Whiting *Merlano/nasello/*in Naples *merluzzo*
Winkles *Lumache di mare*

FRUIT AND NUTS – Il fruttivendolo

Ripe Maturo

Apple Mela
Apricot Albicocca
Banana Banana
Blackberries More di rovo
Cherries Ciliegie
Currents (red, black or
white) Ribes
Dates Datteri
Figs Fichi (sing. fico)
Gooseberries Uva spina
Grapes Uva
Grapefruit Pompelmo
Lemon Limone
Loquat (Japanese
medlar) Nespole di Giappone
Melon Melone

Unripe Non maturo

Melon, water- Cocòmero
Nectarine Pesanoce
Orange Arancia
Peach Pesca
Pear Pera
Pineapple Ananas
Plum Susina
Pomegranate Melagranata
Quince Melacotagna
Raspberries Lamponi
Rhubarb Rabarbaro
Strawberries Fragole
Strawberries, wild Fragole di
bosco
Tangerine Mandurino

NUTS – Noci

Almonds Mandorle
Brazil nuts Noci americani
Chestnuts Castagne
Cobs/hazels Nociolini

Coconuts Noce di coco
Peanuts Arachidi
Walnuts Noci

GENERAL GROCERIES – Lo speziale (generí alimentari/coloniali)

We have compiled the following list from items that we have at one time or another found in grocery shops in Italy. But like their kind everywhere else, not all Italian stores will necessarily stock everything one feels they should or hopes they will.

Very often the most convenient alternative source of supplies has been the nearest *salumeria*. For those in search of the different sorts of ham, sausage and salami we suggest once more that they consult the list of items found on the *Antipasti* and *Piatti freddi* sections in the ON THE MENU section of this book.

Mass-produced foods such as cornflakes are often stocked in these shops, and they are known by their brand-names.

Angelica Angelica domestica
Aniseed Biscotti
Breadcrumbs Pane grattato
Butter Burro
Capers Capperi
Caraway Caro/carvi
Cayenne Pepe di Caienna
Celery salt Sale di sedano
Cheese Formaggio
Chickpeas Ceci
Chocolate Cioccolata
Cinnamon Cannella

Cloves Chiodi di garòfano
Cocoa Cacao
Coffee Caffè
Coffee beans Caffè in grani
Coffee, ground Caffè
macinato
Coriander Coriandro
Cumin seeds Semi di cumino
Curry powder Cari
Egg/eggs Uova/uova
Eggs, hard-boiled Uova sode
Flour Farina

Flour, buckwheat *Farina di grano nero/grano saraceno*
Gherkins *Cetrioli*
Ginger *Zenzero*
Grapefruit juice *Succo di pompelmo*
Ham *Prosciutto*
Ham, cooked *Prosciutto cotto*
Ham, raw *Prosciutto crudo*
Herbs, dried *Erbarrosto (mixed)*
  Basil *Basilico*
  Bayleaf *Alloro/lauro*
  Dill *Aneto*
  Fennel seeds *Semi di finocchio*
  Juniper berries *Ginepro in bacche*
  Marjoram *Maggiorana*
  Marjoram, wild *Origano*
  Rosemary *Rosmarino*
  Saffron *Zafferano*
  Sage *Salvia*
  Savory *Santoreggia, saturcia*
  Thyme *Timo*
Honey *Miele*
Jam *Marmalleta*
Lard *Lenticchie*
Mace *Mace*
Marmalade *Marmellata* (but it is a thin *purée*: not like English marmalade)
Milk *Latte*; in bottles it is *sterilizzato* and keeps for a long time, in cartons it is *pastorizzato* and fresher.

Mustard *Senape*
Nutmeg *Noce moscato*
Oil, olive *Olio* – just that
Oil, groundnut/peanut *Olio di arachide*
Orange juice *Succo d'arrancia*
Paprika *Paprica*
Peas, dried *Piselli secchi*
Pepper *Pepe*
Peppercorns *Pepe in grani*
Pepper, ground *Pepe macinato*
Poppy seed *Semi di papanero*
Rice *Riso*
Rice, ground *Farina di riso*
Rusks *Biscotti di salute*
Salt *Sale* (sold at tobacconists – *tabaccheria* – for reasons too complicated to explain here)
Sugar *Zucchero*
Sugar, lump *Zucchero in pezzi*
Tapioca *Tapioca*
Tea *Tè*
Tomato purée *Conserva di pomadoro*
Tomato juice *Succo di pomadoro*
Tumeric *Curcuma*
Vanilla *Vaniglia*
Vinegar, red wine *Aceto rooso*
Vinegar, white wine *Aceto bianco*
Yeast *Lievito*

POULTRY AND GAME — *Pollame e Salvaggina*

Chicken *Pollo*
  Very young (*petit poussin*) *Pollastrino*
  Spring chicken (1½-3½ lbs) *Pollastro*
  Fat hen *Gallina*
  Capon (3½-5½ lbs) *Cappone*
Duck *Anitra*
Duck, wild *Anitra selvatica*
Duckling *Anatroccolo*
Goose *Oca*
Grouse *Gallo di brughiera*
Guinea-fowl *Faraona*
Hare *Lepre*
Partridge *Pernice/starna*

Pheasant *Fagiano*
Pigeon *Piccione*
Plover *Piviere*
Quail *Quaglia*
Rabbit *Coneglio*
Snipe *Beccaccino*
Teal *Alzávola*
Thrush *Toddo*
Turkey (cock) *Tacchino*
Turkey (hen) *Tacchina*
Turkey (young) *Tacchinotto*
Venison *Selvaggina*
Wild boar *Cinghiale*
Woodcock *Beccaccia*

VEGETABLES AND HERBS – *Erbaiolo* (shop/store),
Piazza delle erbe (market)

Artichokes (globe) *Carciofi*
Artichokes (Jerusalem)
Topinamburi
Asparagus *Asparagi*
Aubergine (US:
eggplant) *Melanzana*
Basil, fresh *Basilico fresco*
Bayleaf *Alloro/lauro*
Beans, broad *Fave*
Beans, French *Fagiolini*
Beans, kidney *Fagioli*
Beetroot *Barbabietola*
Broccoli *Broccoli/cavolo*
romano
Brussels sprouts *Broccoletti/*
cavolini di Brusselle
Cabbage *Cavolo*
Cabbage, red *Cavolo rosso*
Cardoons *Cardi*
Carrots *Carote*
Cauliflower *Broccolo/caval-*
fiore
Celery/Sedano
Chard *Cardo di bietola*
Chicory (UK: endive) *Indiva*
Courgettes *Zucchini*
Cucumber *Cetriolo*
Eggplant (UK:
aubergine) *Melanzana*
Endive (US: chicory) *Cicoria*
Fennel *Finocchio*
Garlic *Aglio*
Gourds *Zucche*
Leeks *Porri*
Lettuce *Lettuga*
Marrows, baby *Zucchini*
Mint *Menta*

Morels (edible
fungi) *Spugnole*
Mushrooms *Funghi* (N.B. Do
not buy them from roadside
stalls: it can be very
dangerous)
Onion *Cipolla*
Parsley *Prezzémolo*
Peas *Piselli*
Peppers, hot *Peperoncini*
Peppers, sweet *Peperoni*
Potatoes *Patate*
Potatoes, sweet *Batate/patane*
Pumpkin *Zucca gialla*
Radishes *Radici*
Rocket *Rucola* (an aromatic
salad green little-known
outside Italy, but worth
travelling a long way to try)
Rosemary *Rosmarino*
Sage *Salvia*
Sea-kale *Cavolo marino*
Shallots *Scalogni/cipolline*
Sorrel *Acetosa*
Spinach *Spinaci*
Squash *Zucca*
Tarragon *Dragoncello*
Thyme *Timo*
Tomatoes *Pomodori/pomidoro*
Truffles, black *Tartifi neri*
Truffles, white *Tartufi*
bianchi
Turnip *Rapa*
Watercress *Crescione d'aqua*
Zucchini (UK: courgettes/
baby marrows) *Zucchini*

INDEX

WINE INDEX

ACKNOWLEDGEMENTS

The authors and publishers would like to express their
thanks to David Gleave and John Francis Phillimore for
their valuable contributions to this new edition of the book;
also to Sheila Brownlee and Peta Miers for their work on
the text; to Margaret Hallam for the layouts; and to the
Italian Trade Centre for their help and advice.